BHARATIYA NAGARIK SURAKSHA SANHITA IN PRACTICE: KEY INSIGHTS AND CRITICAL REFLECTIONS

Editors:

Dr. Aarushi Agarwal

Ananya Dutt

notionpress .com

INDIA · SINGAPORE · MALAYSIA

ISBN
Paperback 979-8-90560-281-8

Contents

RAJESH BINDAL
Judge

SUPREME COURT OF INDIA
TILAK MARG
NEW DELHI - 110 001

FOREWORD

It gives me immense pleasure to write the Foreword to the book *"Bharatiya Nagarik Suraksha Sanhita in Practice: Key Insights and Critical Reflections"* edited by Dr. Aarushi Agarwal and Ms. Ananya Dutt.

The enactment of the Bharatiya Nagarik Suraksha Sanhita, 2023 represents not merely a legislative transition, but a broader institutional attempt to align criminal procedure with technological advancements, a constitutionally conscious society and changing pattern of crime. Laws are enacted to deal with the situations arising out of change in society. If we examine, the old laws were centuries and decades old: the Indian Penal Code 1860, Code of Criminal Procedure 1973 and Indian Evidence Act 1872. Numerous amendments were made during the course of their application as new challenges emerged. With futuristic approach in mind, Criminal Major Acts were replaced in 2024. This is not a solitary attempt to update the laws to cater to the changed situation, we have seen numerous such examples :

- CPC- Code of Civil Procedure 1859 was replaced in 1908 with comprehensive changes.
- Motor Vehicles Act, 1939 was replaced in 1988.
- Companies Act, 1956 was replaced with the 2013 Act.
- Indian Tariff Act, 1934 was replaced with Customs Act, 1952.
- Prevention of Food Adulteration Act, 1954 was replaced with the Food Safety and Standards Act, 2006.
- Income-Tax Act, 1961 was replaced with the Income-Tax Act, 2025

The crime begins with the commission thereof, followed by the registration of FIR. This initiates investigation, which includes various facets including forensics. The process culminates in the presentation of a chargesheet in court, the production of evidence and conclusion with judgment by the court.

BUNGALOW NO. 2, AKBAR ROAD, NEW DELHI - 110011. TEL. NO. (011) 23018043

RAJESH BINDAL
Judge

SUPREME COURT OF INDIA
TILAK MARG
NEW DELHI - 110 001

A perusal of the contents of the book shows that it is divided into four parts. The first deals with structural and institutional reforms; the second deals with police power and accountability; the third deals with the technology and forensic evidence; and the fourth deals with witness protection and other related issues. The process through which a criminal case progresses is discussed in various articles published in the book. Furthermore, with the changing pattern of crime, the manner in which the investigations are carried out and integration of technology have been dealt with elaborately in various parts of the books.

A unique feature of the book is that various chapters have been authored by the law students, providing them a unique learning experience during their course of study. It grants them insight into the niceties of the provision of law, the underlying objectives and how these issues have been dealt with by the courts. Additionally, comparative perspectives from other jurisdictions have also been added.

Collectively, these chapters aim to provide readers with deep insight into the contemporary challenges shaping India's evolving criminal justice system.

I congratulate the editors, contributors, and all those associated with this publication for their commendable efforts. I am confident that this work will stimulate meaningful academic discourse and contribute significantly to the understanding of criminal laws.

I extend my best wishes for the success of this publication.

[Rajesh Bindal]

BUNGALOW NO. 2, AKBAR ROAD, NEW DELHI - 110011. TEL. NO. (011) 23018043

Preface

"The law cannot afford to remain static in a changing society."
—Justice V. R. Krishna Iyer

The transition from the Code of Criminal Procedure (CrPC) to the Bharatiya Nagarik Suraksha Sanhita (BNSS) marks a significant turning point in the evolution of India's criminal justice system. While the CrPC served as the procedural backbone of criminal law for decades, the introduction of the BNSS reflects an effort to modernise procedural mechanisms in accordance with contemporary societal and technological realities. The new framework seeks to address emerging challenges by incorporating provisions relating to digital investigations, electronic evidence, forensic practices, and the use of technology in criminal administration. This transition is not merely legislative reform, but a shift in legal philosophy aimed at making the criminal justice process more efficient, transparent, and responsive to the needs of modern society. At the same time, it places a greater responsibility upon students, practitioners, and scholars of law to understand the changing procedural landscape with clarity and critical insight.

The study of procedural law is indispensable in legal education because it forms the practical framework through which substantive rights and liabilities are enforced. While substantive law defines rights, duties, offences, and liabilities, procedural law provides the mechanism for their implementation before courts and legal authorities. A lawyer may possess thorough knowledge of legal rights and principles, yet without an understanding of procedure, such knowledge cannot be effectively applied in practice. Moreover, in the contemporary legal landscape, procedural law has assumed even greater importance due to the increasing role of technology, digital evidence, forensic science, and electronic governance in the justice system. A sound understanding of procedural law enables law students not only to interpret statutes but also to appreciate the functioning of the legal system as a whole. Therefore, the study of procedural law is essential for every law student aspiring to become a competent, ethical, and effective legal professional.

The chapters authored by legal practitioners, academicians and law students have been arranged in a systematic and thematic manner to provide readers with a comprehensive understanding of the evolving framework of criminal procedure under the Bharatiya Nagarik Suraksha Sanhita (BNSS). The book begins with foundational aspects of criminal procedure, including information to the police, investigation, preliminary inquiry, arrest, police custody, and bail, thereby introducing readers to the core procedural mechanisms governing criminal justice administration.

The subsequent section critically examines the expanding powers of the police and the corresponding need for accountability in a technology-driven legal landscape. These chapters explore important contemporary concerns such as CCTV surveillance in police stations, digital privacy, data protection, state surveillance, videography of crime scenes, and the constitutional implications of technological intervention in criminal investigations. Together, they highlight the growing tension between effective law enforcement and the protection of civil liberties.

The third part of the book focuses on the increasing integration of forensic science and digital technology within criminal procedure. Through discussions on digital forensics, electronic evidence, videography mandates, and virtual courts, the chapters analyse the transformative impact of technological advancements on investigation and adjudication under the BNSS framework.

The final section addresses broader procedural and institutional concerns, including witness protection, online proceedings, virtual courts, and delays within the criminal justice system. Collectively, these chapters aim to provide readers with both doctrinal understanding and critical insight into the contemporary challenges shaping India's evolving criminal procedural regime.

At last, it is sincerely hoped that this book proves useful to students, academicians, practitioners, and all readers interested in criminal law and procedure. It is our earnest desire that readers learn from this work and develop a deeper appreciation of the evolving nature of criminal justice in India.

Dr. Aarushi Agarwal
Ms. Ananya Dutt

Chapter 1

Information to the Police and their Powers to Investigate Under the Bharatiya Nagarik Suraksha Sanhita, 2023

Prateek Som
Advocate, Supreme Court of India.

Sana Sachdeva
Student of BALLB, Maharaja Agrasen Institute of Management Studies, Affiliated to GGSIPU, Delhi.

Abstract

Bharatiya Nagarik Suraksha Sanhita, 2023 (BNSS), transforms the Indian criminal procedure laws through major amendments to the criminal procedure laws related to the police investigation and administration process. Chapter XIII of BNSS, on information to police and the investigation process, is focused on digitisation, systematic police discretion and an efficient investigation process. The present chapter makes a critical analysis of the laws related to the registration of FIRs, preliminary inquiries, custodial inquiries, remand proceedings, witness interrogations and the reports prepared by the police, considering the constitutional provisions contained in Articles

14, 19, and 21 of the Constitution of India. Although BNSS aims at bringing about a transformation in criminal procedure and making the investigation process more efficient, there are fears associated with the increasing discretionary power of the police force concerning arbitrary actions and selective prosecution.

Introduction

Investigation forms the base for the criminal justice system since it is during this stage that the State exercises its coercive powers against the accused. The rules pertaining to registration of information, investigation by the police, custody of persons, and preparation of reports occupy a central place in criminal procedure. Chapter XIII of the Bharatiya Nagarik Suraksha Sanhita, 2023 (BNSS) seeks to overhaul the existing investigative process through digitisation, procedural standardisation, and greater operational autonomy for police authorities.

The chapter attempts to analyse the provisions concerning the investigative framework provided by the BNSS. The key question here is whether the emphasis on efficiency-oriented criminal procedure would provide enough constitutional protection against the abuse of coercive authority.

Section 173: Information in Cognizable Case

Section 173 of BNSS corresponds to Section 154 of the CrPC and governs the recording of information relating to cognizable offences.[1] The provision mandates that every such information, whether given orally or through electronic communication, must be reduced to writing and signed by the informant. Importantly, BNSS explicitly

1 *Bharatiya Nagarik Suraksha Sanhita*, 2023, § 173 (India)

recognises electronic communication, thereby institutionalising the concept of e-FIR and aligning criminal procedure with technological realities.

Preliminary Inquiry and Structured Police Discretion

The provision reinforces the principle that the police are under a statutory duty to register information disclosing a cognizable offence. This duty, though judicially settled under the CrPC regime, has now been reinforced within the statutory framework. The Supreme Court in Lalita Kumari v. Government of Uttar Pradesh[2] held that registration of an FIR is mandatory when information discloses a cognizable offence, subject only to limited exceptions. This principle continues to inform the interpretation of Section 173.

A notable departure under BNSS is sub-section (3), which introduces a structured regime for preliminary inquiry in cases where offences are punishable with imprisonment for three to seven years. The provision requires prior approval from a Deputy Superintendent of Police and permits a preliminary inquiry within a stipulated time frame to determine whether a prima facie case exists. This marks a significant shift from the CrPC position, where preliminary inquiry was purely judge-made and narrowly confined.

Judicial interpretation of Section 173(3) suggests that there are attempts at balancing investigative efficiency with constitutional safeguards. In the case of Imran Pratapgarhi v. State of Gujarat, the Court recognised preliminary inquiry as a narrow statutory exception to the requirement of FIR registration in cases where freedom of speech under Article 19(1)(a) is in issue. At the same time, it is clear

2 *Lalita Kumari v. Government of Uttar Pradesh* (2014) 2 SCC 1

that such discretion cannot be employed in a mechanical manner and can be used to thwart citizens from obtaining justice. Judicial pronouncements reiterated this position by stating that preliminary inquiry should be treated as a narrow exception to FIR registration.

Digital FIRs and Victim-Centric Investigation

This also ensures increased procedural inclusiveness by way of the implied acceptance of Zero FIR and inclusion of protections for vulnerable victims in cases, such as recording statements by female police officers and use of videography under certain conditions.

In 2026, while considering challenges to BNSS provisions, the Supreme Court observed that the Lalita Kumari doctrine had been "misused" in certain contexts, thereby justifying legislative intervention through Section 173(3). This observation is significant, as it signals judicial endorsement of calibrated discretion at the threshold stage.

At the same time, the Court has consistently warned against abuse of this discretion. The Court reiterated that access to justice cannot be compromised by procedural filtering mechanisms and that preliminary inquiry must remain an exception rather than the rule.

Comparative Table: Section 173 Bnss Vs Section 154 Crpc

Aspect	CrPC (Section 154)	BNSS (Section 173)	Judicial Position (2024-2026)
FIR Registration	Mandatory	Mandatory with exceptions	Exception recognised but narrowly construed
Preliminary Inquiry	Judicially evolved	Statutorily codified	Permissible but not universal
Digital FIR	Not explicit	Explicitly recognised	Encouraged for accessibility
Police Discretion	Limited	Structured discretion	Subject to constitutional scrutiny

The comparison highlights that while the BNSS retains the structural foundation of the CrPC, it marks a subtle but significant shift towards embedding calibrated discretion within a traditionally rule-bound system.

Section 173, when viewed collectively, demonstrates a shift in the doctrine from a strict rules-based approach to an approach where police have some degree of discretion in their investigations. Although this discretion can help in screening out cases that do not merit consideration and make the process more efficient, it does pose the problem of selective enforcement, lack of transparency, and the erosion of the clarity that was established in the case of Lalita Kumari v. Government of Uttar Pradesh.

Section 174: Information in Non-Cognizable Cases

Section 174[3] (corresponding to Section 155 CrPC) preserves the traditional distinction between cognizable and non-cognizable offences. While the police are required to record such information, they cannot investigate without the order of a Magistrate. This distinction is rooted in the principle of proportionality, ensuring that coercive police authority is not invoked in cases involving relatively minor offences without judicial oversight.

This provision reflects the principle of limited police intervention in minor offences, thereby safeguarding individuals from unnecessary intrusion. At the same time, the requirement of prior judicial approval may result in procedural delays, particularly in cases where prompt investigation is desirable.

In 2025, the Supreme Court in Om Prakash Ambadkar v. State of Maharashtra[4] recognised that under BNSS, Magistrates are now required to consider the reasons furnished by police for refusal to register FIR before directing investigation. This reflects a significant recalibration of the relationship between police and judiciary, enhancing judicial oversight while respecting investigative autonomy. The requirement of prior judicial authorisation in non-cognizable offences, therefore, reflects an attempt to preserve procedural proportionality

---

3 *Bharatiya Nagarik Suraksha Sanhita*, 2023, § 174 (India).

4 *Om Prakash Ambadkar v. State of Maharashtra & Ors.*, CA No. 352 of 2020, 2025 INSC 139

by preventing excessive police intervention in comparatively minor disputes.

Sections 175–178: Powers and Procedure of Investigation

Section 175[5] affirms the inherent power of police officers to investigate cognizable offences without prior judicial approval, subject to supervisory control of the Magistrate. The Supreme Court in Sakiri Vasu v. State of Uttar Pradesh[6] recognised the wide powers of the Magistrate to ensure proper investigation, including directing registration of FIR and monitoring the process.

Recent jurisprudence interpreting Section 175(3) BNSS has held that applications seeking court-directed investigation must now be supported by affidavits and prior recourse to supervisory police authorities. This requirement introduces procedural discipline by discouraging frivolous applications while ensuring that statutory remedies are exhausted. Section 176 lays down the procedure for investigation, requiring the officer to send a report to the Magistrate and proceed to the spot. This provision ensures early judicial oversight and prevents arbitrary initiation of investigation.

Sections 177 and 178 further regulate the reporting process and codify the power to conduct a preliminary inquiry. The statutory recognition of preliminary inquiry under Section 178 must be read harmoniously with Section 173(3), reinforcing the emerging trend of structured discretion.

---

5 *Bharatiya Nagarik Suraksha Sanhita*, 2023, §§ 175–178 (India).

6 *Sakiri Vasu v. State of Uttar Pradesh*, (2008) *2 SCC 409*

BNSS seeks to preserve police authority, but at the same time ensure that these investigative powers are monitored through some process-oriented measures and court review. Stringent procedures may also result in a delay in accessing the investigation when urgent police intervention is required.

Sections 179–180: Attendance and Examination of Witnesses

Sections 179 and 180 (corresponding to Sections 160 and 161 CrPC) empower the police to require the attendance of witnesses and record their statements during investigation. While these provisions are essential for evidence collection, they have historically been susceptible to misuse.

The Supreme Court in Nandini Satpathy[7] underscored that the right against self-incrimination extends to the stage of police interrogation, thereby placing constitutional limitations on police authority during interrogation.

Statements recorded under Section 180 are not signed and are primarily used for contradiction during trial, reflecting their limited evidentiary value. The integration of technology also introduces questions of data integrity, privacy, and evidentiary admissibility, which remain underdeveloped in the statutory framework.

The provisions relating to attendance and examination of witnesses largely replicate the CrPC framework but operate within an evolving constitutional context. The Supreme Court's jurisprudence continues to emphasise the right against self-incrimination and procedural fairness.

---

7 *Nandini Satpathy v. P. L. Dani*, (1978) *2 SCC 424.*

Recent trends indicate increasing judicial skepticism towards mechanically recorded statements. Courts have repeatedly emphasised that investigative processes must adhere to constitutional standards, particularly in light of technological advancements such as audio-visual recording. Consequently, investigative powers relating to witness examination must increasingly be interpreted through a constitutional lens that prioritizes fairness, dignity, and protection against coercive practices.

Section 183: Recording of Confession and Statements

Section 183[8] (corresponding to Section 164 CrPC) governs the recording of confessions before a Magistrate. The provision retains essential safeguards to ensure voluntariness, including cautioning the accused and providing a reflection period.

Judicial interpretation has consistently emphasised that confessions must be free from coercion. In Dagdu v. State of Maharashtra,[9] the Supreme Court held that any indication of inducement or threat vitiates the confession.[9]

While BNSS retains this framework, it does not significantly strengthen procedural safeguards, thereby missing an opportunity to address longstanding concerns relating to custodial coercion and evidentiary reliability.

8 *Bharatiya Nagarik Suraksha Sanhita*, 2023, § 183 (India).

9 *Dagdu v. State of Maharashtra*, (1977) *3 SCC 68*

Section 184: Medical Examination of Rape Victim

Section 184[10] (corresponding to Section 164A CrPC) mandates prompt medical examination of victims of sexual offences, subject to consent. The provision reinforces victim-centric justice and aligns with constitutional guarantees of dignity and privacy.

Section 187: Investigation Not Completed Within 24 Hours, Custodial Powers and Default Bail

Section 187[11] (corresponding to Section 167 CrPC) is one of the most critical provisions governing police custody and judicial remand. It mandates that an accused must be produced before a Magistrate if the investigation cannot be completed within 24 hours.

Custodial Investigation and Default Bail

The doctrine of default bail, as recognised in Uday Mohanlal Acharya v. State of Maharashtra[12], treats the right to bail upon expiry of the statutory period as an indefeasible right.

A significant doctrinal development emerges from recent rulings dealing with the extension of time for investigation under special statutes. The Court has clarified that such extensions are not automatic and must be based on a reasoned report demonstrating progress of investigation and the necessity of continued detention. In a 2024 decision concerning offences under special legislation, the Supreme

10 *Bharatiya Nagarik Suraksha Sanhita*, 2023, § 184 (India).

11 *Bharatiya Nagarik Suraksha Sanhita*, 2023, § 187 (India).

12 *Uday Mohanlal Acharya v. State of Maharashtra*, (2001) *5 SCC 453*

Court set aside the grant of default bail where statutory conditions for extension had been validly satisfied, underscoring that the right to default bail operates strictly within the statutory scheme and is subject to validly invoked exceptions.

Remand Jurisprudence and Personal Liberty

Equally significant is the Court's insistence on procedural fairness during remand and extension proceedings. In recent 2025 jurisprudence, it has been held that when a court considers an application for extension of time to complete an investigation, the accused must be produced (physically or virtually) and allowed to oppose such extension. The Court recognised that the right to default bail is "intrinsically connected" to personal liberty and cannot be defeated without affording the accused a meaningful hearing.

Further, the Court has moved towards a stricter scrutiny of remand orders, emphasising that judicial custody cannot be authorised mechanically. The broader judicial trend, reflected in contemporaneous constitutional jurisprudence on bail, underscores that "liberty cannot be kept in limbo" and that delays in adjudicating bail or remand matters directly undermine Article 21 protections. This has led to a jurisprudential shift where remand is no longer treated as a routine procedural step but as a judicial act requiring application of mind and recorded reasons.

The Supreme Court has also engaged with the question of computation of the statutory period, reaffirming that the right to default bail accrues immediately upon expiry of the prescribed period and remains enforceable so long as the accused applies before the filing of the charge-sheet. At the same time, the Court has clarified that where the prosecution validly files a charge-sheet within the statutory period or secures a lawful extension, the right does not arise.

Another emerging trend is the Court's concern with prolonged incarceration despite the filing of charge-sheets, particularly in complex economic offences involving voluminous evidence and numerous witnesses. In such cases, the Court has shown willingness to grant interim relief or liberal bail conditions, recognising that continued detention cannot be justified solely on the ground of pendency of trial, However, this liberal approach has been qualified by recent judicial pronouncements by the Supreme Court in Rakesh Mittal vs Ajay Pal Gupta[13] the Supreme Court emphasised that in economic offences involving large-scale financial harm, courts must adopt a cautious approach while adjudicating bail application. This reflects an emerging duality in bail jurisprudence—where personal liberty is balanced against the gravity and societal impact of the offence

Taken together, the post-2024 jurisprudence reflects a clear doctrinal shift: Section 187 BNSS is no longer viewed as a purely procedural provision but as a constitutional safeguard against investigative excess. The courts are increasingly insisting that the State must demonstrate diligence, transparency, and necessity at every stage of detention. Custodial powers are thus being recalibrated within a rights-oriented framework, where default bail operates as a critical check on investigative delay and executive overreach

13 *Rakesh Mittal v. Ajay Pal Gupta @ Sonu Chaudhary & Anr.*, 2026 SC 161

Section 193: Police Report on Completion of Investigation

Section 193[14](corresponding to Section 173 CrPC) constitutes the culmination of the investigation. It requires submission of a comprehensive report containing details of the offence, evidence collected, witness statements, and the opinion of the investigating officer.

The Supreme Court in Bhagwant Singh v. Commissioner of Police[15] held that the Magistrate must give notice to the informant before accepting a closure report, thereby ensuring participatory justice. This is mentioned in 193(3) BNSS as "the officer shall also communicate, in such manner as the State Government may, by rules, provide, the action taken by him, to the person, if any, by whom the information relating to the commission of the offence was first given". A misconception is seen among the Investigating officer that the information/communication to the complainant is to be given only in cases where closure or cancellation reports are filed. It is an erroneous interpretation as the word *shall* communicate is in respect of action taken by him (Investigating officer).

Further Investigation and Accountability Deficit

A significant concern arises from the ambiguous scope of the obligation to 'communicate' action taken. In practice, this has often been narrowly interpreted by investigating agencies as being limited to cases involving closure reports. Such an interpretation is inconsistent with the plain language of the provision and undermines the participatory rights of

14 *Bharatiya Nagarik Suraksha Sanhita*, 2023, § 193 (India).

15 *Bhagwant Singh v. Commissioner of Police*, (1985) *2 SCC 537.*

the complainant. This issue becomes significantly more concerning due to a clear procedural lacuna. If the Investigating Officer fails to comply with the mandate of Section 193(3), particularly by not informing the complainant or victim about the cancellation, closure, or any action taken in the matter, the complainant is effectively left without a judicial remedy against such omission. The situation is further aggravated by the fact that charge sheets are not filed on oath, which, in practice, creates room for misuse.

In practice, investigation agencies often find that Investigating Officers take advantage of this lack of accountability, especially when the complainant has limited recourse and knows that action on the judicial side is not possible against them.

This gap in the procedural framework ultimately results in a scenario where the State machinery, instead of safeguarding the interests of the victim or complainant, operates to their detriment. Addressing this lacuna is therefore essential to ensure fairness, transparency, and accountability in the criminal justice process

A significant development under the BNSS is the explicit recognition of the power of further investigation even after the submission of the police report, subject to judicial supervision. Judicial scrutiny has largely upheld this position against constitutional challenge, emphasising that adequate safeguards exist to prevent its misuse. However, the scope of further investigation remains circumscribed. The Supreme Court has clarified that such an investigation must be confined to specific aspects or leads requiring additional inquiry and cannot be employed as a mechanism for a wholesale re-investigation of the case. This position has been consistently affirmed in *Rama Chaudhary v. State of Bihar* and *Vinay Tyagi v. Irshad Ali.*[16] Despite these doctrinal clarifications, concerns persist regarding the quality of investigation, systemic delays, and the continued over-reliance on police discretion.

Critical Analysis

The investigative system established by the BNSS, 2023, represents a significant step away from the normative model of policing to an investigatory system focused on discretionary investigative powers. Despite the BNSS's attempt to transform India's criminal justice system with electronic reporting, electronic recording, video footage, and a formal preliminary inquiry, several of the measures adopted under the new code have the effect of increasing the power of discretion held by the police force without providing corresponding checks against that power.

The most controversial change made by the BNSS, 2023 is the codification of preliminary inquiry under Section 173(3). Though this change aims to prevent malicious initiation of criminal proceedings, it effectively dilutes the certainty of the law expressed in the landmark case of Lalita Kumari v. Government of Uttar Pradesh, where the Supreme Court held that there was a duty to register the FIR without delay. This change allows for discretionary filtering to take place at the first point of contact, which opens up the possibilities of selective investigation and informal censorship of complaints.

The use of technology in investigating offences in line with BNSS legislation has raised questions related to constitutional concerns. Although electronic FIR, documentation, and court procedures may provide better accessibility for complainants and convenience in

---

16 *Rama Chaudhary v. State of Bihar*, (2009) *6 SCC 346*. *Vinay Tyagi v. Irshad Ali @Deepak*, (2013) *5 SCC 762*.

administering the system, the legislation does not take into account the problems related to data protection, surveillance, cybersecurity, the validity of electronic documentation and evidence, and abuse of digital investigation tools. Without a clear procedural framework that covers collecting, processing, and using digital evidence, technology-enhanced investigation is likely to threaten the privacy of information and fair procedure.

Another institutional problem in BNSS is the lack of reforms in investigation that will shift from policing-centred investigation to institutional reforms in order to enhance accountability and oversight in investigation. While there is judicial supervision through remand and magistrates' review, these checks exist only in theory, as they come at a time when the investigative measures had already been taken. In reality, access to these avenues of redress depends on the complainants'/ accused's knowledge, financial capability, and determination, rendering the checks ineffective as a means of constraining police investigation powers.

Moreover, various sections within the BNSS reflect the legacy of persistent problems with custodial guarantees, forced confession, delayed investigation, and lack of transparency inherent within the CrPC scheme.[17] While introducing new structural and technical changes to the investigative process, the BNSS scheme has not been able to fundamentally re-conceptualise the investigative culture within the country, which has been widely criticised as being susceptible to the abuse of power, use of coercion, and overall lack of accountability.

Based on the trends after the BNSS regime, it appears that constitutional courts have tried to strike a balance between the

17 Law Commission of India. (2018). *Report No. 277: Wrongful prosecution (miscarriage of justice)*. Government of India.

investigative powers and proportionality, fair treatment, and personal liberties as stipulated under Articles 14, 19, and 21 of the constitution. Nevertheless, for the BNSS scheme to maintain its legitimacy in the long run, it cannot merely rely on procedural innovations but should be able to ensure that the exercise of discretion continues to be controlled by constitutional safeguards, judicial oversight, and overall institutional accountability.

Conclusion

The investigative process envisaged in Chapter XIII of the Bharatiya Nagarik Suraksha Sanhita, 2023, is a clear effort to modernise the criminal procedures in India through digitisation, systemisation, and increased procedural flexibility. BNSS has maintained many features of the previous procedural regime; it has, at the same time, widened the ambit of investigative powers at different stages of the criminal process.

In light of this widening of investigative powers, constitutional protections are more important than ever. It is not only necessary that investigative powers exist; it is equally vital that these powers be exercised efficiently and in keeping with the principles of constitutionality and fairness. The emerging judicial position appears to be that the efficiency of the investigation process cannot supersede constitutional values.

In conclusion, the true success of the BNSS will depend on how far investigative power is exercised in accordance with the Constitution.

Chapter 2

A Procedural Pause: Preliminary Enquiry Before Fir Under Bnss, 2023

Kavya Jain
Student of BBALLB, Maharaja Agrasen Institute of Management Studies, Affiliated to GGSIPU, Delhi.

Vamika Misra
Student of BBALLB, Maharaja Agrasen Institute of Management Studies, Affiliated to GGSIPU, Delhi.

Abstract

The Code of Criminal Procedure was enacted in 1898 in British India and was replaced by the new act, namely The Code of Criminal Procedure, 1973. This code underwent several amendments during the course of time. A new bill was further introduced and came into the Statute book as The Bharatiya Nagarik Suraksha Sanhita, 2023. The Sanhita brought a new concept in procedure to prevent false and malicious complaints lacking prima facie substance through Preliminary Enquiry before registration of an FIR. It had many judicial interpretations before the commencement of this Sanhita, which defined and laid down the cases where preliminary enquiry is required. The Sanhita gave statutory recognition to strengthen procedural fairness and credibility. The statute defines procedural standards and accountability mechanisms, and preliminary enquiry can ensure impartial criminal investigation if used cautiously within limited boundaries. Simultaneously, The Bharatiya Sakshya Adhiniyam, 2023 was enacted to replace The Indian Evidence Act, 1872 with the objective of modernizing the law relating to evidence in accordance with technological advancements and contemporary requirements of criminal justice administration. This Adhiniyam recognizes electronic and digital records as significant forms of evidence, emphasizing their admissibility, authenticity and reliability. The provisions directly influence preliminary enquiry, especially in cases involving cyber offences, financial frauds and electronic transactions where verification of digital material becomes essential before formal investigation. Therefore, both frameworks collectively aim to ensure fairness, transparency, accountability and efficiency in the criminal justice system while balancing individual rights with the interests of effective investigation.

Introduction

The Criminal Justice System in India has undergone a significant transformation in response to contemporary and challenging societal needs with a shift from the *Code of Criminal Procedure, 1973*[18], to *the Bharatiya Nagarik Suraksha Sanhita, 2023*[19].

This transition was introduced to ensure speedy justice through use of electronic means and digital evidence, and to make the procedure simple and more citizen-centric. The Sanhita introduced up several new approaches to the criminal justice, one of the most significant concepts is the Preliminary Enquiry, which allows a pause before

18 The Code of Criminal Procedure, 1973 (Act No. 2 of 1947)

19 The Bharatiya Nagarik Suraksha Sanhita, 2023 (Act 46 of 2023)

registration of an FIR in certain cognizable offenses. In many cases concepts can be false, malicious and lack primary facie substance.

Therefore, the need to conduct an enquiry before registering the complaint has become extremely important. The BNSS[20] provides statutory recognition to Preliminary Enquiry, thereby giving legislative backing to concepts that previously existed only through judicial interpretations. However, this transformation also raised concerns relating to the victim's rights, procedural fairness, police discretion, and the credibility of the criminal justice system.

This chapter aims to critically analyses how the shift from the CrPC[21] to the BNSS[22] supports the incorporation of Preliminary Enquiry within the criminal justice framework and examine its implications on the administration of justice.

Evolution Of Preliminary Enquiry Under CrPC

The Code of Civil Procedure, 1973[23], does not specifically provide the concept of preliminary enquiry before the registration of FIR. However, Section 154 of the Code[24], defines the First Information Report (FIR), that it is a mandatory duty of a police officer to register the complaint or information received relating to a cognizable offense.

However, practical issues were created such as false, frivolous matters, civil disputes were presented as criminal complaints. In such situations the court recognised the necessity to keep a check on whether a complaint received having a prima facie substance or not.

20 The Bharatiya Nagarik Suraksha Sanhita, 2023 (Act 46 of 2023)

21 The Code of Criminal Procedure, 1973 (Act No. 2 of 1947)

22 The Bharatiya Nagarik Suraksha Sanhita, 2023 (Act 46 of 2023)

23 The Code of Criminal Procedure, 1973 (Act No. 2 of 1947)

24 The Code of Criminal Procedure, 1973 (Act No. 2 of 1947)

Therefore, judicial support was there to clear the dilemma with the judgement, *P. Sirajuddin v. State of Maharashtra*[25], in which the Supreme Court observed the need of preliminary enquiry to reduce the humiliation faced by public servants while investigating the case on the basis of the registered FIR on received information which has no substance.

With the following landmark judgement, *Lalita Kumari v. Govt. of UP & Ors.*[26], preliminary enquiry is permissible if the information received does not disclose a cognizable offence and such enquiry could be conducted only to ascertain whether a cognizable offence is disclosed and not to ascertain the veracity or otherwise of the information received. At the same time, the Court permitted preliminary enquiry in limited categories of cases, including:

1. Matrimonial disputes,
2. Commercial offences,
3. Medical negligence cases,
4. Corruption cases,
5. Cases involving abnormal delays.

The court further decided that the enquiry should not exceed 7 days and must determine whether the enquiry is disclosing cognizable offense or not.

Thus, CrPC[27] didn't provide any statutory recognition to Preliminary Enquiry, it was only evaluated by judiciary in the procedure.

25 P. Sirajuddin v. State of Maharashtra, 1971 AIR 520

26 Lalita Kumari v. Govt. of UP & Ors., AIR 2014 SC 187

27 The Code of Criminal Procedure, 1973 (Act No. 2 of 1947)

Statutory Recognition Through Bnss

The Bharatiya Nagarik Suraksha Sanhita, 2023[28], formally incorporated the concept of preliminary enquiry within the framework of criminal procedure. Unlike CrPC[29], the legislative expressly recognised the concept through BNSS.

Under BNSS[30], section 173(3) states that *Without prejudice to the provisions contained in section 175, on receipt of information relating to the commission of any cognizable offence, which is made punishable for three years or more but less than seven years, the officer in charge of the police station may with the prior permission from an officer not below the rank of Deputy Superintendent of Police, considering the nature and gravity of the offence,*

i. proceed to conduct preliminary enquiry to ascertain whether there exists a prima facie case for proceeding in the matter within a period of fourteen days; or

ii. proceed with investigation when there exists a prima facie case.

It interprets that the police officer may conduct a preliminary enquiry before the registration of FIR in offenses punishable with imprisonment between three years to seven years. Such enquiry must be conducted with the permission of not below the rank of Deputy Superintendent of Police. The enquiry is generally required to be concluded in fourteen days. The purpose of such enquiry is to determine the sufficient grounds of the offence.

The legislative incorporation of preliminary enquiry reflects the intention of the legislature to prevent the misuse of criminal law

28 The Bharatiya Nagarik Suraksha Sanhita, 2023 (Act 46 of 2023)

29 The Code of Criminal Procedure, 1973 (Act No. 2 of 1947)

30 The Bharatiya Nagarik Suraksha Sanhita, 2023 (Act 46 of 2023)

while ensuring the fair procedure. The BNSS[31], therefore transformed judicial interpretation into the codified safeguard.

The provision seeks to:

1. Prevent false implication,
2. Protect reputation and liberty,
3. Reduce frivolous litigation,
4. Improve efficiency of investigation,
5. Ensure responsible use of criminal machinery.

Recent judicial interpretations have further clarified the scope of Preliminary Enquiry under the BNSS[32]. In *Imran Pratapgrahi v. State of Gujarat*[33], the Supreme Court observed that in the offenses punishable with the imprisonment between 3 years to 7 years, preliminary enquiry may serve as a prudent safeguard particularly in the matters of public expression and free speech. The court emphasized the determination of whether a prima facie case exists before initiating criminal proceedings, therefore protecting individuals from unnecessary prosecution for the false cases and misuse of any law.

Similarly, in *State of Karnataka v. Sri Channakeshava H.D.*[34], the Supreme Court clarified that the Preliminary Enquiry is not a prerequisite in corruption cases under the *Prevention of Corruption Act, 1973*[35]. The Court held that an FIR cannot be quashed merely because the police has failed to conduct the preliminary enquiry where

31 The Bharatiya Nagarik Suraksha Sanhita, 2023 (Act 46 of 2023)

32 The Bharatiya Nagarik Suraksha Sanhita, 2023 (Act 46 of 2023)

33 Imran Pratapgrahi v. State of Gujarat 2025 Live Law (SC) 362 2025 INSC 410

34 State of Karnataka v. Sri Channakeshava H.D. 2025 INSC 471

35 The Prevention of Corruption Act, 1988 (Act No. 49 of 1988)

the information is disclosed as the cognizable offence. The judgment affirmed the requirement should not become an obstacle for the offenses that require the immediate criminal investigation on the material already exists.

These judicial pronouncements demonstrate that although BNSS[36] provide statutory recognition to the preliminary enquiry, the judiciary determines the cautious balance in the application of it. The court attempted to ensure that this principle shall remain a procedural safeguard rather than becoming a procedural mechanism to bind the authorities, which may result in delay in justice or denying access to legal remedies.

However, this codified expression of police discretion under BNSS[37] has also generated the debate regarding accountability and transparency of the fair procedure.

Comparitive Judicial And Legislative Analysis: CrPC v. BNSS

This transformation results in a critical analysis that is a significant shift from CrPC[38] to BNSS[39] regarding the Preliminary Enquiry. Under CrPC[40] the concept was governed preliminary through judicial interpretation, whereas the BNSS provides statutory backing.

This distinction between two frameworks can be highlighted as:

36 The Bharatiya Nagarik Suraksha Sanhita, 2023 (Act 46 of 2023)

37 The Bharatiya Nagarik Suraksha Sanhita, 2023 (Act 46 of 2023)

38 The Code of Criminal Procedure, 1973 (Act No. 2 of 1947)

39 The Bharatiya Nagarik Suraksha Sanhita, 2023 (Act 46 of 2023)

40 The Code of Criminal Procedure, 1973 (Act No. 2 of 1947)

Basis	CrPC, 1973	BNSS, 2023
Legal Recognition	No express statutory provision for Preliminary Enquiry	Statutory recognised under section 173(3) of BNSS, 2023
Source of Authority	Developed mainly through judicial precedents	Incorporated through legislative enactment
Key Judicial Basis	Lalita Kumari v. Government of Uttar Pradesh	Judicial Interpretation along with statutory framework
Nature of FIR Registration	FIR registration generally mandatory in cognizable offenses	Preliminary Enquiry permitted before FIR in certain cases
Scope of Preliminary Enquiry	Limited and Exceptional	Broader and formally recognised
Time Limit for Enquiry	Ordinarily within the 7 days of the information received	Ordinarily within the 14 days of the information received
Applicable Offenses	Specific categories determined by the Judiciary	Offenses punishable with the imprisonment between 3-7 years
Constitution Concerns	Delay in FIR seen as an exception	Concerns regarding excessive police discretion and delay

Basis	CrPC, 1973	BNSS, 2023
Legislative Approach	Victim-Centric approach followed with mandatory FIR principle	Verification-based procedural Approach
Risk Factor	Limited Misuse due to Judicial restrictions	Greater possibility of delay and arbitrary refusal

The comparative framework demonstrates that the BNSS[41] expands the procedural role of preliminary enquiry by converting a judicially evolved exception into a legislatively recognised mechanism. While this shift may strengthen the safeguards against false complaints, it also raises the concerns regarding procedural delay, arbitrariness, increased police discretion and potential barriers to access the justice system.

Judicial Concerns Regarding Preliminary Enquiry

As per the *Bharatiya Nagarik Suraksha Sanhita (BNSS), 2023*[42], the judicial concerns regarding preliminary enquiry under Section 173(3) center on its departure from the principles laid down in the Lalita Kumari[43] precedent.

The provision potentially creates ambiguity by permitting a 14-day delay in FIR registration in cases punishable with imprisonment of

41 The Bharatiya Nagarik Suraksha Sanhita, 2023 (Act 46 of 2023)

42 The Bharatiya Nagarik Suraksha Sanhita, 2023 (Act 46 of 2023)

43 Lalita Kumari v. Govt. of UP & Ors., AIR 2014 SC 187

3–7 years, even where a cognizable offence is prima facie evident. This may weaken the mandatory nature of prompt FIR registration.

The major concerns that were raised, include:

- Conflict with the precedent in Lalita Kumari[44]: Under Section 173(3) of this Sanhita, a preliminary enquiry is permitted for offences punishable with imprisonment of 3–7 years, as recognised by the Supreme Court in *Lalita Kumari v. Government of Uttar Pradesh & Ors.*[45] However, the judgment strictly limits preliminary enquiries to cases where the information does not clearly disclose a cognizable offence. This creates ambiguity regarding the mandatory registration of FIRs in cognizable cases.
- Delayed Access to Justice: The 14-day enquiry period permitted under the BNSS[46], often contrasted with the 7-day guideline recognised in Lalita Kumari[47], may unnecessarily delay the commencement of investigations. Such delays can hinder timely access to justice and increase the risk of destruction, tampering, or loss of crucial evidence relevant to the alleged offence.
- Abuse of Discretion: Section 173(3) grants police authorities the discretion to conduct a preliminary enquiry to determine the existence of a prima facie case, rather than merely verifying whether the complaint discloses a cognizable offence. Such broad discretionary power may create opportunities for arbitrary action, corruption, harassment of informants, or misuse of authority during the enquiry process.

44 Lalita Kumari v. Govt. of UP & Ors., AIR 2014 SC 187

45 Lalita Kumari v. Govt. of UP & Ors., AIR 2014 SC 187

46 The Bharatiya Nagarik Suraksha Sanhita, 2023 (Act 46 of 2023)

47 The Bharatiya Nagarik Suraksha Sanhita, 2023 (Act 46 of 2023)

- Inconsistency with Judicial Precedent: Courts have consistently maintained that a preliminary enquiry is intended only to ascertain whether the information reveals a cognizable offence, and not to examine the truthfulness or veracity of the allegations. Judicial observations in cases such as Smt. *Raveena Meena v. State of U.P.*[48] emphasize that assessing the merits of the complaint at this stage exceeds the permissible scope of enquiry.
- Mandatory Safeguards Required: To preserve constitutional validity and prevent misuse of power, judicial observations emphasize that a preliminary enquiry should be conducted only with prior approval from an officer not below the rank of Deputy Superintendent of Police (SDPO). Additionally, the enquiry process must be properly documented through daily General Diary (GD) entries to ensure accountability, transparency, and procedural fairness during investigation.

Constitutional Implications Of Preliminary Enquiry

Section 173(3) of the Bharatiya Nagarik Suraksha Sanhita (BNSS), 2023[49] introduces a statutory preliminary enquiry for offences punishable with imprisonment between 3–7 years before the registration of an FIR.

The provision seeks to prevent frivolous complaints and unnecessary criminal proceedings. However, by shifting from mandatory FIR registration to a discretionary enquiry mechanism, it raises significant

48 Smt. Raveena Meena v. State of U.P, 202 AHC 70294

49 The Bharatiya Nagarik Suraksha Sanhita, 2023 (Act 46 of 2023)

constitutional concerns relating to equality before law under Article 14[50] and protection of personal liberty under Article 21[51].

Constitutional Concerns and Judicial Interpretation is as follows:

- Departure from the Lalita Kumari Principle[52]: Under the earlier CrPC framework, the Supreme Court in *Lalita Kumari v. Government of Uttar Pradesh & Ors.*[53] permitted a preliminary enquiry only in situations where the information did not clearly disclose a cognizable offence. In contrast, Section 173(3) BNSS[54] authorizes such enquiry even when a cognizable offence appears prima facie evident, provided the offence is punishable with imprisonment of 3–7 years.
- Implications under Article 14: The provision may result in arbitrary or inconsistent police action, as certain complaints may lead to immediate FIR registration while others remain subject to a 14-day preliminary enquiry. Such differential treatment can create concerns regarding equality and uniformity in criminal procedure.
- Implications under Article 21: Although the preliminary enquiry mechanism may protect individuals from wrongful arrest and malicious prosecution, delays in FIR registration may adversely affect victims' access to timely justice. Prolonged enquiry periods can also weaken evidence collection and investigation.

---

50 Art. 14, The Constitution of India as amended by (One Hundred and Sixth Amendment) Act,2023

51 Art. 21, The Constitution of India as amended by (One Hundred and Sixth Amendment) Act,2023

52 Lalita Kumari v. Govt. of UP & Ors., AIR 2014 SC 187

53 Lalita Kumari v. Govt. of UP & Ors., AIR 2014 SC 187

54 The Bharatiya Nagarik Suraksha Sanhita, 2023 (Act 46 of 2023)

- Need for Procedural Safeguards: Judicial observations emphasize that, to preserve constitutional validity, the preliminary enquiry must be completed within the prescribed 14-day period and should be conducted with procedural accountability. The officer-in-charge must promptly decide whether sufficient grounds exist for registration of an FIR.
- Contemporary Judicial Position: Recent judicial observations of the Supreme Court have recognised the necessity of preliminary enquiries in limited categories of offences, particularly those involving speech and expression, to prevent abuse of criminal law. The approach seeks to balance the rights of the accused with the interests of victims and the administration of justice.

Essential Features of Preliminary Enquiry under BNSS, includes:

1. Applicable only to offences punishable with imprisonment between 3–7 years.
2. Requires prior permission from an officer not below the rank of Deputy Superintendent of Police (DSP).
3. Must be completed within 14 days.
4. Intended only to determine the existence of a prima facie case, and not to conduct a detailed investigation.

Constructive Analysis With Suggestions

Building upon these constitutional and procedural concerns, the incorporation of preliminary enquiry under Section 173(3) of the Bharatiya Nagarik Suraksha Sanhita (BNSS), 2023[55] reflects a substantial shift in Indian criminal procedure.

55 The Bharatiya Nagarik Suraksha Sanhita, 2023 (Act 46 of 2023)

The provision departs from the earlier framework established in Lalita Kumari v. Government of Uttar Pradesh & Ors[56]. by introducing a structured and time-bound mechanism for examining certain cognizable offences punishable with imprisonment between 3–7 years before registration of an FIR. While the measure seeks to balance individual liberty with procedural fairness, it also raises practical and constitutional concerns regarding delay, discretion, and access to justice.

Constructive Analysis of Preliminary Enquiry under BNSS[57] comprises of the following aspects:

I. Positive Aspects and Institutional Safeguards:

- Prevention of Frivolous Complaints: The preliminary enquiry mechanism enables police authorities to identify false, malicious, or exaggerated complaints before formal criminal proceedings commence. This may help prevent unnecessary harassment, particularly in personal, matrimonial, or commercial disputes where criminal law is occasionally misused.
- Time-Bound Enquiry Process: Section 173(3) prescribes a mandatory 14-day limit for completion of the preliminary enquiry. The statutory timeline seeks to prevent indefinite administrative delays and ensures that the decision regarding FIR registration is taken within a reasonable period.
- Requirement of Senior-Level Approval: The provision mandates prior permission from an officer not below the rank of Deputy Superintendent of Police (DSP). Such supervisory control aims

56 Lalita Kumari v. Govt. of UP & Ors., AIR 2014 SC 187

57 The Bharatiya Nagarik Suraksha Sanhita, 2023 (Act 46 of 2023)

to reduce arbitrary exercise of police discretion and promote procedural accountability.

- Maintenance of Official Records: Judicial and procedural safeguards further require that all actions taken during the preliminary enquiry be recorded in the General Diary (GD). Proper documentation increases transparency and facilitates future judicial scrutiny where necessary.

II. Concerns and Procedural Challenges:

- Departure from the Lalita Kumari Principle: Although the Supreme Court in Lalita Kumari[58] permitted preliminary enquiry only where the information did not clearly disclose a cognizable offence, Section 173(3) allows such enquiry even where a cognizable offence appears prima facie evident, provided the punishment falls within the 3–7year category. This expansion may conflict with the principle of prompt FIR registration.
- Ambiguity in Determining Prima Facie Case: The BNSS[59] does not clearly define the standard for assessing a "prima facie case" during preliminary enquiry. The absence of a precise threshold may lead to inconsistent police practices and varying interpretations across jurisdictions.
- Risk of Delay and Evidence Tampering: The 14-day enquiry period may create opportunities for destruction, concealment, or manipulation of evidence, particularly in sensitive cases where immediate investigative action is necessary despite the offence falling within the prescribed punishment range.

---

58 Lalita Kumari v. Govt. of UP & Ors., AIR 2014 SC 187

59 The Bharatiya Nagarik Suraksha Sanhita, 2023 (Act 46 of 2023)

III. Suggestions for Improvement:

1. Defined Standards for Prima Facie Assessment

Police manuals and procedural guidelines should clearly specify that the purpose of preliminary enquiry is limited to verifying basic facts and the existence of relevant material, rather than assessing the evidentiary strength or conducting a detailed investigation into the allegations.

2. Mandatory Recording of Reasons

Where the police decide not to register an FIR after completion of the preliminary enquiry, the reasons for such refusal should be recorded in writing and communicated promptly to the informant. This would facilitate effective recourse before the Magistrate under Section 173(4) BNSS[60].

3. Protection of Zero FIR and Serious Offences

Procedural guidelines should expressly clarify that the preliminary enquiry mechanism cannot be used to delay the registration of Zero FIRs or complaints involving serious violence, threats to life, or urgent circumstances requiring immediate police intervention.

4. Electronic Documentation of Enquiry

The preliminary enquiry process, particularly the questioning of complainants or suspects, should be electronically recorded wherever feasible. Video documentation would enhance transparency, reduce allegations of coercion, and ensure procedural fairness during enquiry.

60 The Bharatiya Nagarik Suraksha Sanhita, 2023 (Act 46 of 2023)

5. Judicial Monitoring of Delayed Cases

Cases remaining under preliminary enquiry for extended periods should be periodically reported to the jurisdictional Magistrate. Such oversight would help prevent misuse of discretion, administrative delay, and procedural irregularities in the FIR registration process.

Conclusion

The framework of preliminary enquiry under Section 173(3) of the *Bharatiya Nagarik Suraksha Sanhita (BNSS), 2023*[61] represents both a procedural safeguard and a constitutional challenge within the evolving landscape of Indian criminal law. While the provision aims to prevent misuse of criminal proceedings through a structured and time-bound enquiry process, its departure from the principles established in *Lalita Kumari v. Government of Uttar Pradesh & Ors.*[62] has generated significant debate regarding mandatory FIR registration, police discretion, and access to timely justice.

The analysis demonstrates that the provision possesses certain institutional advantages, including prevention of frivolous complaints, supervisory oversight by senior police officers, and procedural transparency through documentation requirements. However, concerns relating to delay in investigation, ambiguity in determining a prima facie case, possible arbitrariness under Article 14[63], and implications for personal liberty and speedy justice under Article 21[64] cannot be ignored. Excessive discretionary power without clear safeguards may

---

61 The Bharatiya Nagarik Suraksha Sanhita, 2023 (Act 46 of 2023)

62 Lalita Kumari v. Govt. of UP & Ors., AIR 2014 SC 187

63 Art. 14, The Constitution of India as amended by (One Hundred and Sixth Amendment) Act,2023

64 Art. 21, The Constitution of India as amended by (One Hundred and Sixth Amendment) Act,2023

weaken public confidence in the criminal justice system and adversely affect victims' rights.

Therefore, the effectiveness and constitutional sustainability of Section 173(3) depend upon balanced implementation supported by judicial oversight, clearly defined procedural standards, accountability mechanisms, and strict adherence to principles of natural justice. If applied cautiously and within limited boundaries, the preliminary enquiry mechanism can serve as a tool for procedural fairness without undermining the fundamental objective of prompt and impartial criminal investigation.

Chapter 3

Arrest and Investigation Under the BNSS, 2023: A Constitutional Analysis

Aarav Kandoi
Student of B.A.LL.B.(Hons.), Department of Law,
School of Legal Studies, Central University of Punjab, Bathinda.

Abstract

The Bharatiya Nagarik Suraksha Sanhita, 2023 (BNSS) has replaced the Code of Criminal Procedure, 1973 (CrPC) with the stated objectives of efficiency, accountability, and increased protection of individual liberties. This is a significant change in India's criminal procedural system. This chapter of the book critically examines the changing legal framework that governs police investigations and arrests, which are the two of the most significant and repressive elements of the criminal justice system.

The chapter examines the statutory protections, procedural thresholds, and the recalibration of police powers in the context of arrest, with a primary focus on Sections 35 to 62 of the BNSS 2023, which correspond to Sections 41 to 60A of the CrPC. It looks at whether the BNSS merely restates pre - existing protections in a rearranged legislative form or if it advances constitutional demands under Articles 20, 21, and 22 of the Indian Constitution. Additionally, this chapter also contrasts the police investigations under Sections 154 to 176 of the CrPC with Sections 173 to 196 of the BNSS in terms of timeframes, magisterial oversight, investigative discretion, and FIR registrations. It looks into how these restrictions actually affect law enforcement, accused individuals, and victims.

This chapter puts India's procedural changes in context by comparing the provisions of arrest and investigation in England and the United States, and will also focuses on a best practices, rights-based protections, and ways for institutions to be held accountable. Later, this chapter critical thoughts on whether the BNSS signifies a significant change or cautious procedural continuity in India's criminal justice system are included in the chapter's conclusion.

Introduction

The Bharatiya Nagarik Suraksha Sanhita (BNSS) is related to criminal law. Criminal law has evolved due to conflicts in society due to different social, political, and economic issues. When wrongs were committed, society acted against the person committing it and made certain regulations to prevent the repetition of the same. Criminal law begins with the concept of crime itself, which has never been static but rather deeply embedded in the social, political, and economic fabric of society. As **Cesare Beccaria** famously observed: *"It is better to prevent crimes than to punish them."*

The criminal justice system is the main tool used by the state to impose its coercive power on people. It is not only a technical framework for the administration of justice. The most invasive of its many elements are arrest, and investigation which directly violate people's rights, liberties, and dignity. These powers are subject to substantive and procedural restrictions under Articles 20, 21, and 22 of the Indian Constitution. Due to the Supreme Court's repeated emphasis on the need for the legal system to be "just, fair, and reasonable," Article 21 has evolved into a repository of due process protections.

While the government framing of the BNSS highlights modernization and victim-centric justice, the key issue is whether these reforms genuinely modify the procedural safeguards for arrest and investigation or simply integrate existing judicial principles into law. This question holds significant importance in a constitutional democracy, as procedural law should limit arbitrary state actions. **K. I. Vibhute** has argued: *"Criminal procedure is not merely about enforcing law, but it is about controlling the abuse of power by those who enforce it."*

Constitutional Foundations of Arrest and Investigation

The procedural laws in India incorporate various safeguards intended to protect human rights from the moment of arrest through trial and sentencing[65]. In India, the validity of arrest and investigation is supported by both legislative power and constitutional provisions and according to the Constitution's expansive reading of Article 21, every restriction on an individual's freedom must be implemented through a fair, reasonable, and just process, as stated in *Maneka Gandhi v. Union of India*[66].

65 Sharma, A. (2025). TESTING ARREST PROVISIONS IN INDIA AGAINST THE TOUCHSTONE OF HUMAN RIGHTS: A CRITICAL LEGAL STUDY. International Journal of Advanced Research and Multidisciplinary Trends (IJARMT), 2(3), 436-445.

66 Maneka Gandhi v. Union of India, 1978 AIR 597.

The implications of inviolable right are far and wide, for it considers the provisions of the Universal Declaration of Human Rights (UDHR) to which India was also a signatory. The words "No person" does not mean 'only citizens', they include all persons of India irrespective of their nationality, religion or caste. Under the Article 21, the Supreme Court of India evolved several "Rights of the Accused" in various cases: (1) Compensation for illegal detention; (2) Compensation for lock-up death; (3) Free legal aid; (4) Fair and speedy trial; (5) Release of undertrial prisoners; (6) Guidelines in handcuffing.

In *Sunil Batra case*[67], it is already established that these constitutional provisions apply equally to those in custody: Article 14 prohibits arbitrary discrimination whereas Article 19 allows cap on liberty only for the sake of public order, Art. 21 safeguards against cruel or inhumane procedures. In the case of *Prem Shankar Shukla v. Delhi Administration*[68], the Supreme Court focused on the culture that treats humans like animals is fundamentally incompatible with the respect and value that must be afforded to all life even that of a hardened criminal.

Judicial engagement has played a major role in operationalizing fundamental rights. In *D.K. Basu*

v. State of West Bengal[69], the Supreme Court, emphasized on the arrest procedures by creating thorough guidelines to stop abuse while in custody. Similarly, the decision in *Arnesh Kumar v. State of Bihar*[70], reaffirmed the principle that an arrest should not be used as a punitive action prior to a conviction by emphasizing need and proportionality.

67 Sunil Batra Etc. V. Delhi Administration and Ors. Etc, 1978 AIR 1675.

68 Prem Shankar Shukla v. Delhi Administration, AIR 1980 SC 1535.

69 D.K. Basu v. State of West Bengal, (1997) 1 SCC 416.

70 Arnesh Kumar v. State of Bihar, (2014) 8 SCC 273.

Given this constitutional framework, the BNSS must be viewed as both an extension and a break from a robust corpus of rights-based legislation. Effective police arrest and investigation play a crucial role in ensuring justice, maintaining law and order, and successfully prosecuting criminals.[71]

N. V. Paranjape provides that a *"Crime is not merely a legal wrong but a social phenomenon reflecting the failure of societal structures."*

Arrest and Investigation Under the BNSS, 2023

1. Arrest

There is no standard definition of an arrest and no shared nomenclature for the various police practices that start the criminal process and deprive people of their freedom.[72] Although there is no consensus over the definition of arrest, the US common law draws that arrest takes place when a legally authorized person, such as the police, private security, or citizen, puts an individual under custody, especially because of his/her involvement in a crime.[73]

The term "Arrest" is not defined anywhere in the Sanhita. According to the Halsbury's Laws of England, the word arrest means *"the apprehension or restraint or the deprivation of one's personal liberty."*

---

71 Puthalath, S., Sapna, S., & Kumar, P. (2025). Effective Police Investigation Under BNSS 2023: Existing Legal Framework and Challenges. In *Rethinking the Police for a Better Future: Navigating Policing Challenges with Accountability and Trust* (pp. 61-76). Cham: Springer Nature Switzerland.

72 Harmon, R. A. (2016). Why arrest. Mich. L. Rev., 115, 307.

73 Akbas, H. (2019). Power of arrest: Definition, legal justification, and authority. Encyclopedia of security and emergency management, 1-5.

Every deprivation of liberty or physical restraint is not an arrest. Only the deprivation of liberty by legal authority or atleast by apparent legal authority, in a professionally competent and adapt manner amounts to arrest. Further, when the restraint is total and deprivation of liberty is complete that would amount to arrest. Therefore, arrest refers to "*the apprehension of a person by legal authority resulting in deprivation of one's liberty.*"

In the case of *State of Haryana v. Dinesh Kumar*[74], the Supreme Court observed that the term "arrest" was not defined by the Indian Penal Code, the Code of Criminal Procedure, or any other statute dealing to criminal charges. The only indication of what might be deemed an arrest may be found in Section 46 of the Code (Section 43, BNSS), which describes the process for making arrests.

1.1 Bare Provisions (Section 35 – Section 62, BNSS)

a. Section 35 BNSS (Sec – 41, CrPC): A police officer may arrest an individual without a warrant

Section 41 of the CrPC outlines the arrest powers of police without warrants, permitting arrests based on reasonable suspicion while requiring justification for necessity. Amendments to this provision mandate that police document reasons for both arrests made and not made.

It specifies several situations, if:

1. a cognizable offence is committed in the officer's presence;
2. In cases where there is credible information or reasonable suspicion of a cognizable offence punishable by imprisonment of up to seven years, an officer must believe that the arrest is

74 State of Haryana v. Dinesh Kumar, (2008) 3 SCC 222.

essential to prevent further offences, ensure proper investigation, safeguard evidence, prevent witness tampering, or guarantee court attendance.

3. credible information indicates the commission of a cognizable offence punishable by over seven years or carrying a death sentence;
4. the individual is a proclaimed offender;
5. stolen property is found in their possession;
6. they obstruct police duties or escape custody;
7. they are suspected deserters from armed forces;
8. they were involved in acts outside India punishable in India;
9. a released convict breaches conditions;
10. Each arrest must be documented, with reasons recorded in writing.

The BNSS, under Section 35 clause (7), introduces a notable safeguard: "*No arrest shall be made without prior permission of an officer not below the rank of Deputy Superintendent of Police in cases where the offence is punishable with imprisonment for a term less than three years, or where the person is infirm or above sixty years of age.*"

In the landmark judgement of *Joginder Kumar v. State of U.P*[75], the apex court held that the right of a person who has been arrested, to inform someone about his arrest and to consult his lawyer privately, is a fundamental right under Article 21 and Article 22. In the case of *Directorate of Enforcement vs Deepak Mahajan*[76], the court held that in every arrest there is custody but not vice versa and both the words "custody" and "arrest" are not synonymous terms. In *Hema Mishra*

75 Joginder Kumar v. State of U.P., AIR 1994 SC 1349.

76 Directorate of Enforcement v. Deepak Mahajan, AIR 1994 SC 1775: (1994) SC 1775.

v. State of U.P.[77], the SC stated that the Legislation has laid down various parameters, warranting arrest of a person, which itself is a check on arbitrary or unwarranted arrest and the right to personal liberty.

b. Section 36, BNSS (Sec – 41 B, CrPC): Procedure of arrest and duties of officer making arrest

Every police officer making an arrest is under a legal obligation to follow certain safeguards to ensure transparency and must protect the rights of the arrested person. At the time of arrest, the police officer must clearly display accurate and visible identification, including their name, so that their identity can be easily established. Apart from this, the officer is also required to prepare a memorandum of arrest which must be attested by at least one witness, who may be a family member of an arrested person or a respectable person from the locality where the arrest takes place. The memorandum must also be countersigned by the arrested person to ensure that the arrested person is properly documented and acknowledged.

In addition, the police officer must inform the arrested person of their right to notify about their arrest to any person of his choice. This obligation becomes particularly important when the memorandum of arrest is not attested by a family member, thereby ensuring that the arrested person is not kept incommunicado and that their detention is known to someone they trust.

77 Hema Mishra v. State of U.P., AIR 2014 SC 1066.

c. Section 37, BNSS (Sec – 41 C, CrPC): Designated Police Officer

The State Government is required to establish a police control room at both the district and State levels which help information relating to arrests can be centrally monitored and accessed.

Additionally, in every district and police station, a police officer not below the rank of Assistant Sub-Inspector (ASI) must be designated to maintain proper records of arrests. This detail includes the names and addresses of the arrested persons and the nature of the offences with which they are charged. Such information must be prominently displayed, including through digital means, at every police station and at the district headquarters, thereby ensuring that arrest-related information remains accessible and open to scrutiny.

d. Section 38, BNSS (Sec – 41 D, CrPC): Right of arrested person to meet an advocate of his choice during interrogation

When any person is arrested and interrogated by the police, he shall be entitled to meet an advocate of his choice during interrogation, though not throughout interrogation.

e. Section 39, BNSS (Sec – 42, CrPC): Arrest on refusal to give name and residence.

In case of non-cognizable offence, if a person refuses to provide accurate personal details in front of a police officer, they may be arrested for identity verification. Once their identity is confirmed, they can be released on a bond or bail to appear before a Magistrate, requiring Indian residents as sureties for non-residents. If identity confirmation isn't possible within 24 hours, or if the bond is not executed, the individual must be presented before the nearest Magistrate immediately.

f. Section 40, BNSS (Sec – 43, CrPC): Arrest by private person and procedure on such arrest

A private person is allowed to arrest someone who commits a non-bailable and cognizable offence in their presence, or a proclaimed offender. After such arrest, the person must be handed over to the police without unnecessary delay, and in any case within six hours, or taken to the nearest police station.

Once handed over, if the police believe the person falls under the grounds of arrest under Section 35 of BNSS, they will take the person into custody. If the offence appears to be non-cognizable and the person refuses to disclose their true name or address, or gives false information, they will be dealt with under Section 39 of BNSS. However, if there is no sufficient reason to believe that any offence has been committed, the person must be released immediately.

g. Section 41, BNSS (Sec – 44, CrPC): Arrest by Magistrate

When an offence occurs in the presence of a Magistrate within their local jurisdiction, the Magistrate has the authority to arrest the offender personally or direct another to do so. Following the arrest, the offender may be committed to custody in accordance with bail rules. Furthermore, a Magistrate can arrest or direct the arrest of an individual present within their jurisdiction if they have the legal authority to issue a warrant under the circumstances.

h. Section 42, BNSS (Sec – 45, CrPC): Protection of members of Armed Forces from arrest

No member of the Armed Forces of the Union can be arrested for actions performed in the course of their official duties without prior consent from the Central Government. Additionally, State Governments may extend similar protections to specific forces maintaining public order, requiring the State Government's consent for any arrests in those instances.

i. Section 43, BNSS (Sec – 46, CrPC): Arrest how made

While making an arrest, the police officer or any person must physically touch or confine the body of the person, unless thc person willingly submits to custody by words or actions. In the case of a woman, her submission to arrest is generally presumed through oral communication, and unless necessary or unless the officer is female, a male officer should not touch her.

One of the most debated changes under the BNSS is the explicit authorization of handcuffing under Section 43. If the person resists or tries to escape, the police may use reasonable force to complete the arrest. Handcuffs may be used depending on the seriousness of the offence, especially in cases of non – bailable and Cognizable.

This provision introduces clarity but also raises concerns regarding potential misuse. The absence of stringent safeguards or judicial oversight may result in normalization of restraints, undermining the dignity of the accused. The constitutional implications of this provision, particularly under Article 21, are likely to be tested in future litigation. **Michel Foucault** argued that a: *"Punishment has shifted from the body to the soul, but control remains."*

However, the law clearly states that no force can be used to cause the death of a person unless they are accused of an offence punishable with death or life imprisonment. Additionally, women should not be arrested after sunset and before sunrise, except in exceptional circumstances where prior permission of a Magistrate is obtained by a woman police officer.

j. Section 44, BNSS (Sec – 47, CrPC): Search of place entered by person sought to be arrested

When a police officer believes the accused is in a specific location, the individual in charge must permit entry and assist in the search. If entry is denied, the officer is authorized to enter forcibly after informing their authority. If the location has a woman who does not appear publicly and is not the accused, she must be notified and allowed to exit first. Furthermore, officers unlawfully confined during an arrest may break doors or windows to escape or rescue others.

k. Section 45, BNSS (Sec – 48, CrPC): Pursuit of offenders into other jurisdictions

A police officer may, for the purpose of arresting without warrant any person whom he is authorised to arrest, pursue such person into any place in India.[78]

l. Section 46, BNSS (Sec – 49, CrPC): No unnecessary restraint

The person arrested shall not be subjected to more restraint than is necessary to prevent his escape.

m. Section 47, BNSS (Sec – 50, CrPC): Person arrested to be informed of grounds of arrest and of right to bail

Whenever a person is arrested without a warrant, the police officer or the person making the arrest must immediately inform the arrested individual of the full details of the offence or the reasons for the arrest. Further, if the arrest is for an offence that is bailable, the police officer

78 *THE BHARATIYA NAGARIK SURAKSHA SANHITA, 2023*. (2023). https://www.indiacode.nic.in/bitstream/123456789/20099/3/aa2023-46.pdf

must inform the person that they have a right to be released on bail and that they can arrange for sureties on their behalf.

In the landmark judgment of *D.K. Basu v. State of W.B*[79], the SC issued the guidelines that a person who has been arrested and is being in custody, shall be entitled to have one friend or relative or any other person known to him or having interest in his welfare being informed about his arrest.

n. Section 48, BNSS (Sec – 50A, CrPC): Obligation of person making arrest to inform about arrest, etc., to relative or friend

Whenever a person is arrested, the police must inform a chosen relative or friend about the arrest and where the individual is held. The arrested person should be made aware of this right upon arrival at the police station. Additionally, the police are required to record who has been informed. When the arrested person appears before a Magistrate, it is the Magistrate's responsibility to verify that these procedures were correctly followed.

In *Suseela v. Principal Secretary to Govt. of Tamil Nadu*[80], detention order was held illegal as the authorities contended that information of arrest of the detenue was given to his friend through cellphone but there was nothing to show that the telephone number belonged to his friend.

79 D.K. Basu v. State of W.B., (1997) 1 SCC 416.

80 Suseela v. Principal Secretary to Govt. of Tamil Nadu, (2020) CrLJ (NOC) 431 (Mad-DB).

o. Section 49, BNSS (Sec – 51, CrPC): Search of arrested person

When a person is arrested and is not entitled to bail[81], or is unable to provide bail, the police officer may search that person and take into safe custody all items found on them, except necessary clothing. A receipt must be given to the arrested person listing all items taken by the police.

If the person to be searched is a woman[82], the search must be conducted only by another woman and with full respect for decency.

p. Section 50, BNSS (Sec – 52, CrPC): Power to seize offensive weapons

After making an arrest, the police officer or any authorized person may take away any weapons found on the arrested person to ensure safety. All such weapons must then be handed over to the court or the authority before whom the arrested person is to be produced.

q. Section 51, BNSS (Sec – 53, CrPC): Examination of accused by medical practitioner at request of police officer

When a person is arrested and there are reasonable grounds to believe that examining their body may provide evidence of the offence, a registered medical practitioner can conduct such an examination at the request of a police officer. The examination can include necessary tests, and reasonable force may be used if required to carry it out.

In the case of a female, the examination must be conducted only by, or under the supervision of, a female registered medical practitioner.

---

81 Duker, W. F. (1977). The right to bail: A historical inquiry. *Alb. L. Rev.*, *42*, 33.

82 Hanspal, M. S. (2024). *Navigating Legal Changes in BNS, BNSS, and BSA, 2023: A New Era for Women's Safety in India.*

The medical report must be prepared without delay and sent to the investigating officer

r. Section 52, BNSS (Sec – 53A, CrPC): Examination of person accused of rape by medical practitioner

When a person is arrested for rape or attempted rape, a registered medical practitioner, preferably from a government hospital, may examine the accused if a police officer request it. If no suitable doctor is within a 16 km radius, any registered medical practitioner can perform the examination using reasonable force if necessary. The doctor must conduct the examination promptly and prepare a detailed report, including the accused's personal details, injuries, DNA sample information, and the examination times. This report must be sent to the investigating officer and subsequently forwarded to the Magistrate as part of the official case records.

s. Section 53, BNSS (Sec – 54, CrPC): Examination of arrested person by medical officer

When a person is arrested, they must be medically examined as soon as possible by a government medical officer, and if such an officer is not available, by a registered medical practitioner. If needed, further examinations can also be conducted. In the case of a female, the examination must be done only by, or under the supervision of, a female medical officer or female doctor.

The doctor must prepare a report noting any injuries or marks of violence on the arrested person and the approximate time when such injuries were caused and a copy of medical report must be given to the arrested person or to any person nominated by them.

t. Section 54, BNSS (Sec – 54A, CrPC): Identification of person arrested

When an individual is arrested and identification is required for an investigation, the Court can order, at the police's request, the participation of the arrested person in an identification process deemed appropriate. For individuals who are mentally or physically disabled, the identification must take place under a Magistrate's supervision. The Magistrate is responsible for ensuring the process is conducted in a comfortable manner for the individual, and the entire identification procedure should be documented using audio-video means.

u. Section 55 – Section 62, BNSS (Sec – 55 to Section 60A, CrPC)

Sections 55 to 62 of the Bharatiya Nagarik Suraksha Sanhita collectively lay down important safeguards and procedures relating to arrest and custody. Section 55, provides that, when a senior police officer instructs a subordinate to arrest someone without a warrant, he must provide a written order stating the individual's name and the reason for the arrest. The subordinate is required to inform the person of this order prior to the arrest and show it if requested. This procedure does not restrict a police officer's independent authority to arrest without a warrant as outlined in Section 35 of BNSS. Under Section 56, the person having custody of an accused must ensure their health and safety. Section 57 requires that a person arrested without warrant be produced before a Magistrate or the officer in charge of a police station without unnecessary delay. Section 58 ensures that such a person is not detained for more than twenty-four hours without legal authority. Section 59 mandates that police officers report all arrests without warrant to the District or Sub-divisional Magistrate. Under Section 60, a person arrested cannot be released except on bond, bail, or by order of a Magistrate. Section 61 provides that if a person escapes from lawful custody, they may be pursued and re-arrested anywhere in India. Finally, Section 62 emphasizes that every arrest must be made strictly in accordance with the provisions of the Sanhita or any other applicable law, ensuring legality and accountability in the arrest process.

The overall emphasis on technology and updated procedures will modernize the criminal justice system, making it more efficient and aligned with contemporary practices, by replacing the long standing Code of Criminal Procedure, 1973, it seeks to modernize the legal framework, enhance procedural efficiency, and place a greater emphasis on the rights of victims.[83]

2. Investigation

In legal parlance, an investigation refers to a systematic inquiry designed to uncover factual details and collect evidence pertinent to an alleged criminal act.[84] The law governing investigation has undergone more visible changes under the BNSS, particularly in terms of technological integration and procedural streamlining. The provisions corresponding to Sections 154 to 176 of the CrPC have been reorganized under Sections 173 to 196 of the BNSS.

One of the most significant developments is the incorporation of the principle of mandatory FIR registration, as recognized in

83 RAMESH, P. Y. PROCEDURE OF ARREST UNDER BNSS.

84 Mishra, D. (2025). Scope and Extent of Police Powers: A Comprehensive Analysis According to the Bharatiya Nagarik Suraksha Sanhita. *Available at SSRN 5734982.*

Lalita Kumari v. Government of Uttar Pradesh[85]. By embedding this requirement within the statutory framework, the BNSS reduces ambiguity and strengthens the accountability of police officers in the initial stages of criminal proceedings. The introduction of electronic FIRs and digital record-keeping further enhances accessibility and transparency, particularly in a country where access to police stations has historically been uneven.

The BNSS also introduces structured timelines for investigation, particularly in serious offences. While this move is intended to address delays and improve efficiency, it raises concerns regarding the quality of investigations. The imposition of rigid timelines may incentivize superficial or hurried inquiries, potentially compromising the accuracy and integrity of evidence collection.

Magisterial oversight continues to play a central role in the investigative process[86], particularly in matters of remand and custodial interrogation. However, the effectiveness of this oversight remains contingent upon judicial vigilance rather than statutory design. Without strengthening the institutional capacity of Magistrates, procedural safeguards risk becoming symbolic rather than substantive.

The judicial precedent in *State of U.P. v. Sant Prakash*[87], clarified that the fundamental purpose of an inquiry is to gather evidence in relation to suspected misconduct or criminal breaches. The Court emphasised that these functions must be carried out either by a police

---

85 Lalita Kumari v. Government of Uttar Pradesh, (2014) 2 SCC 1:AIR 2014 SC 187.

86 Choudhary, D. Preliminary Enquiry Under Section 173 (3) of the Bharatiya Nagarik Suraksha Sanhita 2023: A Constitutional and Procedural Analysis.

87 State of U.P. v. Sant Prakash, (1976) Cri LJ 274.

officer or by an individual duly authorised by a Magistrate under relevant legal provisions. The process of investigation, therefore, encompasses multiple procedural activities, including the arrest and detention of suspects, examination of witnesses, medical inspection of the accused, evidence collection, and execution of coordinated searches or raids.

The increasing reliance on forensic science and digital evidence represents a progressive shift in investigative methodology. By mandating the use of scientific techniques and videography in certain cases, the BNSS aligns Indian criminal procedure with global standards. Nevertheless, the success of these reforms will depend on the availability of infrastructure, training, and institutional support.

Arrest Laws in India, UK, and USA

When it comes to arrests, a comparative perspective provides valuable insight into how different legal systems balance state power and human liberty. India has progressively strengthened procedural safeguards through legislative codification and judicial engagement[88], while the US and the UK have established stronger accountability systems and enforceable rights-based frameworks.

88 Saunders, C. (2011). 31. Judicial engagement with comparative law. *Comparative Constitutional Law*, 571.

Aspect	India	United Kingdom	United States
Legal Basis of Arrest	Statutory (BNSS Sections 35–62)	Statutory (Police and Criminal Evidence Act, 1984)[89]	Constitutional (4th Amendment)[90]
Arrest without Warrant	Permitted in cognizable offences	Permitted with necessity criteria	Permitted with probable cause
Information of Grounds	Mandatory under Article 22 & BNSS	Mandatory under PACE	Mandatory (due process requirement)
Right to Counsel	Constitutional right (Article 22)	Immediate access to solicitor	Guaranteed under 6th Amendment
Protection Against Self-Incrimination	Article 20(3)	Right to silence[91]	5th Amendment protection
Production before Magistrate/ Judge	Within 24 hours	Prompt judicial oversight	Prompt appearance before magistrate

Aspect	India	United Kingdom	United States
Accountability Mechanism	Judicial review[92] (post facto)	Independent oversight bodies	Strong judicial remedies and civil suits

Conclusion

A detailed analysis reveals that the BNSS primarily serves as a consolidative statute. It codifies existing rights and applies to selected improvements while maintaining the institutional foundation of police discretion. While some of the measures are commendable, such as the digitalization of investigations and prior consent for arrests, they do not substantially alter the power relations. While several provisions have been restructured, the framework relating to proclaimed offenders has been largely retained, with minor procedural refinements. This chapter analyzes and compares the provisions with the earlier CrPC framework, evaluating them considering constitutional mandates and judicial interpretation.

89 Act, C. J. (1984). Police and criminal evidence Act 1984.

90 RAWAT, A. Y. (2024). Comparative Study on Amendment of the Constitution: India, USA, and France.

91 Greer, S. (1990). The right to silence: A review of the current debate. *The Modern Law Review*, *53*(6), 709-730.

92 Prakash, S. B., & Yoo, J. C. (2003). The origins of judicial review. *U. Chi. L. Rev.*, *70*, 887.

When assessing the BNSS, constitutional guarantees must be taken into account. Article 20 forbids self-incrimination, Article 21 ensures due process, and Article 22 provides safeguards against arbitrary arrest. The Supreme Court has expanded fundamental rights through progressive interpretation by emphasizing justice and reason. As Justice P. N. Bhagwati stated: "*The rule of law must run close to the rule of life.*

Chapter 4

Power, Procedure, and Personal Liberty: A Critical Inquiry into the Due Process of Arrest

Mr. Mandeep Baisala
Advocate, High Court of Delhi.

Tapan Nagar
Student of BALLB, Maharaja Agrasen Institute of Management Studies, Affiliated to GGSIPU, Delhi.

Abstract

The rapid increase in reported crime in India—rising by 7.2% to 6.24 million cases—has significantly expanded the scope of arrests by investigative agencies. At the same time, the conviction rate remains approximately 54%, with nearly 29.2% of investigations pending, raising serious concerns about prolonged detention and procedural fairness. In such a context, maintaining a balance between individual liberty and State authority becomes constitutionally imperative. Despite procedural safeguards under the Code of Criminal Procedure, 1973, concerns regarding arbitrary arrests, custodial abuse, and misuse of statutory power persist. The transition to the Bharatiya Nagarik

Suraksha Sanhita, 2023 (BNSS) presents an opportunity to reassess whether legislative reform meaningfully strengthens due process protections in arrest procedures. The Chapter adopts a doctrinal and comparative research methodology, analysing statutory provisions, legislative intent, and judicial precedents relating to arrest powers, with specific focus on Section 35 of the BNSS, which restricts arrest in offences punishable up to seven years unless statutory conditions are satisfied. The provision reinforces the constitutional mandate under Article 21, which guarantees personal liberty and the right to live with dignity, including protection against arbitrary detention and custodial violence. The legislative intent behind Chapter V of the BNSS reflects the principle that the mere existence of power does not justify its exercise. When arrest safeguards are strictly complied with, they prevent unnecessary detention based solely on the cognizable or non-bailable nature of offences, particularly in cases where the likelihood of acquittal is significant and trials are prolonged. Thus, the BNSS seeks to recalibrate the balance between agency powers and constitutional freedoms, though its success ultimately rests on faithful enforcement rather than textual reform alone.

1. Introduction

Arrest represents a critical exercise of state power that directly intersects with individual liberty. Articles 21 and 22 of the Indian Constitution enshrine procedural safeguards to prevent arbitrary detention and uphold the dignity of the individual. Rising crime rates and increased arrests have intensified the need for accountability, transparency, and proportionality in the exercise of this power. The principle of 'Innocent Until Proven Guilty' lies at the heart of our criminal jurisprudence. Read with the constitutional obligation to safeguard personal liberty, it requires that police powers be exercised sparingly and only after striking a careful balance between the authority of the State and the cherished fundamental right to personal liberty. Any deviation must be justified by strong, compelling, and exceptional reasons.

This chapter critically examines the constitutional and statutory framework governing arrests, the procedural safeguards embedded in BNSS and CrPC, and the jurisprudence that ensures the protection of fundamental rights, highlighting the delicate balance between law enforcement and personal liberty.

2. Constitutional Mandate and Protection of Personal Liberty

Fundamental Rights occupy a place of pride in the Indian Constitution. The framers of the Constitution enshrined **Articles 21 and 22** within **Part III** to safeguard individual liberty. Consequently, procedural requirements—such as informing an arrested person of the grounds for their arrest—are not mere formalities; rather, they impose a mandatory **constitutional obligation** upon the State. Article 22 (1) is the fundamental right of every person arrested and detained in custody to be informed of the grounds of arrest. For instance if the grounds are not informed it would not only violate the Article 22 (1) but also amount to depriving the arrestee of his liberty protected under Article 21, the term "procedure established by Law" also includes what is provided under Article 22 (1). Article 21 Article 21 guarantees the right to life and personal liberty, which include guarantee against torture & assault by state. The Cr.P.C. contains analogous provisions but our Constitution-makers were anxious to make these safeguards an integral part of fundamental rights. This is what **Dr. B.R. Ambedkar** said while moving for insertion of article 15A (as numbered in the Draft Bill of the Constitution) which corresponded to present article

22 : *"Article 15A merely lifts from the provisions of the Cr.P.C. two of the most fundamental principles which every civilised country follows as principles of international justice. It is quite true that these two provisions contained in clause (1) and clause (2) are already to be found in the Cr.P.C. and thereby probably it might be said that we are really not making any very fundamental change. But we are, as I contend, making a fundamental change, because what we are doing by the introduction of article 15A is to put a limitation upon the authority both of Parliament as well as of the Provincial Legislature not to abrogate these two provisions, because they are now introduced in our Constitution itself."* referred by Supreme Court[93].

In the time when crime is increasing rapidly, the number of arrests made by Investigation agencies are also rising. Increased torture and Custodial Violence affecting the credibility of Rule of Law. In line to protect the Constitutional as well as Statutory mandates under BNSS/ CrPC it advocates for the strict compliance to protect the fundamental right provided by the Constitution to the Citizens. No doubt the power to make arrest is part of investigation but the existence of the power of arrest is one thing and its justification for the exercise of it is quite another as held in ***Joginder Kumar v. State of Uttar Pradesh***[94]. ***Crime Report 2023***[95] showing the increase in crime by 7.2% by reaching 6.24 million cases has significantly expanded the scope of arrests by investigative agencies. At the same time, the conviction rate remains approximately 54%, with nearly 29.2% of investigations pending, raising serious concerns about prolonged detention and procedural fairness. To maintain the balance between the power of state and

93 In the Matter of Madhu Limaye and Ors.1969 Cr LJ 1440 (SC), MANU/ SC/0047/1968

94 Joginder Kumar v. State of Uttar Pradesh MANU/SC/0311/1994)

95 National Crime Records Bureau (NCRB)

societal order. Legislation tried to incorporate Constitutional mandate along with judicial pronouncement in Chapter V of BNSS.

3. Impact of Arrest on Individual and Society

The word '**arrest**' is derived from the French word "**Arreter**" meaning 'to stop or stay'. It is clear that the word 'arrest', when used in its ordinary and natural sense, means the apprehension or restraint or the deprivation of one's personal liberty. Apex Court in the catena of Judgment explains the Impact of Arrest. Arrest not only affects the individual himself but also impacts persons associated with him by affecting their physiological balance, social well-being, stigma attached to arrest, which causes irreversible damage to reputation and standing of individuals in society. Arrest has multidimensional impacts not limited to societal impact but also extended to the physical and mental health due to depression aggravated by inadequate conditions in prison, even becoming worse when it leads to Custodial. Violence. Therefore no arrest can be made in a routine manner on a mere allegation of commission of an offense made against a person. It would be prudent for the police officer in the interest of the protection of the constitutional right if a citizen and perhaps in his own interest that no arrest should be made without reasonable satisfaction reached after some investigation as to the genuineness and bona fide of a complaint and a reasonable belief both as to person's complicity and even so as to the need to effect arrest.

4. Legal Framework Governing Arrest: When and How Arrest is Made

Section 35 of BNSS (Correspond to Section 41 & 41A CrPC) - Right to live with dignity and Personal Liberty is the most sacrosanct fundamental right guaranteed under Articles 20, 21 & 22 of the

Constitution. Any Attempt to encroach upon this fundamental right has been frowned upon by this court in catena of judgment, for this regard we refer to ***Roy V.D. v. State of Kerala***[96]. Arresting a person without any justification is perhaps one of the most serious encroachments upon the liberty of the subject which can be contemplated. Principle in ***Joginder Kumar (Supra)***, where the Court held that arrest must be justified, not routine. Rule 26.1 contained in the Punjab Police Rules, Vol.3 lays down that the authority given under Section 35, BNSS (correspond to Section 41 of CrPC) to the Police officer to arrest without warrant is permissive and not obligatory and whenever escape from justice or inconvenient delay is likely to result from the police failing to arrest, they are bound to do so; but in no other cases, the law allows a police officer to apply to a Magistrate for a warrant or a summons instead of making the arrest immediately, and this discretion shall be exercised whenever possible and expedient as held in ***Ram Pyare Lal v. Om Prakash***[97].

4.1 Arrest in Non-Cognizable Offences-

In Non-Cognizable Offences arrest can't be made without the warrant or order of a magistrate as given in the Section 35 (2) of BNSS, unless it falls under Section 39 of BNSS. Section 39 provides that when any person has committed the non-cognizable offence in presence of a police officer and such person refuses to provide his name and address or such officer has reason to believe that provided name and address are false then he may be arrested by officer. Clause 2 of Section 39 states that arrested person shall be released on bond or bail bond on asserting the name and address.

96 Roy V.D. v. State of Kerala, MANU/SC/0693/2000

97 Ram Pyare Lal v. Om Prakash, 1977 Cr 1984 (Del.)/ MANU/DE/0114/1977

4.2 Arrest in Cognizable Offences-

Arrest without warrant or permission of Court is governed by the Section 35 BNSS, if any one of the circumstances specified in any of the clauses of Section 41(1) is non-existent, the arrest purporting to be under that section would be illegal. After the several recommendation of **Law Commission**[98], Parliament introduced value of proportionality permeating the amendment relating to arrest under the clause (b) in Section 35(1). Section 35(1)

(b) provides that in offences punishable up to 7 year of imprisonment, accused shall be arrested only on the satisfaction of condition provided i.e., to prevent further offence, prevent tempering of evidence, prevent from making any inducement to any person acquainted with facts and to secure his presence in court. Such condition comes into play when officer has reason to believe that such person has committed the offence based on credible information. Proviso of Section 35(1)(b) provides that Police officer shall record the reason for making arrest in writing or for not making under this sub-section. Even if serious crime takes place resulting in the unfortunate death, all efforts must be made to apprehend the culprits involved in the crime. But that does not entitle the police to exercise the power under section 35 arbitrarily and to trample the dignity and liberty of the citizens' safeguard of which is guaranteed under our Constitution. On mere suspicion, police must not arrest a person unless suspicion is well founded as observed in ***Kajal Dey v. State of Assam***[99]. Sub Clause (C) of Section 35(1) provide the any person committed the offence punishable with imprisonment for more than 7 years, but that power should be exercised only when officer has reason to believe that such person has committed such offence and the same shall be based upon the credible information. Merely the

98 152nd, 154th & 177th Report of Law Commission

99 Kajal Dey v. State of Assam, 1989 Cr LJ 1209 (Gau), MANU/GH/0078/1989)

offence is cognizable and punishable for imprisonment for more than 7 years, officer can't make arrest unless the twin conditions in clause (C) are satisfied. The emphasis is on unless "Credible Information" is received observed by Supreme Court in Para 8 of ***Vihaan kumar v State of Haryana & ors***[100]. **Walmsley, J.,** In ***Subodh Chandra Roy Chowdhry vs. Emperor***[101] explain the expression "Credible and reasonable" must refer to the mind of the person by whom the information is received, and mere assertions cannot form the material for the exercise of an independent judgment, by such person. In cases, where High Court is convinced that power to arrest by officer exercised wrongly in violation of Section 41(1)(a), the High Court can always issue a Writ of Mandamus under Article 226 restraining the officer from misusing his legal power, held in **Ram Lal Yadav v. State of U.P**[102].

Section 35(3) provides that when arrest is not made in sub-section (1), officer shall issue the notice of appearance before police as specified in such notice. No arrest shall be made in respect of offence referred in notice unless such person failed to comply with the notice. In ***Arnesh Kumar***

v. State of Bihar[103] Supreme Court notice the mechanically reproducing most of reasons in case diary given in Section 35 for making arrest should be discouraged, therefore further directed Police officer do not arrest unnecessarily until satisfy them about urgency of arrest, if not doing so, **Notice of appearance** in terms of Section 35(3) of BNSS be served on the accused within in two weeks from institution

100 Vihaan kumar v State of Haryana & ors MANU/SC/0161/2025

101 Subodh Chandra Roy Chowdhry vs. Emperor 52 Cal 319, MANU/WB/0577/1924

102 Ram Lal Yadav v. State of U.P, 1989 Cr LJ 1013 (All), MANU/UP/0576/1989

103 Arnesh Kumar v. State of Bihar MANU/SC/0559/2014

of case punishable up to 7 year of imprisonment and magistrates also directed to do not authorize arrest mechanically.

4.3 How arrest made?

Section 43 states the procedure to carry out the arrest, making arrest actually means to touch or confine the body of a person to be arrested unless submission of body by words and submission of women on oral intimation shall be presumed unless contrary circumstances. Unless exceptional circumstances, women can't be arrested after the sunset and before the sunrise unless the written report prepared by women police officer and obtaining prior permission from JMFC within whose local jurisdiction offence is committed or arrest is to be made. If the arrest of accused is illegal and in contravention with provisions of CrPC/BNSS, then even if force is used by the accused in their rescue, they cannot be held guilty of the offense under Section 353, IPC as held in ***Sagwan Pasi v. State of Bihar***[104]. While making arrest if no effort is made to join any independent witness even though number of them were present and no plausible explanation from the side of prosecution s forthcoming for not joining the independent witnesses, this, by itself, is a circumstance throwing doubt on the arrest as held in ***Pawan Kumar v. Delhi Administration***[105].

4.4 Use of Handcuff during arrest-

Sub-Section (3) of Section 43 introduced new statutory provision in BNSS which provide not to use handcuff while making arrest or producing before court unless such person is habitual or repeated offender, or escaped custody, involved in organise crime, terror, drugs,

---

104 Sagwan Pasi v. State of Bihar, 1978 Pat LJR 275/ MANU/BH/0190/1977

105 Pawan Kumar v. Delhi Administration, 1989 Cr LJ 127 (Del.)/ MANU/DE/0045/1987

arms and ammunition, murder, rape and other heinous offences against the state. By adding this provision in the BNSS, the law gives the police very wide power to use handcuffs, even though the Supreme Court had earlier practically prohibited or severely restricted the routine use of handcuffs. Further the term repeated offender is not explained in the provision whether it includes only the repeated offender of serious offences or it includes petty offender for the purpose of Section 43(3) of BNSS. However it is important to note that CrCP did not contain any provision regarding use of handcuff, it developed through the judicial pronouncement in line with Article 21. In ***Sunil Batra v. Delhi Admn.***[106], Supreme Court held that use of handcuff within or without prison is violative to the fundamental right provided by Article 14, 19 & 21 as it is against human dignity and Indian Culture. In ***Prem Shankar Shukla v. Delhi***[107], Supreme Court held that routine, public handcuffing is a *prima facie* inhuman and arbitrary violation of **Article 21**, as security can be maintained through less undignified measures. Handcuffing is permissible only in extreme cases where the escorting authority records contemporaneous reasons and obtains judicial approval. It has to be remembered that an accused in a criminal trial is presumed to be innocent and it is for the prosecution to prove its case against him beyond reasonable doubt. The intendment of law must be kept in view and needless harassment to a citizen must always be scrupulously avoided. It is fallacious to equate the question of custody or restraint with the handcuffing of the person concerned as held in ***Prabhunarayan v. State of M.P***[108].

106 Sunil Batra v. Delhi Admn., (1978) 4 SCC 494

107 Prem Shankar Shukla v. Delhi Administration, 1980 (3) SCR 855

108 Prabhunarayan v. State of M.P., 1987 Cr LJ 339 (MP) : 1987 MPLJ 53

5. Procedural Safeguard During Arrest

Major safeguards provided under BNSS were developed after Landmark Judgment of Supreme Court in ***DK Basu v State of West Bengal***[109], after rapid increase in cases of custodial violence, torture and death in custody. Supreme Court remarked on this condition as alarming proportion that it is affecting the credibility of the Rule of Law and administration of Criminal Justice. Supreme Court judgment in ***DK Basu*** brings accountability and transparency in case of arrest and detention. Supreme Court issued guidelines that were eventually codified into statute following amendments to CrPC. Guidelines given in ***DK Basu*** shape the safeguards in form of duty of officer at time of arrest to bear accurate, visible and clear identification and name tag to facilitate easy identification to curb illegal detention. After the identification, ***DK Basu*** guideline constitute framework for **arrest memo** by the police at time of arrest which shall contain the time of arrest and shall be attested by the at least one family member of arrested person or any respected person of locality where arrest is made along with the countersigned by the arrestee. In any case an arrest memo is not attested by a family member, the arrestee shall be entitled to have family/friends named by him to be informed about his arrest. Duty to bear identification and issue arrest memo today took the shape of statutory duty under Section 36 BNSS, providing the mandatory duty of officer to bear clear identification and provide arrest memo attested by the arrested person and his family member.

109 DK Basu v State of West Bengal, MANU/SC/0157/1997

5.1 Role of Designated Police Officer and Control Rooms-

Police officer not below the rank of ASI designated under Section 37 BNSS by State Govt. along with the establishment of Police Control room in every District and at State level. Designated officer shall maintain the record of names, addresses of arrested person and nature of offence with which charged. Which shall be displayed at all Police Station and at district headquarter, displaying name at Police Station and district headquarter will act as detterent for the Police Officials from hiding the details of the arrestee and avoid illegal detention. This Statutory safeguard was developed after ***DK Basu*** guidelines which mandate officer making an arrest to inform within 12 hours regarding the arrest and display the same at a conspicuous board at Control Room.

5.2 Right to Inform a Relative or Friend-

Today this obligation is statutory in nature but takes its place as statute by virtue of ***DK Basu*** guidelines which mandated that an arrested person is entitled to have one relative/friend informed about the arrest and place where the arrested person is being held. Further officer shall make a diary entry at place of detention regarding arrest, which also contains the name of person who has been informed about the arrest along with details of officer in whose custody arrestee is. In BNSS Section 48 create this statutory duty on officer making arrest to forthwith inform the relative/friend of arrestee about the arrest (entry of same fact shall be made in a book) and place of detention along with designated officer appointed under Section 37. Officer informed the arrestee about this right as soon as brought to Police Station. Further magistrate shall also have the duty to satisfy himself that statutory mandate given in subsection (2) & (3) is achieved, otherwise further arrest leads to illegal detention and it is duty of magistrate to keep eye on police and provide the statutory safeguards to the arrested person.

5.3 Right to Legal Representation-

The right to meet an advocate during arrest and interrogation—though not necessarily throughout the entire interrogation—evolved significantly following the landmark ***D.K. Basu*** guidelines. These safeguards were established to curb illegal arrests and ensure that every arrestee is informed of their rights and available remedies.

Today, this has been codified as a statutory right under **Section 38 of the BNSS** (which was originally introduced into the CrPC following the *D.K. Basu* ruling. This right derives its primary value from **Article 22** of the Constitution, which enshrines the fundamental right to consult and be defended by a legal practitioner of one's choice. By ensuring access to legal support, this provision empowers the arrested person to seek appropriate legal remedies and effectively challenge the grounds of their arrest. A person in custody charged with an offence is always permitted reasonable facilities to consult his professional legal adviser, and when the legal adviser interviews him, the interview should take place in such a manner that the confidential nature of the communications between him and his lawyer is not violated as held in ***Sudha Sindhu Dey vs. Emperor***[110].

Other guidelines given in ***DK Basu*** were focused on maintaining accountability through mandatory diary entries that record the arrestee's details, the specific individual notified of the arrest, and the officers responsible. Additionally, the procedural right to a medical check-up ensures that an **inspection memo** is generated, creating a

110 Sudha Sindhu Dey vs. Emperor, AIR 1935 Cal 101, MANU/WB/0180/1934

signed record by both parties of the arrestee's physical condition at the time of detention.

5.4 Grounds of Arrest: A Fundamental Safeguard-

One of most important safeguard provided to the arrestee against the arrest is Grounds of Arrest, which prevent the arbitrary arrests and leads to arrest only in situations where it is required and same will be mentioned in the grounds of arrest. Information of arrest along with the grounds of arrest to person himself along with his family or friend to enable the arrestee to challenge his arrest and even press for bail. When the grounds of arrest are not communicated to the arrestee then it will become problematic for him to figure out why he was arrested? And how will he be able to secure the bail when he does not know the grounds of arrest and further what acts he should be avoiding if released on Bail. Section 47 makes it mandatory in case of arrest without warrant, officer making arrest shall forthwith communicate the full particulars of offence and grounds for such arrest. If the mandate of Section 47 is not fulfilled by not communicating the ground of arrest then it will render the arrest as illegal arrest and the arrestee will be released due to illegal arrest. The term "forthwith" used in Section 47 was explained in Report of Joint Committee[111] The Joint Select Committee added this word in subsection (1). This makes it clear that the communication of full particulars of offence or the grounds of arrest must be made immediately at the time of making the arrest. Section 47(2) provides the right of an arrested person to be informed about his entitlement for bail in case of bailable offence to prevent unnecessary incarceration. Section 47 of BNSS is a corollary to and is based on Article 22 (1) of the Constitution, Article 22(1) provides that no person who is arrested shall be detained in custody without being informed, as soon as may be, of the grounds for such arrest.

111 (1980) 1 CHN 365.

5.5 Lacuna in Statute-

Section 47 of the BNSS remains silent regarding the specific mode, nature, and stage at which the grounds of arrest must be communicated. This procedural gap has been addressed through judicial pronouncements. In ***Harikisan vs. The State of Maharashtra and Ors.***[112] the Constitutional bench held that for the arrestee's right to be meaningful, the grounds must be furnished in a language they understand and a script they can read. This principle was later reiterated in ***Lallubhai Jogibhai Patel vs. Union of India***[113]. The jurisprudence regarding the mode of communication evolved significantly with P**ankaj Bansal v. Union of India**[114], in this case Supreme Court held that informing the grounds of arrest to the arrested person is a fundamental right, so the mode of conveying the grounds must necessarily be meaningful to serve the purpose. The Supreme Court also provides **two reasons** why the mode of conveying the grounds of arrest should be in writing. The **first reason** is that it creates a definitive record, minimizing disputes over whether Article 22(1) was complied with, as in oral mode there will be a high chance for dispute. The **second reason** is to actualize the constitutional right to legal counsel by providing the specific factual basis needed to challenge the arrest. Same principle reiterated by Supreme Court in ***Prabir Purkayastha v. State (NCT of Delhi)***[115]**,** further held that reasons for arrest are formal in nature and can be generally attributed to any person arrested on accusation of an offense whereas the 'grounds of arrest' would be personal in nature. The ration laid down by the Supreme Court in Pankaj Bansal and Prabir Purkayastha has interpreted the provision

112 Harikisan vs. The State of Maharashtra and Ors., MANU/SC/0154/1962

113 Lallubhai Jogibhai Patel vs. Union of India, (MANU/SC/0216/1980)

114 Pankaj Bansal v. Union of India, MANU/SC/1076/2023

115 Prabir Purkayastha v. State (NCT of Delhi), MANU/SC/0435/2024

of statute in context of constitutional scheme and has laid down that the grounds of arrest have to be in writing, therefore said ratio becomes the binding law by virtue of Article 141. In ***Vihaan Kumar (Supra),*** Supreme Court explains the mode, manner and method to communicate the grounds of arrest. Grounds of Arrest should be communicated to the arrested person in a way that sufficient facts constituting the grounds are imparted and effectively in the language which he understands. Mode and method of communication must be such that the object of constitutional safeguard under Article 22 is achieved. Said objective further fulfilled by providing the written grounds of arrest to the relative/friend of the arrested person along with the arrested person, to provide necessary opportunity to him through relatives to secure his release at earliest possible for actualising his right under Article 21.

Recently, in ***Mihir Rajesh Shah v. State of Maharashtra & Ors.***[116], Supreme Court held that the objective of the Constitutional mandate would not be fulfilled by mere reading out the grounds of arrest to the arrested person. There is no harm in providing the grounds of arrest in writing in the language the arrestee understands, this approach would not only fulfill constitutional mandate but also be beneficial to investigating agencies to prove that the grounds of arrest were informed to arrestee. Further clarified that in every case registered under the IPC or BNS, the grounds of arrest must be provided in writing within a reasonable timeframe.

In exceptional circumstances such as offences against body or property committed in flagrante delicto, where informing the ground in writing is rendered impractical, it shall be sufficient for person making arrest to orally convey the same at time of arrest and later, a written

116 Mihir Rajesh Shah v. State of Maharashtra & Ors., MANU/SC/1492/2025

grounds shall be furnished at least two hours prior to production before magistrate but this is applicable only in a case where accused is caught red handed and it is not a universal rule for every arrest.

From the ratio given by the Supreme Court in the catena of judgment, it is evident that the written grounds of arrest is not only statutory but also a constitutional obligation. Oral form is not reliable as at time of arrest, the arrestee is not in a calm or state of mind that can understand the true meaning of grounds read out to him in oral mode. Further this would also disable the person from seeking further legal remedy to challenge his arrest.

6. Rights After Arrest

6.1 Production Before Magistrate Within 24 Hours-

In cases of arrest without warrant in absence of any remand order, the most vital safeguard is incorporated under **Section 58 of BNSS.** Section 58 provides that in any case the officer shall not detain the person for more than 24 hours after excluding the time for the journey from the place of arrest to the magistrate's court. Further, officers have to produce the arrested person before the magistrate irrespective of jurisdiction within 24 hours as per section 58 and no person shall be detained for more than 24 hours without the order of magistrate. Safeguard incorporated under Section 58 of BNSS is not merely a statutory right, rather it also has the Constitutional Value under the Article 22(2) which makes it a fundamental right of an arrested person. Article 22(2) provides provision to produce arrested person before magistrate within 24 hours after the arrest excluding time for travel to court of magistrate and no person shall be detained for more than 24 hours without the order of magistrate.

This safeguard protects the arrested person from continuous illegal detention and give him a chance to oppose the further remand at time of production before the magistrate within 24 hours of arrest. It is also the high time for magistrate to not authorize the detention mechanically if the magistrate found illegality in arrest memo, informing the nominated person about the arrest, grounds of arrest, reason of arrest and not producing before the magistrate within 24 hours after making the arrest. If any illegality is found in abovementioned safeguard then the magistrate becomes duty bound to release the arrested person and declare the said arrest illegal. In ***Pankaj Bansal (Supra)***, it was contended that the mere passing of successive remand orders would not be sufficient to validate the initial arrest, if such arrest was not in conformity with law.

6.2 Health and Safety of arrested person-

BNSS provides the statutory mandatory duty of person having custody to take reasonable care of the health and safety of an accused under Section 56 of BNSS. By virtue of this section, it protects the arrested person from the violence caused by Police in the pretext of investigation and so-called punishment given by them. The power to award punishment rests solely with the judiciary. Any encroachment by the executive through custodial violence risks shifting the Rule of Law toward a Police State, which is fundamentally repugnant to a democratic society.

7. Compensation in Case of Custodial Violence

There is indeed no express provision in the constitution of India for grant of compensation for violation of a fundamental right to life, nonetheless, Supreme Court has judicially evolved a right to compensation in cases of established unconstitutional deprivation of personal liberty. In **Neelabati Bahera v. State of Orissa[117],** Supreme Court held that it is on prison authority or police to ensure that a person in custody is not deprived of his right to life. The duty of care on the part of the State is strict without any exceptions and wrongdoer is accountable and state is responsible if any person in custody deprived of his life except according to law. Power of enforcement imposed a duty to "forge new tools", of which compensation was an appropriate one where that was the only mode of redress available. This remedy is based on Public Law based on the principle of strict liability to which the defence of sovereign immunity does not apply. In **State of Madhya Pradhesh v. Shyamsunder Trivedi & Ors[118],** case related to Custodial death, Supreme Court directed the accused police officer to pay up to Rs. 50,000 as compensation to the heir of deceased.

8. Conclusion

Safeguards during arrest provided under the Chapter V of BNSS does not have any major upgradation from the safeguards incorporated under CrPC. After the ***DK Basu*** judgment, several safeguards were codified in CrPC after the amendment in it. Law makers introduce minor changes in the process and safeguards of arrest by codifying the **sub-section 3 of Section 43**, which provides the specific circumstances i.e, heinous crimes in which investigation agencies can use the handcuff but Apex Court at several instances disgraced the use of handcuff as it is against human dignity. Section 35(7) of BNSS, include new provision for arresting a person above the age of 60 years or infirm person in cases punishable up to 3 years of imprisonment after the prior permission

117 Neelabati Bahera v. State of Orissa MANU/SC/0307/1993

118 State of Madhya Pradhesh v. Shyamsunder Trivedi & Ors,. MANU/SC/0722/1995

from at least DSP. Other improvement is visible in **Section 37 of BNSS**, in which law makers tried to improve the transparency during arrest by appointing designated officers not below the rank of ASI at each and every Police Station and district, officer shall maintain the record of person arrested, nature of offence and address of arrestee. Said Information shall be displayed (include digital mode) at all police stations and district headquarters. The Corresponding Section in CrPC was 41C, which does not contain provision to appoint designated officers and records of arrested persons were maintained at district and state level nor at Police Station Level. Law makers in BNSS codified many judicial safeguards into clearer statutory duty, While the Code of Criminal Procedure also incorporated some safeguards, BNSS **structures them more systematically**.

Chapter 5

Police Custody Under the Bharatiya Nagarik Suraksha Sanhita: Flexibility or Erosion of Safeguards

Kunal Verma
Student of BALLB, Maharaja Agrasen Institute of Management Studies, Affiliated to GGSIPU, Delhi

Abstract

The right to default bail is a predominant part of India's criminal procedure. It has since long served as a mechanism to prevent indefinite investigative detention. Under the Section 167(2) of CrPC, 1973 an accused had the right to be released on bail if the charge sheet is not filed within sixty days or ninety days (depending on the severity of the offence). This right has cemented its place as an "indefeasible right" flowing from the protection of life and liberty in the constitution. This meant that once the statutory period expired and the accused applied for bail, the right could not be defeated by subsequent filing of the charge sheet.

The BNSS, 2023 under Section 187(3) retains the skeletal structure of the right but introduces a significant modification in the remand scheme. Section 187 now permits the police custody of up to fifteen days to be taken "in whole or in parts" at any time during the first forty or sixty days of detention. Even though the statutory timelines remain intact, the flexibility granted to agencies may affect the balance between investigation and protection of liberty.

This chapter undertakes a comparative examination between the aforementioned provisions of the CrPC, 1973 and the BNSS, 2023. It also analyses these developments with the context of India's rising undertrial population. The chapter also delves into the friction between efficiency driven reforms and the constitutional grant of personal liberty.

Introduction

The code of criminal procedure, 1973 was replaced by the Bharatiya Nagrik Suraksha Sanhita, 2023 on July 1, 2024. The New criminal procedure code brought several changes in provisions related to arrest, detention, investigation etc. One such major change took place in the provision related to remand which was earlier given under section 167 of CRPC, 1973[119] and is now governed by section 187 of BNSS, 2023. This paper delves into the constitutional link of this provision and explores how the contours of the provision have been altered, and what effect would such alteration cause. It also explores the friction between investigative efficiency and personal liberty of the accused.

119 Code of Criminal Procedure, 1973.

Remand and the Right to Default Bail Under Section 167 CRPC, 1973

The heading of Section 167 of CRPC reads as Procedure when investigation cannot be completed in twenty-four hours. The section works in a tandem with Section 57 of the CRPC which contains the provision titled person arrested not to be detained more than twenty-four hours. (Code of Criminal Procedure, 1973, Sections 167 and 57) Section 167 deals with the grant of Police and judicial custody and the powers of the magistrate on the same subject. 167(2) grants the power to authorise police or judicial custody of the accused to the magistrate, not exceeding fifteen days in the whole, the proviso A to this subsection states that after the expiry of 15 days, if adequate grounds exist, the magistrate may authorise judicial custody for the accused person, but the total period of custody shall not exceed 90 days, in case of an investigation which is related to an offence punishable with death, imprisonment for life or imprisonment for a term of not less than 10 years or 60 days, in case of an investigation which is related to any other offence, on the expiry of the aforementioned total custody period the accused person shall be released on bail if he is prepared to and does furnish bail. The legislative intent is clear from the presence of the word shall in this proviso, which makes it a binding provision. Proviso B requires the accused to be physically present in front of the magistrate for the grant of police custody or its extension thereof, while the medium of electronic video linkage is deemed sufficient for the extension of judicial custody. Under section 167(2) the default by the investigating agency in the completion of the investigation within the stipulated time creates a right to default bail for the accused that is indefeasible in nature as stated in Uday Mohanlal Acharya v. State of Maharashtra[120]. The right under this section has evolved to be a

120 Uday Mohanlal Acharya v. State of Maharashtra, (2001) 5 S.C.C. 453.

predominant factor in the personal liberty discussion through several judicial pronouncements.

Judicial Interpretation of Default Bail

The right to default bail under section 167(2) of CRPC existed since it's very inception, but was later amended in 1978 (Code of Criminal Procedure (Amendment) Act, 1978) to contain the 60/90 day distinction. Such distinction was necessary in order to grant sufficient time for the completion of investigation of offences that were of heinous nature. The right has since been refined explored and linked to liberty, by the way of judicial pronouncements.

Evolution and the nature of the right to default bail

The object behind the statutory enactment of section 167 was that the accused shall not be detained for any unreasonably long period pending investigation therefore, it was necessary to prescribe an outer limit for such detention in order to safeguard the rights of the accused. Therefore, even though it is often mistakenly construed as a provision for grant of bail, it is better portrayed as the maximum period an accused shall be kept in custody pending filing of the charge sheet. The proviso to section 167 (2), on account of a default by the investigating agency, grants and indefeasible right to an accused person as stated in Hitendra Vishnu Thakur v. State of Maharashtra[121], 1994, the court in cases of like nature is obligated to inform the accused of his right to bail in order to enable him to make an application in that behalf as stated Hussainara Khatoon v. State of Bihar, 1979[122] the right to be under this proviso has been termed to be absolute and the court has gone on to an even greater in order to state that the magistrate has no

121 Hitendra Vishnu Thakur v. State of Maharashtra, (1994) 4 S.C.C. 602.

122 Hussainara Khatoon (I) v. State of Bihar, A.I.R. 1979 S.C. 1369.

power to remand a person beyond the stipulated period or delve into the merits of the case at this stage. Aslam Babalal Desai v. State of Maharashtra, 1992[123] the provision, therefore is in consonance with the legislative intent of having the investigations completed at the earliest, and to avoid the accused being detained for an unnecessary prolonged period of time, pending investigation. The right albeit being indefcasible when certain conditions are met has its own limitations pertaining to the filing of the challan all the charge sheet as rightfully conceded by Shri Kapil Sibal in Sanjay Dutt versus state[124], where stated that once the Chalaan is filed the question of grant of bail does not rise under this particular provision. The right, therefore has evolved to be an indefeasible right wherever applicable but not without the aforementioned limitations, these principles were built upon in later judicial pronouncements.

Enforcement of the right and prevention of frustration

The right given under the proviso of section 167(2) is a right that is predominant for ensuring that the personal liberty of accused is safeguarded which makes the role of the courts to rightfully enforce it, very important. The role to prevent frustration of the said right therefore, substantially lies with the courts. It was noted that a practice had developed where some courts, in order to defeat the right of the accused to bail under the proviso, had kept the bail applications pending for some days till the charge sheets had been submitted. This practice was condemned by the court[125].

123 Aslam Babalal Desai v. State of Maharashtra, (1992) 4 S.C.C. 272.

124 Sanjay Dutt v. State through CBI, Bombay, (1994) 5 S.C.C. 410.

125 Mohamed Iqbal Madar Sheikh v. State of Maharashtra, (1996) 1 S.C.C. 722.

Clarification of time limits under section 167(2) of CrPC

The legislative intent has always been that the investigation related to an offence shall be concluded within 24 hours failing which it could have been completed within 15 days under the code of criminal procedure, 1898. Subsequently, the period was extended to 60 days under the code of criminal procedure, 1973, and was further amended to its final form of 90 days in case of offences punishable with death, imprisonment for life or imprisonment for a term of not less than 10 years and 60 days in case of all other offences as stated in Rakesh Kumar Paul v. State of Assam[126].

Default Bail : A fundamental right

The right to default bail under the proviso of section 167(2) is held to be equivalent to a fundamental right given to the accused pending investigation if certain conditions are met. The right is not merely a statutory right, but is recognised as a fundamental right under article 21 of the Constitution of India[127].

Framework of Section 187 of Bnss

The BNSS or the Bharatiya Nagrik Suraksha Sanhita, 2023 came into force on July 1, 2024. It replaced the CrPC, 1973 as the Indian criminal procedure code, this was done for several reasons, including the need for faster, criminal justice, Inc Corporation of technology, the strengthening of investigation powers plan to update the colonial framework. It also has a better harmonisation when working in tandem with the new criminal laws. Section 187 of the BNSS, 2023

126 Rakesh Kumar Paul v. State of Assam, (2017) 15 S.C.C. 67.

127 Bikramjit Singh v. State of Punjab, (2020) 10 S.C.C. 616.

has replaced section 167 of the CRPC,1973 as the provision related to remand when investigation cannot be completed in 24 hours. The first subsection contains the procedure as to what needs to be done when it appears that the investigation cannot be completed within the period of 24 hours. It states that if the officer in charge of the police station or the police officer making the investigation if he's not below the bank of sub Inspector believe that the accusation or information is well founded and there are grounds for believing the same, he shall transmit a copy of the entries in the diary and the accused to the nearest magistrate. subsection 2 of section 187 is where we see the alteration in law from what It was in the CrPC, it states the provision that empowers the magistrate to remand the accused to either police or judicial custody, the provision has been altered in the sense that the police custody can now be sought for a period of 15 days in the whole or in parts at any time during the initial 40 days. In case of offences where the detention period is 60 days and 60 days in case of offences where the detention period is 90 days. The third subsection contains the provision for default bail which has not been altered from CrPC. Subsections 4 to 10 contain provisions related to the production of the accused before the magistrate, powers of the magistrate of second class under this provision, detention of women under the age of 18, powers of an executive magistrate under the section, copy of the remand order to be sent to the chief judicial magistrate, upper limit of six months of investigation in case of summon cases and the power of the sessions judge in such cases[128]. The new remand framework is deemed to aid in ensuring the efficiency of investigations and may even expedite investigation due to the ability of the prosecution to seek police custody in parts for a combined period of 15 days in the initial

128 Bharatiya Nagarik Suraksha Sanhita, 2023, Section 87.

40 or 60 days as the case may be but it raises several questions related to its impact on personal liberty.

Comparative Analysis of Section 167 CRPC and Section 187 BNSS

Both the provisions, namely section 167 of criminal procedure code, 1973 and section 187 of BNSS 2023, deal with the procedure when investigation cannot be completed in twenty-four hours. Both of them contain the provision that is exercised when the investigation related to a crime in which an accused has been arrested. Cannot be completed in the first 24 hours and further remand needs to be sought. Such remand may be in the form of either Judicial or Police custody. The continuity from CRPC to BNSS is exhibited by the similarities between the two provisions, they are similar van dealing with the production of the accused within 24 hours, the supervision of the magistrate, continuation of default bail etc.

The key differences can be seen in the following frameworks:-

a. Police custody framework - under section 167 of CRPC Police custody could only be sought in the first 15 days within the total custody period of 60/90 days, depending on the offence for a combined period of 15 days in the whole. Under section 187 of BNSS, the same Police custody can now be sought for a total period of 15 days either in whole or in parts within a 40 day window in case of offences where the total custody period is 60 days or within a 60 day window in case of offences where the total custody period is 90 days.

b. Role of the magistrate - the aforementioned change in the provision from CRPC to BNSS raises questions regarding the increased role and responsibility of the magistrate in the grant of Police custody, whereas earlier under the CRPC framework, the magistrate could only grant Police custody within a period of 15 days and for a period of 15 days in the whole, now, under the BNSS framework, the magistrate can grant police custody for a period of 15 days in the whole or in parts during the first 40 or 60 days from a period of 60 or 90 days depending on the office. This clearly exhibits an increased discretion on part of the magistrate while deciding the period of police custody due to the very nature of the provision under the BNS.

c. flexibility in investigation - the motive behind the change in the provision is clearly to accommodate for a higher flexibility when an investigation is being conducted. The said flexibility accrues due to the investigating agency now being able to seek the police custody in parts and for a longer period since earlier, the period in which Police custody could be sought was only limited to 15 days, but has now been extended to 40/60 depending on the offence.

d. strategic use of custody - a highly strategic use of custody has now been made possible due to the change in the provision. Since the investigating agency can strategically divide the custody they require in parts that total up to 15 days into a period of 40/60 days depending on the office. The said change will aid in investigation, but on the other hand, it also raises questions regarding the effect on the personal liberty of the accused and the consequential effects on his fundamental rights.

Therefore, even though there is noted continuity in section 187 of BNSS from the earlier provision under section 167 of CRPC there also exist a fundamental shift in the nature of police custody. The said shift needs to be analysed critically in order to avoid any instances where the provision is utilised in a manner that makes it liable for risks related to its misuse or prolonged investigative control. What makes the updated provision prone to such risks is the shift of the long kept Balance towards investigating agencies in order to aid them in the investigation. Another topic that needs to be analysed. Critically is the constitutional dimension attached to this section since the right that arises under this section is not nearly a statutory right but is right of fundamental nature[129].

Implications for Personal Liberty Under Article 21

The right to default bail that was earlier granted under the proviso to section 167(2) of the CRPC and is now governed by section 187 of BNSS has repeatedly been held to be a fundamental right under Article 21 by the apex court of India. The right operates as a safeguard to make sure that the accused is not deprived of his personal liberty, and that the custody is only exercised within the permissible limits. Therefore, the right is not merely a statutory right, but he is a right of fundamental nature that comes under the definition of procedure established by law under article 21[130]. The meaning of liberty shall not be restricted to the singular dimension as to whether the detention that has been ordered in a particular case is lawful or not, but also extends to the dimension of ensuring that the said custody stays under the law, fully prescribed time limits, this ensures that the custody is only granted up to the point where it's requirement is directly relative to the investigation and does not extend to the point where it becomes unnecessary and roaches upon a person's fundamental right of personal liberty under Article 21. It is pertinent to mention

129 Bikramjit Singh v. State of Punjab, (2020) 10 S.C.C. 616.

130 Bikramjit Singh v. State of Punjab, (2020) 10 S.C.C. 616.

that although it is necessary to ensure the time limits adhered to, it is also necessary that the incarceration itself is lawful. The provision for default bail ensures that the delay in investigation is attributable to the investigating agencies and the said delay is minimised through the use of efficient and time-saving measures in order to ensure that the time limits are adhered. It also allows a cheque to be accessed on arbitrary detention by the investigating agencies and empowers the accused against any bills to arbitrarily detain him. There is a large amount of population of under trials in India, and the said provision ensures that the legal system is able to expedite their trial and avoid incarceration of indefinite nature. Any bids to illegally extend the time limits given under section 187 of BNSS in order to get an extension for the filing of the chargesheet, whether it be by the way of keeping the default bail application pending or otherwise, shall be thwarted as rightly done so in the case of Mohamed Iqbal Madar Sheikh[131]. Such a dilution of the right may lead to its frustration and may also contravene on the individuals, personal liberty, and article 21. The said provision of default bail is therefore predominant factor in order to ensure fairness to the accused, ensure his personal liberty granted to him by the Constitution of India is not contravened upon, and that the rule of law is maintained. This is done through keeping a check on the power of the investigating agencies in order to Balance, their power against the rights of the accused, which prevents indefinite incarceration.

131 Mohamed Iqbal Madar Sheikh v. State of Maharashtra, (1996) 1 S.C.C. 722.

Balancing Investigative Efficiency and Procedure Safeguards

The section on default bail is often considered a fundamental right given to the accused in order to ensure his personal liberty's protected such a right due to its very nature holds predominant position in the sense that it thwarts any attempt at an overreach by the investigating agencies. The aforementioned section has gone through a change since the police custody that was earlier granted only in the initial 15 days of the total custody period could now we taken in whole or in parts during the first 40/60 days out of the total custody period of 60/90 days, this change took place when the CRPC, 1973 was replaced by the BNSS, 2023. This particular change erodes the 15 days safeguard since the custody can now be spread over a longer period of time that is 40/60 days. The erosion of the side safeguard brings with it, several challenges related to investigative overreach. It also weakens a boundary that had long existed and was a bar that if crossed could have resulted in a breach of the fundamental right of the accused, the reasoning offered as to why this took place was that it would assist the investigating agency in ensuring an efficient and meaningful investigation, and while it may offer certain benefits in that domain, it does not justify any contravention of a fundamental right that is given to the accused under Article 21 of the constitution. The accused under the procedure laid out in section 187 of BNSS repeatedly be brought back into the police custody in the initial 40/60 days of the custody for a combined period of 15 days , this brings with it a greater risk of coercion by the investigating agency on the accused, or the advent of some pressure tactics at play by the investigating agency or may even open the door to the abuse of the custodial process. This disrupts the long maintained balance between police custody, and the rights of the accused. The greater discretion with the investigating agency and the magistrate also leads to a dilution of the fundamental rights of the accused in the sense that he faces uncertainty related to his custody, which may take the form of arbitrariness against him. Such a dilution of the protection offered by Article 21 to the personal liberty of the accused is not fair just and could not be considered reasonable since the investigating agencies would have a discretionary power related to custody, which would contravene on the fundamental right to personal liberty of an individual. The psychological pressure, that an accused may face due to the uncertainty of being taken back into police custody over and over again over a period which may extend to 60 days in case of certain offences, is what tilts the scale that have long maintained a balance between the powers of the investigating agencies and the personal liberty of the accused. The said disruption of Balance is detrimental to the rights of the accused that are given to him by the Constitution of India under Article 21. It also weakens judicial custody as a safeguard against Police influence or any sort of coercion or pressure by the investigating agency. It would also further burden the judicial system by increasing the workload of the magistrates, who now have to consider several more factors while granting police custody and may also result in higher number of requests for police custody by the investigating agencies. The objective of the alteration in this section as has been stated time and again is to improve the efficiency of investigation by the investigating agencies, but the benefit accrued due to the alteration is not enough to justify the contravention on the fundamental rights and the personal liberty of the accused. The shift to a flexible custody system has raised several serious concerns related to the personal liberty and fundamental rights of the accused.

Conclusion

The section 167 of CRPC contained time limits that were a safeguard against arbitrary detention and were rooted in the fundamental rights that are given to an accused. The purpose of this time limits was that the accused does not face any coercion or pressure by the investigating agency. The shift under BNSS that introduces a framework that makes the police custody flexible and opens the door to making the accused vulnerable and the investigating agencies more influential than they already are, which disturbs the proportionality in this domain. Contravening liberty for achieving investigative efficiency is not ideal and exhibits a shift in the commitment to the fundamental right of personal liberty.

Chapter 6

Bail in India: A Comprehensive Legal Analysis

Himanshu Bodwal
Advocate, High Court of Delhi.

Divya
Student of BALLB,
Maharaja Agrasen Institute of Management Studies

Abstract

Bail is a significant part of the criminal justice system in India as it helps in protecting the personal liberty of an accused person while ensuring their presence before the court during trial. The idea of bail is very corresponding to the Article 21 of the Constitution of India, which guarantees the right of life and personal liberty. The rules of justice and fairness have been repeatedly emphasized by the Indian courts against the unnecessary detention of an accused person. Indian bail law has evolved over the years by means of several statutes and judgments. The Bharatiya Nagarik Suraksha Sanhita (BNSS), 2023, has made significant changes in criminal procedure, covering numerous aspects such as bail, undertrial detention, rights of accused persons, etc. Some of these changes are designed to be more efficient, but still protect individual rights in the criminal justice system. The paper explores the concept and legal provisions of bail in India as laid down in the Code of Criminal Procedure, 1973 and Bharatiya Nagarik Suraksha Sanhita, 2023. It covers various forms of bail, key legislation and case law decisions of the Supreme Court that have influenced the bail jurisprudence. The study also brings to the fore the recent reforms of the BNSS, 2023 and its effect on personal liberty and criminal justice administration.

Introduction

"The issue of bail is one of liberty, justice, public safety and burden of the public treasury, all of which insist that a developed jurisprudence of bail is integral to a socially sensitized judicial process."[132]

– Justice V. R. Krishna Iyer

Bail is one of the most fundamental concepts in criminal law and procedure. It refers to the conditional release of an accused person from custody, upon furnishing a bond (with or without sureties), undertaking to appear before the court at all future hearings. The word '**BAIL**' is derived from the Old French word ***'bailler'*** meaning ***'to give away or deliver'***. According to **Section 2 (1) (b)** of the **Bharatiya Nagarik Suraksha Sanhita (BNSS), 2023**, the term means *"release of a person accused of or suspected of commission of an offence from the custody of law upon certain conditions imposed by an officer or court on execution by such person of a bond or bail bond."*[133]

132 *Gudikanti Narasimhulu v. Public Prosecutor*, (1978) 1 SCC 240.

133 Bharatiya Nagarik Suraksha Sanhita, 2023, § 2(1)(b).

The constitutional underpinning of bail flows from **Article 21** of the Constitution of India, the Right to Life and Personal Liberty[134]. The Supreme Court has consistently held that deprivation of personal liberty without just cause is a violation of this fundamental right. Bail jurisprudence thus attempts to balance the state's interest in ensuring the accused's presence at trial against the individual's right to liberty.

India's bail provisions underwent a landmark transformation with the enactment of the *Bharatiya Nagarik Suraksha Sanhita (BNSS), 2023*, which replaced the *Code of Criminal Procedure (Cr.P.C.), 1973*[135]. Similarly, the *Bharatiya Nyaya Sanhita (BNS), 2023* replaced the *Indian Penal Code (IPC), 1860*[136], redefining offences and their classifications, which directly impacts bail decisions.

Types of Bail

Bail can be classified along several dimensions depending on the stage of criminal proceedings, the nature of the offence and the discretion of the Court or Police Officer. The following is a comprehensive taxonomy:

Classification Based on Nature of the Offence

a. Bail in bailable Offences (Section 436 Code of Criminal Procedure (Cr.P.C.), / Section 478 of Bharatiya Nagarik Suraksha Sanhita (BNSS), 2023)[137]

134 Constitution of India, art. 21.

135 Bharatiya Nagarik Suraksha Sanhita, 2023 (India); Code of Criminal Procedure, 1973 (India).

136 Bharatiya Nyaya Sanhita, 2023 (India); Indian Penal Code, 1860 (India).

137 Code of Criminal Procedure, 1973, § 436; Bharatiya Nagarik Suraksha Sanhita, 2023, § 478.

b. Bail in Non-Bailable Offences (Section 437 Cr.P.C/ Section 480 of Bharatiya Nagarik Suraksha Sanhita (BNSS), 2023)[138]

A bailable offence is one where bail is a matter of right. Under Section 436 Code of Criminal Procedure (Cr.P.C.), (corresponding to Section 478 of Bharatiya Nagarik Suraksha Sanhita (BNSS), 2023, a person accused of a bailable offence or arrested without a warrant in a bailable matter is entitled to be released on bail as a matter of right. Neither the police officer nor the Magistrate has any discretion to refuse bail in such cases.

Persons covered under Section 436 Code of Criminal Procedure (Cr.P.C.), / Section 478 BNSS

- Persons accused of bailable offences.
- Persons arrested in a matter where no cognizable offence is involved (e.g., under Sec-41(1)(b) to (i) and S. 151 Code of Criminal Procedure (Cr.P.C.), / S. 35 BNSS).[139]

Release on Bond without Sureties (S. 436(1) Proviso / S. 478 BNSS)[140]

The police officer or Court may, if they think fit or shall if the person is indigent and unable to furnish surety, release such person on executing a bond without sureties. An Explanation clarifies that a person unable to give bail within one week of arrest can be presumed to be indigent.

138 Code of Criminal Procedure, 1973, § 437; Bharatiya Nagarik Suraksha Sanhita, 2023, § 480.

139 Code of Criminal Procedure, 1973, §§ 41(1)(b)–(i), 151; Bharatiya Nagarik Suraksha Sanhita, 2023, § 35.

140 Code of Criminal Procedure, 1973, § 436(1) proviso; Bharatiya Nagarik Suraksha Sanhita, 2023, § 478.

- For **NON-BAILABLE** offences, bail is discretionary and not a matter of right. **Section 437** Code of Criminal Procedure (Cr.P.C.), (S. 480 BNSS) governs this discretion.

Key provisions under S. 437 of Code of Criminal Procedure (Cr.P.C.), / S. 480 BNSS

- **Section 437(1):** A police officer or Magistrate may grant bail to an accused person in non-bailable offence cases, unless the offence is punishable with death or life imprisonment and there are reasonable grounds to believe the accused is guilty.[141]
- **Section 437(2):** The Court shall impose conditions including appearance, not tampering with evidence, not influencing witnesses, etc.[142]
- **Section 437(6):** If the trial of an accused in non-bailable offence is not concluded within 60 days from the first date fixed for taking evidence, the Magistrate shall release the accused on bail if the accused has been in custody throughout that period. (Default Bail Condition)[143]
- **Section 437(7):** After conclusion of trial but before pronouncement of judgment, the court may grant bail if it considers that there are reasonable grounds for believing that the accused is not guilty.[144]

141 Code of Criminal Procedure, 1973, § 437(1).

142 Code of Criminal Procedure, 1973, § 437(2).

143 Code of Criminal Procedure, 1973, § 437(6).

144 Code of Criminal Procedure, 1973, § 437(7).

Classification Based on Stage of Criminal Proceedings

a. Pre-Trial/ Pre-Conviction Bail[145]

PROVISION	BNSS 2023 EQUIVALENT	NATURE
S. 436 Code of Criminal Procedure (Cr.P.C.),	S. 478 BNSS	Mandatory (Bailable offences)
S. 436 A Code of Criminal Procedure (Cr.P.C.),	S. 479 BNSS	Mandatory (Half-sentence undergone)
S. 437(1) Code of Criminal Procedure (Cr.P.C.),	S. 480(1) BNSS	Discretionary (Non-bailable)
S. 437(2) Code of Criminal Procedure (Cr.P.C.),	S. 480(2) BNSS	Discretionary with conditions
S. 437(6) Code of Criminal Procedure (Cr.P.C.),	S. 480(6) BNSS	Default Bail (Trial not concluded in 60 days)
S. 438 Code of Criminal Procedure (Cr.P.C.),	S. 482 BNSS	Anticipatory Bail

145 Code of Criminal Procedure, 1973, §§ 436, 436A, 437, 438, 439, 167(2); Bharatiya Nagarik Suraksha Sanhita, 2023, §§ 478–483, 187(2).

PROVISION	BNSS 2023 EQUIVALENT	NATURE
S. 439 Code of Criminal Procedure (Cr.P.C.),	S. 483 BNSS	Special Powers of High Court/ Sessions Court
S. 167(2) Code of Criminal Procedure (Cr.P.C.),	S. 187(2) BNSS	Default Bail (Chargesheet not filed)

b. Post-Trial Bail (S. 437(7) Code of Criminal Procedure (Cr.P.C.), / S. 480(7) BNSS)[146]

Granted after conclusion of trial but before pronouncement of judgment. The court may grant bail if there are reasonable grounds to believe the accused is not guilty of the offence alleged. This provision bridges the gap between conviction and appeal.

c. Post-Sentence / Appellate Bail (S. 389 Code of Criminal Procedure (Cr.P.C.), / S. 430 BNSS)[147]

Section 389(3) Code of Criminal Procedure (Cr.P.C.), (S. 430(3) BNSS) provides that if a convict satisfies the convicting Court that he intends to file an appeal, and the sentence of imprisonment does not exceed three years, the convicting Court shall grant bail to the convict.[148]

146 Code of Criminal Procedure, 1973, § 437(7); Bharatiya Nagarik Suraksha Sanhita, 2023, § 480(7).

147 Code of Criminal Procedure, 1973, § 389; Bharatiya Nagarik Suraksha Sanhita, 2023, § 430.

148 Code of Criminal Procedure, 1973, § 389(3); Bharatiya Nagarik Suraksha Sanhita, 2023, § 430(3).

For longer sentences, the Appellate Court exercises discretion under Section 389(1) Code of Criminal Procedure (Cr.P.C.).[149]

Special Types of Bail

a. Anticipatory Bail (Section 438 Code of Criminal Procedure (Cr.P.C.), / Section 482 BNSS)

b. Default Bail / Compulsory Bail (Section 167(2) Code of Criminal Procedure (Cr.P.C.), / Section 187(2) BNSS)

c. Transit Bail (Section 81(1) Code of Criminal Procedure (Cr.P.C.), / Section 187(1) BNSS)

d. Interim Bail

e. Regular Bail

f. Bail under Section 436A Code of Criminal Procedure (Cr.P.C.), / Section 479 BNSS (Half-Sentence Bail)

A. Anticipatory Bail (S. 438 Code of Criminal Procedure (Cr.P.C.), / S. 482 BNSS)[150]

Anticipatory bail is a direction to release a person on bail in anticipation of an arrest. Section 438 Code of Criminal Procedure (Cr.P.C.), (S. 482 BNSS) empowers the High Court or Court of Session to grant anticipatory bail when a person apprehends arrest for a non-bailable offence. It is a pre-arrest bail and operates as a direction to release even before formal arrest.

149 Code of Criminal Procedure, 1973, § 389(1).

150 Code of Criminal Procedure, 1973, § 438; Bharatiya Nagarik Suraksha Sanhita, 2023, § 482.

Key conditions imposed under S. 438 Code of Criminal Procedure (Cr.P.C.),:

- The person must make himself available for interrogation by a police officer as and when required.
- The person must not leave India without the prior permission of the Court.
- The person must surrender his passport to the investigating authority.
- The person shall not, directly or indirectly, make any inducement, threat or promise to any person acquainted with the facts of the case to dissuade them from disclosing facts to the Court or police.

B. Default Bail / Compulsory Bail (S. 167(2) Code of Criminal Procedure (Cr.P.C.), / S. 187(2) BNSS)[151]

Under Section 167(2) Code of Criminal Procedure (Cr.P.C.), (S. 187(2) BNSS), when an accused is remanded to custody pending investigation, and the police fail to file the chargesheet (final report) within the specified time limit, the accused becomes entitled to default bail as a matter of indefeasible right.

151 Code of Criminal Procedure, 1973, § 167(2); Bharatiya Nagarik Suraksha Sanhita, 2023, § 187(2).

TIME LIMIT FOR CHARGESHEET	APPLICABLE OFFENCE
90 days	Offences punishable with death, life imprisonment, or imprisonment for a term of not less than 10 years
60 days	All other offences
On expiry of period	The Magistrate is bound to release the accused if he is prepared to and does furnish bail

C. Transit Bail (S. 81(1) Code of Criminal Procedure (Cr.P.C.), / S. 187(1) BNSS)[152]

When a person is arrested for an offence committed beyond the jurisdiction of the court where he is arrested, and has to be transported to the appropriate jurisdiction, a transit bail may be granted. This is a temporary bail to facilitate the lawful transit of the arrested person.

D. Interim Bail

Interim bail is a temporary bail granted for a short period pending the hearing and disposal of a regular bail application. Courts have inherent power to grant interim bail to prevent irreparable harm to the accused or to preserve the status quo. The Supreme Court in *Siddharam Satlingappa Mhetre v. State of Maharashtra* recognized the power to grant interim anticipatory bail.[153]

---

152 Code of Criminal Procedure, 1973, § 81(1); Bharatiya Nagarik Suraksha Sanhita, 2023, § 187(1).

153 *Siddharam Satlingappa Mhetre v. State of Maharashtra*, (2011) 1 SCC 694 (India).

E. Regular Bail

After arrest and formal remand, the accused may apply for regular bail before the appropriate Magistrate or Court under S. 437 Code of Criminal Procedure (Cr.P.C.), (S. 480 BNSS) or before the Sessions Court or High Court under S. 439 Code of Criminal Procedure (Cr.P.C.), (S. 483 BNSS).[154] This is the most common form of bail sought after arrest.

F. Bail under S. 436A Code of Criminal Procedure (Cr.P.C.), / S. 479 BNSS (Half Sentence Bail)[155]

Section 436A Code of Criminal Procedure (Cr.P.C.), (S. 479 BNSS) provides that where a person has been in detention during the period of investigation, inquiry or trial for a period extending up to one-half of the maximum period of imprisonment specified for that offence (other than an offence for which the punishment of death has been specified as one of the punishments), the Court shall release the accused on bail.

Bharatiya Nagarik Suraksha Sanhita (BNSS), 2023 expanded this significantly: Section 479 BNSS now extends this benefit to first-time offenders (those who have not been previously convicted of any offence) where the period of detention during investigation, inquiry or trial has reached one-third (instead of one-half) of the maximum imprisonment.[156]

154 Code of Criminal Procedure, 1973, §§ 437, 439; Bharatiya Nagarik Suraksha Sanhita, 2023, §§ 480, 483.

155 Code of Criminal Procedure, 1973, § 436A; Bharatiya Nagarik Suraksha Sanhita, 2023, § 479.

156 Bharatiya Nagarik Suraksha Sanhita, 2023, § 479.

Landmark Cases in Bail Jurisprudence

1. Maneka Gandhi v. Union of India (1978) 1 SCC 248[157]

The Supreme Court held that the right to personal liberty under Article 21 is not merely procedural but substantive. Any procedure restricting liberty must be just, fair, and reasonable. This case forms the bedrock of bail jurisprudence — deprivation of liberty through prolonged detention without bail violates Article 21.

2. Hussainara Khatoon v. State of Bihar (1979) 3 SCC 544[158]

A landmark PIL where the Supreme Court directed the release of thousands of under-trial prisoners who had been in jail for periods exceeding the maximum sentence for the offences they were charged with. The Court held that speedy trial is a fundamental right under Article 21, and failure to provide bail in such circumstances is unconstitutional. This directly led to the introduction of Section 436A Cr.P.C.

3. Sanjay Chandra v. CBI (2012) 1 SCC 40 (2G Spectrum Case)[159]

The Supreme Court, while dealing with bail in the 2G spectrum case, reiterated that 'bail is the rule and jail is the exception' even in economic offences. The Court held that the purpose of bail is not punitive and that financial capacity and seriousness of charge alone cannot be the basis for denial of bail.

---

157 *Maneka Gandhi v. Union of India*, (1978) 1 SCC 248 (India).

158 *Hussainara Khatoon v. State of Bihar*, (1979) 3 SCC 544 (India).

159 *Sanjay Chandra v. CBI*, (2012) 1 SCC 40 (India).

Key Cases on Section 437 CR.P.C. (Non-Bailable Offences)

1. State of U.P. v. Amarmani Tripathi (2005) 8 SCC 21[160]

The Supreme Court laid down the triple test for bail in non-bailable offences: (1) Likelihood of fleeing from justice; (2) Likelihood of tampering with evidence or influencing witnesses; and (3) Likelihood of repeating the offence. These factors remain the cornerstone of all bail decisions under Section 437 Cr.P.C. / Section 480 BNSS.

2. Arnesh Kumar v. State of Bihar (2014) 8 SCC 273[161]

Addressed the power of arrest under Section 498A IPC / Section 85 BNS. The Supreme Court directed that police must apply the tests under Section 41 Cr.P.C. before effecting an arrest, and Magistrates must satisfy themselves before authorizing detention. This case significantly restricted mechanical arrests and thereby preserved the right to bail in many matrimonial cases.

3. Dataram Singh v. State of U.P. (2018) 3 SCC 22[162]

The Supreme Court reaffirmed that bail is the rule and jail is the exception. The Court held that a bail order cannot be cancelled merely because the prosecution moved a revision — there must be supervening circumstances such as misuse of liberty, violation of conditions, or fresh material. Courts must be sensitive to the deprivation of personal liberty.

160 *State of U.P. v. Amarmani Tripathi*, (2005) 8 SCC 21 (India).

161 *Arnesh Kumar v. State of Bihar*, (2014) 8 SCC 273 (India).

162 *Dataram Singh v. State of U.P.*, (2018) 3 SCC 22 (India).

Key Cases On Anticipatory Bail (S. 438 CR.P.C. / S. 482 BNSS)

1. Gurbaksh Singh Sibbia v. State of Punjab (1980) 2 SCC 565[163]

This is the landmark Constitution Bench judgment on anticipatory bail. The Supreme Court held that Section 438 Cr.P.C. must be liberally construed and courts should not impose unduly restrictive conditions. The anticipatory bail operates from the moment of arrest. Courts cannot impose the condition of surrendering to custody before seeking anticipatory bail.

2. Siddharam Satlingappa Mhetre v. State of Maharashtra (2011) 1 SCC 694[164]

The Supreme Court comprehensively discussed anticipatory bail and held that courts should lean in favour of granting anticipatory bail unless there are very strong reasons to the contrary. The Court also clarified that anticipatory bail can be granted for an indefinite period and need not be limited to a brief period. Interim anticipatory bail pending hearing is permissible.

3. Sushila Aggarwal v. State (NCT of Delhi) (2020) 5 SCC 1[165]

A Constitution Bench of the Supreme Court held that anticipatory bail granted under Section 438 Cr.P.C. does not automatically end upon the filing of a chargesheet or framing of charges.

---

163 *Gurbaksh Singh Sibbia v. State of Punjab*, (1980) 2 SCC 565 (India).

164 *Siddharam Satlingappa Mhetre v. State of Maharashtra*, (2011) 1 SCC 694 (India).

165 *Sushila Aggarwal v. State (NCT of Delhi)*, (2020) 5 SCC 1 (India).

It can be absolute (without time limit) unless the court expressly limits it. The court can impose conditions while granting anticipatory bail.

Key Cases On Default Bail (S. 167(2) CR.P.C. / S. 187(2) BNSS)

1. Rakesh Kumar Paul v. State of Assam (2017) 15 SCC 67[166]

The Supreme Court held that the right to default bail under Section 167(2) Cr.P.C. is an indefeasible right that accrues on non-filing of chargesheet within the prescribed period. Once the accused exercises this right, it cannot be extinguished even by subsequent filing of chargesheet. The bail cannot be cancelled on this ground alone.

2. Uday Mohanlal Acharya v. State of Maharashtra (2001) 5 SCC 453[167]

The Supreme Court clarified that the right to bail under Section 167(2) Cr.P.C. is an inviolable right. Even if bail is not availed within a certain period, the right does not lapse unless there is a deliberate waiver. The accused can exercise this right at any time before a chargesheet is filed.

166 *Rakesh Kumar Paul v. State of Assam*, (2017) 15 SCC 67 (India).

167 *Uday Mohanlal Acharya v. State of Maharashtra*, (2001) 5 SCC 453 (India).

Key Cases on Special/Stringent Bail Laws (PMLA, NDPS, UAPA)

1. Union of India v. K.A. Najeeb (2021) 3 SCC 713[168]

The Supreme Court held that even under the stringent UAPA (Unlawful Activities Prevention Act), the constitutional court (High Court or Supreme Court) can grant bail under Article 32/226 if the accused has been in prolonged custody and the trial is unlikely to conclude soon, as continued incarceration would violate Article 21.

2. Vijay Madanlal Choudhary v. Union of India (2022) 4 SCC 321[169]

The Supreme Court upheld the twin conditions of PMLA (Prevention of Money Laundering Act) bail — (1) the court must be satisfied that there are reasonable grounds for believing the accused is not guilty, and (2) that the accused is not likely to commit any offence while on bail. These conditions are constitutionally valid.

3. Nikesh Tarachand Shah v. Union of India (2017) 18 SCC 372[170]

The Supreme Court struck down the provision in PMLA that denied bail on the basis of prior conviction in a scheduled offence, holding it unconstitutional under Articles 14 and 21. This was the first major case striking down a bail restriction provision.

---

168 *Union of India v. K.A. Najeeb*, (2021) 3 SCC 713 (India).

169 *Vijay Madanlal Choudhary v. Union of India*, (2022) 4 SCC 321 (India).

170 *Nikesh Tarachand Shah v. Union of India*, (2017) 18 SCC 372 (India).

Conclusion

Bail law in India reflects a careful constitutional balance between the state's interest in prosecuting crime and the individual's fundamental right to personal liberty under **Article 21**. From the mandatory bail in bailable offences to the discretionary regime in non-bailable offences, from anticipatory bail to default bail, the law provides multiple safeguards at each stage of criminal proceedings. The enactment of the BNSS, 2023 has introduced significant modernizations, particularly the liberalization of the half-sentence default bail rule in favour of first-time offenders (Section 479 BNSS), the introduction of electronic monitoring as a bail condition, and enhanced procedural safeguards around arrest. The BNS, 2023 has also redefined several offences and their classifications, directly impacting bail eligibility.

The overarching principle emerging from decades of Supreme Court jurisprudence from '*Hussainara Khatoon*' to '*Sanjay Chandra*' to '*Dataram Singh*', is that ***"Bail is the rule, Jail is the exception"***.[171] Under-trial detention must be the last resort, not the default. Courts are duty- bound to consider bail applications expeditiously and liberally, reserving incarceration only where the interests of justice inescapably demand it.

---

171 *Hussainara Khatoon v. State of Bihar*, (1979) 3 SCC 544 (India); *Sanjay Chandra v. CBI*, (2012) 1 SCC 40 (India); *Dataram Singh v. State of U.P.*, (2018) 3 SCC 22 (India).

Chapter 7

Judicial Mandates Vs. Ground Reality: Enforcement of CCTV Installation in Police Stations

Mr. Mandeep Baisala
Advocate, High Court of Delhi.

Priyanshi Gupta
Student of BALLB, Maharaja Agrasen Institute of Management Studies, Affiliated to GGSIPU, Delhi.

Abstract

Powers given to the investigation agencies are only limited to the investigation and collecting evidence, but in reality, it is not limited to it. Agencies are misusing their power and several times accused in their custody face force, injury, or in some serious cases, it leads to custodial death. This Chapter focus on the Custodial Violence and Enforcement of Judicial Mandate by state and its functioneries. In the past few years, over 11,600 custodial deaths have been reported in India, which is completely against Article 14 and 21 of our constitution. Apex Court in Paramvir Singh Saini vs. Baljit Singh & Ors. 2020 gave directions that all the Police Stations in the country, must be entirely covered by CCTV cameras equipped with microphones and night vision to prevent such incidents and increase accountability of agencies. After several years of these directions, their effective enforcement is missing, despite these directions being in furtherance of the fundamental rights of each citizen of India guaranteed under Article 21. Article 21 guarantees the right to life and personal liberty, which includes freedom from torture and other cruel, inhuman, or degrading treatment or punishment. Delhi, being the capital of the country, lacks its effective implementation; as per RTI information received out of 224 Police Stations, only 204 have made the compliance of these directions. Police Stations in Gautam Budh Nagar have only 5 cameras in each station under their jurisdiction to cover the entire Police Station, and several Police Stations in Ghaziabad have only 2 cameras installed, which also lack proper working and microphone facilities. In recent times, several incidents are reported of violation of human rights of citizens inside Police Stations, so the effective implementation of these directions is crucial in light of the statutory duty u/s 56 BNSS to take reasonable care of the health and safety of the accused.

Introduction

In the criminal justice system, the powers conferred upon investigative agencies are limited to the investigation and collecting the evidence to help prosecutor to prove the alleged offense against the accused beyond reasonable doubt. Indian criminal jurisprudence does not formally define the term 'custodial violence, the term combines ***custody*** (meaning lawful detention or safekeeping) with *violence*, referring to physical or psychological harm inflicted on a person in police or judicial custody. During the 2023-2024 National Human Right Commission received almost 2,346 new intimations concerning death in judicial custody, and 160 intimations of death in police custody, which constitutes a violation of Articles 14 and 21 of the Constitution. This brutal state of custody might be due to several reasons such as Belief in Force by Officials, Weak Training of officials, Corruption, Social Approval, Poor working conditions and High Pressure, etc. To bring the accountability and transparency in investigation, inquiry etc during Police Custody, Supreme Court in 2020 with aim to increase accountability and transparency issued directions to install the CCTV Cameras in all Police Stations in India covering all the parts of Police Station equipped with microphone and night vision. Direction given by Supreme Court were essential to protect fundamental right to life and dignity enshrined under Article 21 of Constitution. In recent months, there has been a noticeable surge in violence by Police officials inside the Police Station. It is become very important to make the officials accountable for their fault and bring transparency into the criminal justice mechanism to maintain the Rule of Law. This Chapter aims to examine the effectiveness of CCTV surveillance in police stations as a tool for ensuring accountability, and to analyse the gaps in its implementation across jurisdictions

Need for Cctv Cameras in Police Station

In recent time several incidents have been reported of Custodial Violence which is violation of statutory rights, fundamental rights and international conventions. The Power to investigate vest with the agencies who usually misuse them by physically/mentally harassing them, torturing them, sometimes they step into the shoes of judiciary by giving punishment to them without trial. Fundamental Rights of accused or arrested persons are also protected and agencies cannot encroach upon them. Most commonly during the police custody agencies attempt to pressurize the accused for making the confession statement by using force also but that confession does not have any evidentiary value as per Section 181 of BNSS. Article 20(3): Protects an individual from being compelled to be a witness against themselves. This provision directly addresses the issue of forced confessions extracted under torture or coercion, which are a common feature in custodial interrogations. In **D.K. Basu etc. v. State of West Bengal**[172], Supreme Court described 'custodial torture' as a naked violation of human dignity and degradation that destroys self-esteem of the victim and does not even spare his personality. Custodial torture observed the Court is a calculated assault on human dignity and whenever human dignity is wounded, civilization takes a step backwards. Even the **Third Report of the National Police Commission in India** expressed its deep concern with custodial violence and lock-up deaths, also mentioned that the power to arrest without warrant mechanically giving rise to the chances of corruption. Article 21 of Indian Constitution states that no one shall be deprived of life and personal liberty, expression **"Life and Personal Liberty"** has been held to include the right to live with human dignity and thus it would also include within itself a guarantee against torture and assault by the state or its functionaries. The Universal Declaration of Human Rights in 1948, which marked the emergence of a worldwide trend of protection and guarantee of certain basic human rights, stipulates in Article 5 that "No one shall be subjected to torture or to cruel, inhumane or degrading treatment or punishment". Despite the pious declaration and fundamental right, the crime continued unbated. We can at least put some resistance to it by installing CCTV Cameras in Police Stations and Prisons.

172 D.K. Basu etc. v. State of West Bengal etc. MANU/SC/0157/1997

Judicial Mandate

Supreme Court, in case of **Paramvir Singh Saini vs. Baljit Singh and Ors[173].**, delivered by three judge bench of apex court in furtherance of fundamental rights of each citizen of India guaranteed under Article 21 laid down specific guidelines to install the CCTV Cameras equipped with the microphone and night vision and that CCTV cameras are installed at all entry and exit points; main gate of the police station; all lock-ups; all corridors; lobby/the reception area; all verandas/ outhouses, Inspector's room; Sub-Inspector's room; areas outside the lock-up room; station hall; in front of the police station compound; outside (not inside) washrooms/toilets; Duty Officer's room; back part of the police station etc. in all police stations and offices of other investigation agencies in country. Further Apex Court Constituted the oversight committee at state and district level to ensure the installation and effective working of those cameras along with monitoring the non-reported violation of human rights. At Police Station Level, Station House officer (SHO) shall be responsible for the proper working of CCTVs and if any fault arises it shall be duty of SHO to immediately report to District Committee. Recording of the CCTVs shall be stored for the 18 months and in any case it shall not be below 1 year and backed by centralized monitoring system. Adequate funds for the same, which must be done by the States'/Union Territories' Finance Departments at the very earliest.

Human Rights Court- Apex Court further held that there must be setup of Human Right Court in every district as per Section 30 of Protection of Human Right Act, 1993. In case of any violence in custody resulting into the injury or custodial death, such person may report the issue to State Commission or Court. Such court then

173 Paramvir Singh Saini vs. Baljit Singh and Ors, MANU/SC/0908/2020

immediately summon the footage of the incident for its safe keeping, which may then be made available to an investigation agency in order to further process the complaint made to it.

Role of Technology in Criminal Justice System- Installation of CCTV Cameras in Police Station was developed to bring accountability and transparency in system and if any violence or abuse of Human right ever happens, in such case victim shall have an option to report such incident and get the CCTV footage as evidence, by the videography, crucial evidence can be captured and presented in a credible manner. For fulfilling the mandate of Section 65B(4) for its admissibility as evidence, Supreme Court in **Shafhi Mohammad and Ors. vs. The State of Himachal Pradesh and Ors.**[174] held that legal position on the subject on the admissibility of the electronic evidence, especially by a party who is not in possession of device from which the document is produced. Such party cannot be required to produce certificate Under Section 65B(4) of the Evidence Act. The applicability of requirement of certificate being procedural can be relaxed by Court wherever interest of justice so justifies. Effective implementation of this will definitely lower the corruption, illegal detention or arrest, violence and abuse etc. This direction given by the Apex Court in **Paramvir Singh Saini** (*Supra*) was developed from catena of judgments advocating for the usage of technology in criminal system to procure and preserve evidence. Supreme Court noted in **K.H. Shekarappa V State of Karnataka**[175], it is "distressing" that torture continues to take place under the "shield of uniform and authority" within the four walls of a police station where victims are helpless.

---

174 Shafhi Mohammad and Ors. vs. The State of Himachal Pradesh and Ors. MANU/SC/0331/2018

175 K.H. Shekarappa and Ors. Vs. State of Karnataka, MANU/SC/1974/2009

In **Ziyauddin Burhanuddin Bukhari v. Brijmohan Ramdass Mehra and Ors**[176]**.,** Apex Court noted that new techniques and devices are the order of the day. Audio and video tape technology has emerged as a powerful medium through which a first-hand information can be gathered and can be crucial evidence. In **Ram Singh and Ors. v. Col. Ram Singh**[177]**,** Three Judge bench of Supreme Court discussed the issue of use of technology in evidence by referring to certain English and American judgments. **English** Judgments in **R. v. Maqsud Ali**[178], and **R. v. Robson**[179], and American Law as noted in **American Jurisprudence**[180], it will be wrong to deny to the law of evidence advantages to be gained by new techniques and new devices, provided the accuracy of the recording can be proved. Such evidence should always be regarded with some caution and assessed in the light of all the circumstances of each case. Electronic evidence was held to be admissible subject to safeguards adopted by the Court about the authenticity of the same. In **Tukaram S. Dighole v. Manikrao Shivaji Kokate**[181], the same principle was reiterated. This Court observed that new techniques and devices are order of the day. A Constitution Bench of Supreme Court in **Karnail Singh v. State of Haryana**[182] noted that technology is an important part in the system of police administration. Later in 2018 Supreme Court in **Shafhi Mohammad (***Supra)* the time is ripe that steps are taken to introduce videography in investigation, particularly for crime scene as desirable and acceptable best practice as

176 Ziyauddin Burhanuddin Bukhari v. Brijmohan Ramdass Mehra and Ors., MANU/SC/0277/1975

177 Ram Singh and Ors. v. Col. Ram Singh, MANU/SC/0176/1985

178 R. v. Maqsud Ali, (1965) 2 All ER 464

179 R. v. Robson, (1972) 2 ALL ER 699

180 2d (Vol. 29) page 494

181 Tukaram S. Dighole v. Manikrao Shivaji Kokate, MANU/SC/0086/2010

182 Karnail Singh v. State of Haryana, MANU/SC/1323/2009

suggested by the Committee of the MHA to strengthen the Rule of Law. Further Supreme Court constituted the Central Oversight Body (COB) and also directed that the COB to issue appropriate directions so as to ensure that use of videography becomes a reality in a phased manner. Prior to **Paramvir Singh Saini** Judgment, Supreme Court in **Dilip K. Basu Vs. State of West Bengal and Ors.**[183] directed State Governments to take steps to install CCTV cameras in all the prisons in their respective States, within a period of one year from today but not later than two years and also consider to install CCTV Cameras in Police Stations in phased manner. SC in judgment categorically stated that "CCTV cameras will help go a long way in preventing violation of human rights of those incarcerating in jails". It will also help the authorities in maintaining proper discipline among the inmates and taking corrective measures wherever abuses are noticed.

Implementation of Paramvir Singh Saini Judgment

Even after Supreme Court directions, custodial violence is still happening because CCTV rules are not properly followed. Despite direction given by Supreme Court in **Paramvir Singh Saini** (*Supra)* and **Dilip K. Basu Vs. State of West Bengal** (*Supra)* to install CCTV cameras to prevent the custodial violence and protect the human rights of citizens. Considerable amount of time has passed after giving judgment but no effective implementation has been observed. Supreme Court had to take Suo Moto Writ Petition namely **"IN RE: LACK OF FUNCTIONAL CCTVs IN POLICE STATIONS"** has been registered pursuant to the cognizance taken on News Paper report, as per report around 11 lives were in police custody in Rajasthan but the efforts to procure CCTV footage from the police stations concerned,

183 Dilip K. Basu Vs. State of West Bengal and Ors. MANU/SC/0799/2015

proved futile because the information was denied/not provided on frivolous grounds as has been delineated in the order. Response-Affidavit has been filed by the State of Rajasthan on 12th October 2025, showing shocking state of Compliance, around 135 Police Station are not equipped with CCTV Cameras, no CCTV cameras installed in the interrogation rooms,video footage recorded through the installed CCTV cameras is preserved only for a period 45 days and not centralized monitoring system. At present Suo Moto Writ is pending for adjudication before Supreme Court.

The condition of CCTV surveillance in the National Capital Region (NCR) is far from satisfactory, as per RTI information received there are 224 Police Stations in Delhi and out of 224 only 204 are covered with CCTV coverage[184]. That 204 police stations are also not fully complied with Paramvir Singh Saini (Supra) judgment, on visiting several stations in Delhi all area of Police Station as mentioned in Judgment are not fully covered by CCTV cameras. Condition becomes more alarming when we move towards the Ghaziabad and Gautam Budh Nagar districts of NCR, as per RTI information in Ghaziabad each police station have been covered by only 'Two CCTVs' and in worst case those Two CCTVs are also not functioning in few Police Stations of Ghaziabad. PS Muradnagar have only 2 unit those are also not functioning, PS Nawada have 6 units, PS Masuri have only 5 units, PS Ko Nagar have only 4 units, PS Crossing Republic and PS Wave City have only 3 units, PS Sahibabad, Khoda & Link Road have only 5 units each, PS Indrapuran only have 6 units, PS Tronica City and Loni do not have microphone and night vision facility[185]. RTI information received for Gautam Budh Nagar reveals that all

184 RTI information vide letter dt. 15.01.2026 bearing no. 251226/DEPOL/R/E/25/11518/126

185 RTI information dt. 28.01.2026 bearing letter no. 353/05/(1594)/2025

station in Gautam Budh Nagar have only 5 unit in each Station[186]. It is very strange to observe that how can two CCTV Cameras are able to fully comply with the SC judgment which says that from Cabins to back door all area must be under surveillance of CCTV Cameras equipped with microphone and night vision. In Gautam Budh Nagar all Police Stations are having Five CCTV Cameras installed to Cover whole police station which is practically impossible to cover whole Police Station with help of five cameras. Inquiries into districts like Lucknow, Kanpur, Ghaziabad, Bahraich, and Lakhimpur Kheri painted a picture of administrative apathy. Instead of the mandated 12–18 months of storage, police stations reported retention periods that are practically useless for any victim seeking justice: Kanpur (Naubasta Police Station): A meager seven days of retention, Kanpur (Barra Police Station): Fifteen days, Lucknow (Chowk Police Station): Thirty days, Unnao (Kotwali Police Station): Forty-eight days and at other Police Station most of CCTV cameras are not functioning[187]. This information indicates shocking state of lack of action on the part of executive to strictly comply with the order of Judiciary in time bound manner, even in those cases which are directly concerned with the Fundamental Right should not be delitescent by authorities. Further this raise serious question, **Are CCTV cameras really effective, or are they just for formality?**

Examination of witnesses by the police under Section 180 of the Bharatiya Nagarik Suraksha Sanhita (BNSS) is generally conducted during investigation, often within police stations. Statements recorded under this provision do not have independent evidentiary value, as clarified under Section 181 of BNSS; however, they assume significance

186 RTI information dt. 29.01.2026 bearing letter no. RTI No. 415/2025

187 Article on Live Law by title- Custodial Violence And The CCTV Mirage: Why Rule Of Law Is Faltering In Uttar Pradesh

during trial for the limited purpose of establishing contradictions or omissions. In practice, there have been several instances where witnesses are subjected to coercion or pressure by police officials while recording such statements. The proviso to Section 180(3) permits recording of statements through audio-video electronic means, which reflects legislative intent to ensure transparency in the process. In this context, installation of CCTV cameras equipped with audio facilities in police stations can play a crucial role in capturing the circumstances under which such statements are made.

This becomes particularly important in light of judicial precedents such as *Parvat Singh and Ors. v. State of Madhya Pradesh*, where it has been reiterated that statements recorded during investigation can only be used for contradiction or omission. Therefore, CCTV surveillance can act as an effective safeguard against coercion, prevent tampering, and enhance accountability in the recording of witness statements.

Another significant concern is the misuse of police powers, including refusal to register FIRs, arbitrary detention, harassment of victims, and instances of mental and physical cruelty. Such abuse is often aggravated by corruption, where officials demand or accept bribes to perform—or refrain from performing—their legal duties, thereby subjecting individuals to further exploitation. The installation of CCTV cameras equipped with audio recording facilities, including within officials' cabins, can serve as an effective deterrent against such practices. Continuous digital recording creates a permanent record of police conduct, thereby discouraging misconduct due to the fear of accountability. Moreover, the availability of such electronic evidence can empower victims to report instances of abuse and strengthen their complaints by providing credible proof. In this way, CCTV surveillance can play a crucial role in promoting transparency, curbing corruption, and ensuring responsible exercise of police powers.

The most significant advantage of installing CCTV cameras in police stations lies in their potential to curb custodial violence, including assault and custodial deaths. It is a statutory duty of police officials to ensure the health and safety of persons in custody, as mandated under Section 56 of the Bharatiya Nagarik Suraksha Sanhita (BNSS). CCTV surveillance can effectively assist in monitoring compliance with these safeguards and ensure that such obligations are not violated in practice. In cases where incidents of custodial violence occur, the availability of CCTV footage provides victims with a reliable means to report such misconduct before a court of law and seek appropriate remedies. The presence of digital evidence significantly strengthens the credibility of such claims and reduces the possibility of denial or suppression by authorities.

Thus, the creation and preservation of electronic records not only facilitate accountability but also act as a strong deterrent against the misuse of power, ultimately contributing to the protection of fundamental rights within the criminal justice system.

Challenges in Effective Implementation of CCTV Surveillance

Effective implementation of CCTV Cameras in Police Station will definitely help in bringing the accountability and transparency in Criminal Justice machinery. At same time we have to be careful with subject the issues which can arise if ignored and such issues are Privacy, Tampering / disabling of CCTV (practical issue), Lack of independent monitoring, and Lack of technology-Electricity, storage and internet. Cyber activities are advancing day by day so we have to be very careful for the effective implementation of CCTV Cameras.

Privacy- Installation of CCTV Cameras inside Police Station equipped with microphone and night vision which simply means that it will record each and every moment inside the Police Station. Police Station is the place where most of investigation is carried out and strategies for law and order are prepared by Officials. If anything compromises these footages and recording it will hamper the privacy of official as well as arrested persons. As cybercrime is also at its peak, fraudsters are now using AI tools in crime so if they get access to these CCTV Cameras then it will affect the privacy of officials involved and integrity of investigation process which is something which need careful implementation and cyber security system for this CCTV infrastructure. Privacy no donut is one of the facets of Right to Life and Personal Liberty under Article 21 as held by Constitutional Bench held in **Justice K.S. Puttaswamy and Ors. Vs. Union of India (UOI) and Ors[188] MANU/SC/1054/2018.**

Tampering/ Disabling of CCTV- Idea to curb custodial violence and act as deterrent for corruption will become dormant if the person responsible (Station House Officer) for the maintenance of CCTV Cameras temper the recording, change the view angle of the Camera towards total stillness, not reporting the non-functional Cameras to District Committee. This issue if arises and left ignored by authorities will leave the whole idea paralysed.

Lack of independent monitoring- To make this judicial incentive to be more fruitful and effective authorities may constitute the independent committee to monitor the CCTV Footage of Police Station to curb the custodial violence and corruption. Independent committee can work with the help of the Human Right Committee

188 Justice K.S. Puttaswamy and Ors. Vs. Union of India (UOI) and Ors MANU/SC/1054/2018

which can take action if any mishappening happens inside the Police Station.

Lack of technology- Electricity, storage and internet; As per the Supreme Court guideline the recording shall be stored for the 18 months to 12 months for every police station. This needs a good quality and quantity of storage system which can store such large size of footage for 18 months. Such storage system also needs to be safe and secure so that no tampering or manipulation can be done. To work effectively such system needs continuous electricity or good backup during disturbed supply of electricity, any mishappening can also happen during the time when CCTV are not working due to disturbed supply of electricity. For pan India implementation of CCTV cameras need 24 hours supply of electricity with backup to work effectively. Along with electricity and storage CCTV Cameras needs high speed internet to work in a system, at present at Pan India level some part of India needs access to high-speed internet. State should take effective action to comply with the Judgment of Supreme Court.

Chapter 8

Between Cybercrime Enforcement and Digital Surveillance: Data Protection and Privacy Under the BNSS, 2023

Sakshi Rewaria
Faculty Member, Indian Institute of Management (IIM), Rohtak & practising Advocate, Supreme Court of India.

Abstract

The exponential rise of cybercrimes in India ranging from financial frauds and identity theft to cyberstalking, data breaches, ransomware attacks, and online radicalisation has fundamentally altered the landscape of criminal investigation and prosecution. As offences increasingly migrate to digital spaces, the Bharatiya Nagarik Suraksha Sanhita, 2023 introduces a technologically driven procedural regime that expands the use of electronic evidence, digital documentation, audio-video recording of investigations, and online proceedings. While these reforms are presented as necessary responses to emerging cyber threats, they simultaneously intensify pressing concerns about data protection. This chapter critically examines how the BNSS addresses cybercrime investigation while assessing whether adequate safeguards exist to prevent excessive data extraction, prolonged retention of digital records, intrusive surveillance practices, and unchecked police access to personal information. The absence of clearly articulated data governance standards, retention limits, and independent oversight mechanisms under BNSS is examined as a structural vulnerability that may normalise expansive surveillance under the justification of combating cybercrime. The study finds that although BNSS strengthens procedural tools to tackle digital offences, it does not sufficiently embed proportionality, necessity, and accountability safeguards into its technological framework. The chapter concludes that effective cybercrime control must coexist with enforceable privacy protections and transparent surveillance regulation to preserve the constitutional promise of a citizen-centric criminal justice system.

1. Introduction: Cybercrime and the Procedural Turn in Criminal Law

India is slowly realising one thing: crime is now online. As many aspects of daily life (phone usage, app usage, cloud-based data storage, social media) have become more common, so have criminals. Recent reports from the National Crime Records Bureau (NCRB) show drastic increases in reported cyber complaints and shifting trends regarding the types of cyber offences occurring in India's cities and states. These statistics tell two stories: one of increasing victimisation (the trend towards greater and more serious cybercrime) and the other of an inadequately prepared system striving to address the problem.[189]

189 National Crime Records Bureau. (2026). *Crime head-wise and State/UT-wise cyber crimes – IT Act cases during 2023*. Open Government Data (OGD) Platform India, Ministry of Home Affairs, Government of India. https://www.data.gov.in/resource/crime-head-wise-and-stateut-wise-cyber-crimes-it-act-cases-during-2023

The Indian legislature has made major reforms to the structure of the legal system in response to this gap in the existing legal framework. The Bharatiya Nagarik Suraksha Sanhita, 2023 (BNSS) is a complete overhaul of the criminal procedure code designed to allow law enforcement agencies to conduct investigations using the latest technological developments. It brings criminal procedures into line with modern times by providing for the use of electronic evidence in investigations. It outlines provisions regarding audio-video recordings, digital documentation, and video/telephone hearings to obtain evidence as quickly as possible and to ensure the integrity and uniformity of the manner in which evidence is handled by law enforcement agencies.

This change in procedures is essential, given that digital criminal activity can occur anywhere in the world and the relevant evidence may be stored on servers far from the crime scene. The existing options of a search warrant and a paper record are nowhere near sufficient.[190] Most criminal investigators today depend on forensic science, digital device imaging, and metadata analysis to gather evidence for prosecution.

Modern technology doesn't just change how things are done; it changes how power works. Governments can use the enormous amount of information they have available through huge data sets, devices and the metadata associated with them to monitor you every single day at an unprecedented level. Passage of BNSS expands the criteria (i.e. the basis) on which law enforcement can employ digital searches and/or use electronic information as evidence at court. These powers may become standard if strong protections are not put in place to limit them. If so, they could create an imbalance between individual rights and state powers.

190 Dhaker, A. K. (2025). Artificial Intelligence and the Evolution of Criminal Trial Procedures: A Comparative Study of CRPC, 1973 And BNSS, 2023. *Anusandhanvallari*, 3555-3562.

The Indian Constitution provides that every person has the fundamental right to informational privacy, as set out by the Supreme Court of India in K.S. Puttaswamy v. Union of India[191]. The interpretation of privacy as founded upon the constitutional right to be free from interference by others holds that the government has legitimate reasons for intruding into individual privacy, and any such intrusion will be subject to the principles of legality, necessity, and proportionality in law.[192] Consequently, the principles established by Puttaswamy will apply to the interpretation of BNSS as a constitutional instrument.

2. The Expanding Landscape of Cybercrime in India

India's digital journey has been nothing short of exceptional; there are now over 850 million internet users with 88.25 million users at the end of March,23 which lead to yearly growth of 6.83% from 2022[193]; substantial growth in UPI payments; onboarded almost 376 banks to facilitate 730 crore transactions in volume worth Rs. 11.9 lakh Crore[194], and mobile devices are now ubiquitous, making it very easy for people to communicate with one another through email, text message, and social media. However, it also means that criminals now

191 *K.S. Puttaswamy (Retd.) v. Union of India*, (2017) 10 SCC 1 (Supreme Court of India)

192 Chatterjee, S. (2019). Is data privacy a fundamental right in India? An analysis and recommendations from policy and legal perspective. *International Journal of Law and Management*, *61*(1), 170-190.

193 Telecom Regulatory Authority of India. (2024). *The Indian telecom services performance indicators (Yearly performance indicators 2022–2023)*. Government of India. https://www.trai.gov.in/sites/default/files/PIR_12032024_0.pdf

194 Ministry of Electronics and Information Technology. (n.d.). *Growth story*. Government of India. https://www.digitalindia.gov.in/growth-story/

have a larger area to operate in, which has increased the number of cyber crimes committed over the last few years and how frequently they occur. Cyber crimes are no longer a specialty; they are one of the fastest-growing types of crime committed in the country.[195]

The National Crime Records Bureau (NCRB) reports that in 2022 there were 65,893 recorded cyber crime occurrences.[196] In 2021, the total number of reported cybercrimes was only 52,974[197]. The rate of reported cyber crimes (4.8 per lakh population) has continued to increase significantly. More than 60 percent of known cyber crimes were committed for profit. The fact that these are not isolated events; they represent an ongoing effort to exploit the technological infrastructure for profit[198]. I4C (Indian Cyber Crime Coordination Centre), which operates under the Ministry of Home Affairs, recognizes how large the threat is. In 2023, the government reported to Parliament that more than 13 lakh complaints were filed on the National Cyber Crime Reporting Portal related to financial cyber fraud in a single year, resulting in reported losses of many thousands of crores, and that

---

195 Tripathy, S. S. (2025). A comprehensive survey of cybercrimes in India over the last decade. *arXiv preprint arXiv:2505.23770.*

196 Press Information Bureau. (2024, February 7). *Increase in cyber crimes.* Ministry of Home Affairs, Government of India. https://www.pib.gov.in/PressReleaseIframePage.aspx?PRID=2003505

197 Press Information Bureau. (2024, February 7). *Increase in cyber crimes.* Ministry of Home Affairs, Government of India. https://www.pib.gov.in/PressReleaseIframePage.aspx?PRID=2003505

198 National Crime Records Bureau. (2022). *Crime in India 2021 (Vol. II).* Ministry of Home Affairs, Government of India. https://ncrb.gov.in/uploads/nationalcrimerecordsbureau/custom/1678700177Crime%20in%20India%202021%20Vol %202.pdf

this number had increased to more than 24 lakh as of 2025.[199] By using the 1930 Helpline and Citizens' Reporting of Financial Fraud Systems, law enforcement agencies were successfully able to secure more than Rs. 8,19 Crore in more than 23.61 Lakh complaints.[200] This demonstrates both the extent of damage as well as the need for prompt responses to incidents.

2.1 Financial Frauds, Identity Theft and Phishing

Financial fraud dominates the cybercrime profile in India, with the majority of cases involving cheating and online fraud. This includes OTP fraud, UPI scams, fake investment apps, harassment from loan apps, and impersonating as a bank official.

The Ministry has issued numerous warnings about fraudsters exploiting the digital payment ecosystem. For instance, billions of UPI transactions processed each month in 2023-24 means any percentage of users that misuse the service could be responsible for a significant amount of fraud.[201] Fraudsters also use phishing, fake KYC alerts and remote access applications to obtain a user's banking credentials.

Another area of increased concern is Identity theft. The use of Aadhaar for fraud and SIM swapping, and fake social media accounts have become popular tools to defraud others. Over 50 lakh mobile connections connected through fake documentation have been

---

199 Press Information Bureau. (2026, February 11). *Cyber crime reporting and investigation*. Ministry of Home Affairs, Government of India. https://www.pib.gov.in/PressReleasePage.aspx?PRID=2226441

200 Press Information Bureau. (2026, February 11). *Cyber crime reporting and investigation*. Ministry of Home Affairs, Government of India. https://www.pib.gov.in/PressReleasePage.aspx?PRID=2226441

201 Reserve Bank of India. (2024). *Annual report 2023–24*. Government of India. https://www.rbi.org.in

blocked according to enforcement actions with the Department of Telecommunications on investigation of cyber fraud.[202] These statistics illustrate the presence of organized networks rather than independent criminals. Financial cybercrime is attractive due to its scalability.

2.2 Ransomware, Data Breaches and Cyber Terrorism

India is one of the most frequent targets of ransomware attacks worldwide.[203] The extent of this threat was highlighted in the 2023 Annual Report from CERT-In which documented more than 1.5 million cybersecurity incidents over the previous twelve months.[204] These incidents encompassed various forms of malicious activity, including malware infections, phishing campaigns, adversary-induced intrusions into websites, and ransomware attacks.

Ransomware attacks have affected many sectors, including hospitals, schools, and public sector organizations. In many cases, the attackers encrypted the databases containing highly sensitive information before demanding ransom payments in cryptocurrency. CERT-In reports that modern ransomware actors are increasingly using "living off the land" techniques, which leverage legitimate administrative tools to evade detection. As worrisome as ransomware attacks are,

202 Press Information Bureau. (2023, August 17). *Two reforms introduced for mobile user protection and prevention of telecom fraud.* Department of Telecommunications, Ministry of Communications, Government of India. https://www.pib.gov.in/PressReleasePage.aspx?PRID=1949957

203 Sabharwal, S., & Sharma, S. (2019). Ransomware attack: India issues red alert. In *Emerging Technology in Modelling and Graphics: Proceedings of IEM Graph 2018* (pp. 471-484). Singapore: Springer Singapore.

204 Indian Computer Emergency Response Team. (2023). *Annual report 2022.* Ministry of Electronics and Information Technology, Government of India. https://www.cert-in.org.in

data breaches are even worse. Sensitive personal information, health records, and financial information have all been found for sale on dark web marketplaces.[205] When government databases are compromised, the cost of a data breach is much higher than simply the privacy costs experienced by individuals.[206]

2.3 Platform-Based Crimes and Transnational Dimensions

Most cybercrime is driven by the platforms on which they happen. For example, the misuse of social media, encrypted messaging applications, video game consoles, and marketplaces is common.[207]

Cyber fraud networks often operate across state borders as well as between countries. The flow of money is often routed through a series of mule accounts on a non-disclosed basis. The use of cryptocurrency wallets obfuscates the identities of those committing the fraud.[208] The servers that host these accounts typically exist outside of India and a large number of requests for Mutual Legal Assistance from other jurisdictions may take a long time to process. As a result, by the time the relevant data arrives, it may have already been erased.

---

205 HIPAA Journal. (2026, February 26). *Healthcare data breach statistics.* https://www.hipaajournal.com/healthcare-data-breach-statistics/

206 Tanwar, S., Paul, T., Singh, K., Joshi, M., & Rana, A. (2020, June). Classification and imapct of cyber threats in India: a review. In *2020 8th International Conference on Reliability, Infocom Technologies and Optimization (Trends and Future Directions)(ICRITO)* (pp. 129-135). IEEE.

207 Gordon, S., & Ford, R. (2006). On the definition and classification of cybercrime. *Journal in computer virology*, *2*(1), 13-20.

208 Atrey, I. (2023). Cybercrime and its Legal Implications: Analysing the challenges and Legal frameworks surrounding Cybercrime, including issues related to Jurisdiction, Privacy, and Digital Evidence. *International Journal of Research and Analytical Reviews*, *10*(3).

The Ministry of Home Affairs advised Parliament that it has traced several large classified cyber fraud rings to major organised international Networks which proves that cybercrime can not necessarily be categorised strictly as domestic and has an international dimension as well.[209] Digital platforms create substantial complexity with respect to regulatory matters including the following three issues: (1) intermediaries; (2) data accessibility; and (3) encryption policies; all of which compel law enforcement officials to operate within the constraints of the existing laws in an effort to achieve timely access to digital evidence.

3. Investigative Challenges in Digital Environments

Technical knowledge is required for analysing cybercrime. Digital evidence can change quickly, so logs can be deleted within seconds and data can be stored on the cloud at several locations in different jurisdictions.[210] The chain of custody needs to be preserved, and forensic imaging must be accurate, as even a tiny procedural mistake can result in weakening a prosecution.

Gaps in capacity must be addressed; police departments do not have evenly distributed cyber forensic laboratories across the nation, and officers need training on an ongoing basis. The government is investing in I4C cyber forensic training programmes, but there is

209 Press Information Bureau. (2026, February 11). *Cyber crime reporting and investigation*. Ministry of Home Affairs, Government of India. https://www.pib.gov.in/PressReleasePage.aspx?PRID=2226441

210 Karia, T. D. (2008). Digital Evidence: An Indian Perspective. *Digital Evidence & Elec. Signature L. Rev.*, *5*, 214.

currently an enormous demand for that training, and the programme's capacity cannot keep pace.[211]

The Supreme Court's decision in Justice K.S. Puttaswamy v. Union of India (2017)[212] established that there is a fundamental right to possess and control one's personal information. Furthermore, if the state wishes to intrude upon one's right to privacy, it must do so in a manner that is lawful, necessary, and proportionate to its goal; therefore, this framework is crucial in the context of cybercrime. The ability to expand police investigative powers must not undermine constitutionally guaranteed rights. The number of cybercrimes committed within India has been steadily increasing over time. The government has consistently monitored these changes with its own data, and its research has verified that cases of cybercrime are on the rise.[213] We are also seeing a large amount of financial loss and an increase in reported cases of cyber security incidents.

4. Procedural Modernisation Under the Bharatiya Nagarik Suraksha Sanhita, 2023

India's criminal process has undergone a transformation with the introduction of the Bharatiya Nagarik Suraksha Sanhita, 2023 (BNSS), which replaces the old colonial Criminal Procedure Code, 1973. This new law does not simply replace old words for new ones;

211 Prakash, N., & Duhan, D. R. (2020). Computer forensic investigation process and judicial response to the digital evidence in India in light of rule of best evidence. *International Journal in Management and Social Science*, *8*(05).

212 *K.S. Puttaswamy (Retd.) v. Union of India*, (2017) 10 SCC 1 (Supreme Court of India)

213 Iqbal, J., & Beigh, B. M. (2017). Cybercrime in India: Trends and challenges. *International Journal of Innovations & Advancement in Computer Science*, *6*(12), 187-196.

rather, it replaces the way things used to be done. Crime has now become digital, as has evidence for prosecution and communication between parties. Therefore, it follows that courts should no longer rely solely on paper to conduct their business.

4.1 Recognition of Electronic Evidence

The BNSS brings together provisions on crime under the Criminal Procedure Code (CrPC) and the Evidence Act. Under the new Indian Evidence Act, electronic records are now admissible as evidence. Examples of electronic records are emails, CCTV footage, server logs, call detail records, metadata and digital files.[214] Section 176 of the BNSS authorises police officers to enter and search premises and seize evidence from digital devices. Digital devices can now form the basis of prosecution; for example, laptops, mobile phones and storage devices.[215]

Judicial recognition has already been given to the important role played by electronic evidence. In Anvar P.V. v. P.K. Basheer (2014)[216], the Supreme Court held that electronic evidence must meet the statutory certification requirements. In Arjun Panditrao Khotkar v. Kailash Kushanrao Gorantyal (2020)[217], the Court reaffirmed that there are strict evidentiary requirements of compliance with Section 65B of the Evidence Act. The decisions of the Supreme Court indicate that whilst digital evidence is powerful, it must comply with

214 Karia, T., Anand, A., & Dhawan, B. (2015). The Supreme Court of India re-defines admissibility of electronic evidence in India. *Digital Evidence & Elec. Signature L. Rev.*, *12*, 33.

215 The Bharatiya Nagarik Suraksha Sanhita, 2023, § 176 (India).

216 *Anvar P.V. v. P.K. Basheer*, (2014) 10 SCC 473 (Supreme Court of India).

217 *Arjun Panditrao Khotkar v. Kailash Kushanrao Gorantyal*, (2020) 7 SCC 1 (Supreme Court of India).

procedural requirements. The BNSS creates an enhanced framework for investigating electronic evidence. The BNSS acknowledges that, in today's world, the serious crimes take place on a computer instead of at the street.

4.2 Digital Documentation and e-Records

The foundation of Criminal Procedure is built upon the documentation created in furtherance of its processes. Previously, the majority of documentation used in Criminal Procedure, including FIR's, Statements, and Case Diary notes, was comprised primarily of handwritten documents. Consequently, there were frequently complaints of delay and malfeasance related to the submission and completion of documentation in Criminal Procedure.

Section 173 of the BNSS authorises the registration of an FIR in electronic format, thereby legitimising the registration of an FIR electronically.[218] This provision is indicative of the current state of the National Crime Reporting Portal and state-level e-FIR systems, both of which are already operational. In addition, the provisions of Section 193 permit the submission of an Electronic Police Report (Charge Sheet) to the Court, reducing paperwork and increasing the ability to trace documents under the Criminal Procedure.[219] Digital records allow for audit trails of documentation and are less susceptible to modification, therefore creating greater evidentiary integrity and institutional accountability. The creation of digital case diaries will provide additional transparency in Criminal Procedure; senior members of law enforcement will be able to supervise and monitor the creation of electronically generated documentation in "real-time."

218 The Bharatiya Nagarik Suraksha Sanhita, 2023, § 173 (India).

219 The Bharatiya Nagarik Suraksha Sanhita, 2023, § 193 (India).

4.3 Audio-Video Recording of Investigation and Statements

The federal BNSS has made significant reforms by requiring that audio and video recordings in investigations be documented. This can be done using mobile or other electronic recording devices when conducting searches and seizures under section 176(3) of BNSS. The purpose of this amendment is to minimize incidents of false evidence or coercion being accused by the police or investigators.[220]

In addition, section 183 of BNSS provides for the use of audio visual and electronic devices to record witness testimony.[221] This will also improve the reliability of evidence. It will limit later arguments concerning whether a witness provided testimony voluntarily. The Supreme Court's primary concern has been that investigations be conducted fairly. In Shafhi Mohammad v. State of Himachal Pradesh (2018)[222] the court strongly encourages the use of technology to enhance transparency during criminal proceedings. The use of audio and video recordings meets the court's objective.

This reform will help to protect defendants by enabling the police or investigators to have contemporaneous documentation of actions taken during the investigation of an offence. At the same time, a contemporaneous record will limit the likelihood of abuse of persons in custody. The reliance on objective evidence will also reduce the chances of subjectively documented evidence being produced.

---

220 The Bharatiya Nagarik Suraksha Sanhita, 2023, § 176(3) (India).

221 The Bharatiya Nagarik Suraksha Sanhita, 2023, § 183 (India).

222 *Shafhi Mohammad v. State of Himachal Pradesh*, (2018) 2 SCC 801 (Supreme Court of India).

4.4 Online Proceedings and Virtual Hearings

The digitalisation of court processes has been accelerated due to the pandemic. Most courts had continued with virtual trials and hearings. Digital hearings create much less delay than physical hearings. They also increase the ability to access witnesses at long distances. They also reduce transportation/transportation-related costs and risks for witnesses.[223] Video production or hearings provide significant logistical savings for under trial prisoners. The establishment of protective measures is very important for using video conferencing for trial/hearings. The equal access to technology must be provided to all persons. Confidentiality of communication between the client and their lawyer must still be provided to the client. Cybersecurity must be guaranteed for all parties. Procedural efficiency cannot override a person's right to a fair trial when the trial is concluded.

4.5 Digital Summons, Warrants and Case Management

Historically, the service of summonses has taken a long time due to a number of factors: physical delivery could be unsuccessful, or the accused could avoid being served altogether. Section 63 of the BNSS[224] now allows for electronic service of summonses : namely email, text messages and other digitally-based means of communication, using established protocols. This approach is consistent with present-day communications systems. Likewise, electronic issuance and transmission of warrants or other court-related documents are permitted. By incorporating aspects such as e-signature and secure

223 Press Information Bureau. (2026, February 12). *Digitization of courts.* Ministry of Law and Justice, Government of India. https://www.pib.gov.in/PressReleasePage.aspx?PRID=2227226

224 The Bharatiya Nagarik Suraksha Sanhita, 2023, § 63 (India).

platforms, this enables a faster and more reliable mechanism for creating court processes.

Electronic case tracking also increases transparency in the litigation process, allowing litigants to track their case's progress online, and judges to manage their dockets more efficiently. As with all service types, digital service must ensure compliance with the fundamental principles of procedural fairness, including providing verifiable proof of delivery[225].

5. Data Protection Concerns Under the BNSS Regime

The 2023 BNSS (Bharatiya Nagarik Suraksha Sanhita) is a complete transformation of criminal procedure, including the recognition of E-Records, the requirement to record searches in audio and video formats, and the incorporation of new technologies such as electronic filing and online trials. These updates are necessary due to the evolving nature of crime, including a growing number of crimes occurring on the internet, with much of the evidence related to those crimes being stored digitally. Law enforcement needs to rely on more than just paper records to operate efficiently. However, there are additional implications beyond just a change to how evidence is stored when digitizing criminal procedure in India. The change due to digitization is fundamentally changing the volume of data collected by the state. For instance, one mobile device may hold years of stored messages, photographs and financial records (and usually substantial amounts of data related to where that mobile device has been in the physical world).

225 Press Information Bureau. (2026, February 12). *Digitization of courts.* Ministry of Law and Justice, Government of India. https://www.pib.gov.in/PressReleasePage.aspx?PRID=2227226

Likewise, because CCTV systems generate near-continuous video feeds of criminal acts, this form of digital evidence will dramatically increase the state's data collection.

The expansion of data collection procedures increases the overall volume of personal information collected on individuals, raising varied data protection issues highlighted in CERT-In's Annual Report 2023, which showed that over 1.5 million cybersecurity breaches were reported during a one-year period alone.[226]

According to the BNSS, the authorities are given broader authority to conduct searches, seizures, and recordation of data. Nevertheless, the new BNSS does not provide sufficient guidance regarding data governance concepts. It does not define levels of data sensitivity, specify encryption standards, or require anonymisation (where applicable).

Retention of digital evidence poses a significant challenge. Digital evidence has an indefinite shelf life, unlike tangible assets, making it very low cost and easy to maintain. This leads many agencies to keep large amounts of digital evidence for future use (just in case). Retention of data also leads to fighting against cybersecurity risks, as governments are targeted for data breaches. The number of reports issued by CERT-In on data breach incidents will be very high if agencies continue to retain large volumes of data. Increased exposure to risk occurs with increased amounts of data. The technical capacities & financial resources to preserve and maintain secure storage are not standardized across individual police services.

---

226 Press Information Bureau. (2026, February 12). *Digitization of courts.* Ministry of Law and Justice, Government of India. https://www.pib.gov.in/PressReleasePage.aspx?PRID=2227226

Collaborative investigations are a new trend for modern investigative processes. The Indian Cyber Crime Coordination Centre (I4C) is tasked with coordinating between law enforcement agencies. Suspicious financial transactions are tracked by financial intelligence units, and CERT-In provides alerts when cyber crime suspects are found. Banks and telecom providers share intelligence with each other when an investigation progresses. Inter-agency collaboration is an element of many jurisdictions where cyber crimes are often committed. Therefore the ability for law enforcement to work across many jurisdictions relies on structured access control. There is no detailed requirement for access to seized digital evidence in the BNSS and there are no requirements for role-based access control.[227]

The digital environment allows for instant creation of duplicates and a single unauthorized download could potentially destroy sensitive and confidential materials forever. When data is collected for one purpose and used later on for another, this is termed function creep. Function creep is an inherent risk in data governance theory. Digital investigative systems create considerable datasets. These datasets may include biometric data, geolocation data, communication logs, and behaviour-related data. Agencies can always identify secondary uses for these same datasets over time.

In Anuradha Bhasin v. Union of India (2020)[228], the Supreme Court held that any restriction on a person's digital rights must be temporary, necessary, and proportionate, and therefore the same logic applies to surveilling individuals.

227 Sarmah, A., Sarmah, R., & Baruah, A. J. (2017). A brief study on cyber crime and cyber laws of India. *International Research Journal of Engineering and Technology (IRJET)*, *4*(6), 1633-1640.

228 *Anuradha Bhasin v. Union of India*, (2020) 3 SCC 637 (Supreme Court of India).

The Digital Personal Data Protection Act, 2023 (DPDP Act) has been enacted by India to regulate the use of personal data.[229] In doing so, new principles of purpose limitation, data minimisation, accuracy and limited storage have been introduced. The Act lays out responsibilities on data fiduciaries.

In contrast, however, the DPDP Act also provides exemptions under which data may be processed by the state in areas of state sovereignty, state security, and law enforcement. These exemptions are based on practical necessity, but they do not extinguish the constitutional protections that remain.[230] In addition, even where there is a statutory exemption, Article 21 continues to apply.[231] As such, the doctrine of proportionality continues to exist. Therefore, compliance with the obligation of data minimisation is both statutory and mandated as part of the constitution.

Coordination between the BNSS and DPDP is necessary. Data-safe and secure policing requires that all investigative powers associated with police investigations have limits on the retention and use of stored data, clear standards for secure storage, and a clear mechanism for enforcing accountability for the use of the data.[232] The BNSS has updated its process and acknowledges the reality of the digital world, the expansion of procedures alone without a data governance strategy in place introduces risk. There are very legitimate fears about the data

229 *Digital Personal Data Protection Act, 2023*, No. 22 of 2023, India.

230 Jha, A. (2024). THE DPDP ACT 2023: CRITICAL INSIGHTS INTO ITS LEGAL FRAMEWORK AND PRACTICAL IMPACT. *Bulletin of Pure & Applied Sciences-Zoology, 43.*

231 Constitution of India, Article. 21.

232 Malhotra, C., & Malhotra, U. (2024). Putting interests of digital nagriks first: digital personal data protection (dpdp) act 2023 of India. *Indian Journal of Public Administration*, *70*(3), 516-531.

protection implications of the BNSS; and these fears are based on technology, scale, and constitutional principles. The Supreme Court has repeatedly stated that sacrificing liberty for the sake of an efficient process is not justified.

6. Conclusion: Towards a Citizen-Centric Digital Criminal Procedure

Cyber Security & Civil Liberties are not necessarily fixed points of reference concerning either legislative action or courts' rulings. They represent a continuum of ongoing constitutional negotiations between all parties to such relationships. As technology evolves, new threats emerge, and thus must replacement laws and policy protections/ mitigations (which we refer to as cyber security & civil liberty protections).

The state's responsibility to safeguard its citizens from cyber-related harm must be balanced with its duty to uphold the dignity and autonomy of those citizens. State power has been greatly enhanced by the usage of digital tools. These advances have made it possible for law enforcement to increase the speed and efficiency of their investigations through improved search capabilities, the ability to obtain information from a much greater number of sources, the capacity for continuous monitoring of a subject's activity, and the ability to analyse large amounts of data using algorithms. Digital tools, in and of themselves, are not necessarily harmful. In fact, many times they are essential tools for combatting criminal activity.

A recalibration of the balance of political power therefore requires that both the State has a responsibility to exercise their power against criminals, and to limit their use of power in relation to their citizens. The privacy of individuals should be protected by obtaining appropriate, limited authority to conduct digital searches. Digital records should not be retained forever. A lawful government search should not result in the development of ongoing surveillance of an individual. Excessive or bulk data collection without proper authority undermines the constitutional foundations of our democracy.

Speed is promised by technology and E-FIRs (electronic First Information Report) do help reduce delays. The ability to record audio and video adds to the level of confidence people have in using e-Courts for their legal needs. Online hearings have made legal hearings more accessible. Digital case management systems like e-Courts have significantly reduced the number of pending cases. The e-Courts Mission Mode Project and National Judicial Data Grid have demonstrated how digital infrastructure can improve openness. Public access to information about all pending cases is easily viewable.

Cybercrime is going to evolve; therefore new threats will emerge through the use of artificial intelligence; deepfake technology will also impede evidence analysis; while cryptocurrencies may create difficult issues with tracking criminal transactions; furthermore, Cloud Computing will continue to create further blurring of jurisdictional lines. India must be proactive with its response. Training and capacity-building are extremely important. There is a need for police to receive specialised training in cyber forensics. Judiciaries and prosecutors need to have enhancement of digital literacy.

Lastly, international collaboration will also play an important role in shaping the future of crime. Cybercrime does not occur in a vacuum; therefore, mutual legal assistance processes must keep pace. Standard protocols must be established for handling digital evidence. A citizen-centric digital criminal/law enforcement system places citizens at the center of the changes that will occur due to advancing technology. It asks whether everyone will feel more secure because of more technology, or whether the same society will continue to feel less secure from criminals because technology is used to restrict individuals' freedom. Therefore, it is important to note that the use or implementation of new technologies for law enforcement will not result in the militarization of criminal processes.

Chapter 9

Digital Evidence, Surveillance and Privacy Under the Bharatiya Nagarik Suraksha Sanhita: Emerging Challenges in Technology-Driven Criminal Investigations

Dr. Manindra Singh Hanspal
Assistant Professor, Presidency University, Bengaluru.

Abstract

The passage of the Bharatiya Nagarik Suraksha Sanhita, 2023 (BNSS), that replaces the Code of Criminal Procedure, 1973, is the largest legislative change to the criminal procedure in India in fifty years. One of the most significant of its innovations is the inclusion of the digital technology in the criminal investigation and trial architecture, which includes the following provisions: the requirement to record the statements of the survivor in audio and video under the Section 173(3), the requirement to conduct a forensic investigation on the serious offence under the Section 176(3), the express admission of the electronic records under the Section 530, and the official All of these provisions are indicative of the shift by legislators to recognize that contemporary criminal justice cannot exist outside the digital infrastructure. But this technological embrace also has pressing and under-investigated questions of the defense of the rights of individuals in the shadow of massive state investigative authority. The chapter critically analyzes the digital evidence, surveillance, and privacy aspect of the BNSS in the light of the constitutional jurisprudence of India with the most notable case of Justice K.S. Puttaswamy (Retd.) v. Union of India (2017), that acknowledged the right to privacy as a fundamental right and subjected state encroachment on personal realms to a three-pronged test of legality, Based on the comparative analysis of the digital evidence frameworks in the United States, the United Kingdom, and the European Union and the authenticated data of the National Crime Records Bureau (NCRB), the Law Commission of India, and international organizations, the chapter charts the operational and constitutional loopholes that the technology provisions of BNSS do not fill: failure to oversee surveillance activities by the judicial system, lack of a forensic science infrastructure, and It contends in the chapter that the BNSS is making positive strides to technological modernisation, but these are not accompanied by a sufficient rights-protective structure, and suggests a five dimensional reform agenda based on judicial modernisation, standardisation of chain of custody, and constitutional proportionality.

1. Introduction

A police officer investigating a cognizable offence at the time the Code of Criminal Procedure was introduced in the year 1973 was provided with a paper case diary, face-to-face interviews with the witnesses and physical evidence was kept in sealed envelopes which were presented to a magistrate. The same officer is 50 years later, and he/she is carrying a smartphone, can record a statement of the victim in a video, can access call data records at a telecom server, and could have access to geolocation information, social media data, and facial recognition results before a court has been requested to examine a single detail of the investigation. This changed investigative reality is, in a significant sense, the legislative recognition of this new investigative reality with the Bharatiya Nagarik Suraksha Sanhita, 2023, which will take the place of the CrPC, starting July 1, 2024.

The BNSS imposes a new codified criminal procedure, as by no previous law, an express requirement of audio-video recording of statements by the survivors of a specified offence (Section 173(3))[233], a legislative mandate of forensic investigation in serious offences (Section 176(3)), introduction of electronic filing of complaints and reports (Section 173(1))[234] and structure of virtual court proceedings and electronic service of These are not aesthetic alterations. They are indicative of a policy choice to incorporate digital technologies into the procedural DNA of Indian criminal justice, a choice which has its own repercussions on investigation efficiency as well as the rights of the accused, victims and the integrity of the criminal justice record.[235] But the involvement of the BNSS in technology, regardless of its aspiration, is not quite comprehensive in some crucial aspects. It requires investigations through forensics without the construction of the infrastructure to facilitate it.[236] It accepts electronic records without determining the live issues concerning certification, authenticity and

233 *Bharatiya Nagarik Suraksha Sanhita, 2023*, § 173(3), No. 46 of 2023, India.

234 *Bharatiya Nagarik Suraksha Sanhita, 2023*, § 173(1), No. 46 of 2023, India.

235 Bansal, S., Nayak, S. S., & Dave, I. (2024). The role of forensic science and digital technology in enhancing investigation efficacy: an analytical study. *Cuestiones De Fisioterapia*, *53*(03), 2332-2359.

236 Puthalath, S., Sapna, S., & Kumar, P. (2025). Effective Police Investigation Under BNSS 2023: Existing Legal Framework and Challenges. In *Rethinking the Police for a Better Future: Navigating Policing Challenges with Accountability and Trust* (pp. 61-76). Cham: Springer Nature Switzerland.

chain of custody, which have bedevilled Indian courts in the last twenty years. It allows remote adjudication without touching upon the issue of dignity and due process of remote adjudication. And it increases the practical scope of state surveillance by its provisions as to search, seizure, and interception without any independent means of oversight that the Supreme Court, in Puttaswamy, found constitutionally indispensable.

2. Digital Evidence and Technology-Driven Investigation: The Conceptual Landscape

The digital evidence, or to be more precise, any information that can be probative and is represented in a binary format, has unique features that make it unlike traditional physical or documentary evidence.[237] According to Casey (2011), four important properties are listed, including its volatility (an electronic data can be overwritten, corrupted, or wiped in a few seconds when a device is seized); its volume (a single smartphone can store hundreds of thousands of data points, which can be vital to an investigation); its duplicability (a forensic copy of a digital device is bit-identical to the original, unlike a photo.[238] Such properties create a unique bundle of evidentiary issues. Since the date of the introduction of the Information Technology Act, 2000, the question of admissibility and reliability of electronic records has been a subject of debate in Indian courts, with often no definitive answer found to it, as the provisions have since been reflected in the

237 Salkute, S. R. (2026). Trial Court as Guardian of Electronic & Digital Record Under Section 63 of the Bharatiya Sakshya Adhiniyam, 2023: A Modern Approach--[Part-II]. *AIJFR-Advanced International Journal for Research*, 7(1).

238 Casey, E. (2011). *Digital evidence and computer crime: Forensic science, computers, and the internet.* Academic press.

Bharatiya Sakshya Adhiniyam, 2023 (BSA) the third of the legislative trinity with the BNSS and the The provisions of the BSA (Section 63, which replaces Section 65B of the Indian Evidence Act, 1872)[239] on admissibility of electronic records demands a certificate by a responsible official that the computer was operating properly, that the record is complete and accurate, and that the copy is accurate. The Supreme Court has been to this requirement several times, including in Anvar P.V. v. P.K. Basheer, (2014)[240], Shafhi Mohammad v. State of Himachal Pradesh, (2018)[241], and Arjun Panditrao Khotkar v. Kailash Kushanrao Gorantyal, (2020)[242] where it has, every time, attempted to strike a balance between the strictness of the certification requirement and the practicability of investigations and prosecutions.

The principle of the so-called chain of custody, the recorded process of custody, control, transfer, analysis, and disposition of evidence, is especially critical in the digital environment.[243] Digital evidence can also be modified without an externally visible indication of being tampered with, unlike physical evidence, which has visible evidence of such actions. This is, unless cryptographic hashing verification is used.[244] Although the BNSS focuses heavily on forensic investigation, it does not put a legislative standard in place as to the digital chain of custody, nor does it leave the issue to the procedural manuals and forensic science laboratory (FSSL) guidelines, which have no statutory

239 *Bharatiya Sakshya Adhiniyam, 2023* (Section 63).

240 *Anvar P.V. v. P.K. Basheer*, (2014) 10 SCC 473 (India).

241 *Shafhi Mohammad v. State of Himachal Pradesh*, (2018) 2 SCC 801 (India).

242 *Arjun Panditrao Khotkar v. Kailash Kushanrao Gorantyal*, (2020) 7 SCC 1 (India).

243 Prayudi, Y., & Sn, A. (2015). Digital chain of custody: State of the art. *International Journal of Computer Applications*, *114*(5).

244 Hargreaves, C. J. (2009). Assessing the reliability of digital evidence from live investigations involving encryption.

weight. It is against this background that the BNSS can be seen as a considerable, albeit partial, legislative interest in the digital evidence problem. Table 1 below aligns the important digital evidence and technology provisions of the BNSS with the corresponding CrPC provisions, and it is found that the changes made are either in nature or scope.

Table 1- BNSS 2023 vs. CrPC 1973 — Key Digital Evidence and Technology Provisions

Subject Matter	CrPC, 1973 (Relevant Section)	BNSS, 2023 (Relevant Section)	Nature of Change
Electronic Records as Evidence	S. 65B, Indian Evidence Act[245]	S. 530, BNSS[246] (read with Bharatiya Sakshya Adhiniyam, 2023, S. 63)	Mandatory electronic filing; admissibility of electronic records expanded; certificate requirement retained but digitally executable
Audio-Video Recording of Statements	No express provision	S. 173(3) Mandatory audio-video recording of statements of survivors of specified offences[247]	Entirely new provision; creates evidentiary obligation; no pre-existing counterpart in CrPC

Subject Matter	**CrPC, 1973 (Relevant Section)**	**BNSS, 2023 (Relevant Section)**	**Nature of Change**
Trial via Video Conferencing	S. 273 (presence of accused at trial, interpreted by courts)[248]	S. 530 read with S. 316[249], 530(1)(b)[250] n Virtual trials and proceedings expressly authorised	Codifies Supreme Court guidelines; replaces case-by-case judicial extension
Search and Seizure of Electronic Devices	S. 96–105 (general search; no express electronic device provision)	S. 94 BNSS specifically covers documents and electronic devices	Electronic devices expressly included in the search and seizure framework; chain of custody obligation is implied
Use of Forensic Science in Investigation	No mandate express	S. 176(3) — Forensic investigation mandatory for offences punishable with 7+ years' imprisonment	First legislative mandate for forensic deployment; includes mobile forensics and digital data recovery

Subject Matter	**CrPC, 1973 (Relevant Section)**	**BNSS, 2023 (Relevant Section)**	**Nature of Change**
Zero FIR and E-FIR	No provision; developed by courts	S. 173(1) proviso BNSS E-FIR through electronic communication is expressly recognized	Codifies judicial innovation; enables digital first-contact policing; raises authentication challenges
Transit Remand and Electronic Communication	S. 167 — physical or virtual production permitted[251]	S. 187 BNSS — transit remand; production via electronic means permitted[252]	Reduces physical movement; raises questions about identity verification and coercion detection

245 *Indian Evidence Act, 1872*, Section 65B.

246 *Bharatiya Nagarik Suraksha Sanhita, 2023*, Section 530.

247 *Bharatiya Nagarik Suraksha Sanhita, 2023*, Section 173(3).

248 *Bharatiya Nagarik Suraksha Sanhita, 2023* (Section 273).

249 *Bharatiya Nagarik Suraksha Sanhita, 2023* (Section 316).

250 *Bharatiya Nagarik Suraksha Sanhita, 2023* (Section 530(1)(b)).

251 *Bharatiya Nagarik Suraksha Sanhita, 2023* (Section 167).

252 *Bharatiya Nagarik Suraksha Sanhita, 2023* (Section 187).

Table 1 has a number of observations that are worth highlighting. First, the forensic requirement of Section 176(3) BNSS is literally new; there is no such parallel legislative pressure in the CrPC, although its practical effectiveness is wholly dependent on the capacity of forensic science. Second, the audio-video recording component of Section 173(3), though safeguarding the dignity of victims and possibly beneficial to the integrity of the evidence, imposes a significant digital records management burden on police stations that do not have the infrastructure to store, secure, and transmit large video files. Third, the introduction of electronic filing and e-FIR into Section 173(1) is a very welcome modernization, but creates authentication issues, i.e. how can a magistrate be sure that a complainant has filed electronically, or that a statement made via a digital medium was not made under duress?

3. The Constitutional Framework: Privacy, Surveillance, and the Puttaswamy Standard

Justice K.S. Puttaswamy (Retd.) v. Union of India, (2017)[253] completely transformed the constitutional architecture that regulates the use of digital evidence and surveillance in India. The decision by the nine-judge constitutional bench was the first one since the right to privacy is a fundamental right enshrined in Article 21 of the Constitution of India, which clearly and without qualification affirmed the constitutional right to privacy.[254] Although the case adjudicated in its immediate contextual context was the attack on the Aadhaar scheme, its dogmatic scope stretches much further and to all the other aspects of state intrusion within the personal lives of the individuals including

253 Justice K.S. Puttaswamy (Retd.) v. Union of India, (2017) 10 SCC 1

254 Arun, P. (2021). In pursuit of personal data: A survey on state surveillance and democracy in India. In Companion to Indian Democracy (pp. 234-255). Routledge India.

the most crucial, the surveillance and investigational procedures that BNSS enabled.

The Puttaswamy case created a three-pronged test of reviewing the constitutionality of any state action interfering with the privacy right. First, it must have a law that has authorised the act like the need of legality, without which executive action cannot be taken without any statutory ground. Second, the action should seek a legitimate state purpose, the need of legitimate purpose. Third, and above all in the present analysis, the means used should be in accordance with the end pursued - the proportionality requirement, which presupposes that the intrusion of the state should not be higher than the requirements of the military of the accomplishing of the legitimate purpose.[255] This three-part standard possesses both the direct and indirect implications to the provisions of digital investigation in the BNSS. Think of the issue of surveillance. Intercepting communications under the Indian Telegraph Act, 1885, as amended, and the Information Technology Act, 2000 demands the permission of the Secretary of the Ministry of Home Affairs or other equivalent by state law an executive, and not a judicial, official.[256] Following the Puttaswamy, the reasonableness of this executive authorisation regime should be evaluated in relation to the proportionality test. Even the Supreme Court in its own observation in Puttaswamy states that a system of state-surveillance is easily transformed into authoritarianism when it does not face sufficient constitutional protection can be understood as a scathing remark about a system where the executive makes its own surveillance

255 Chandrachud, D. Y. (2017). Supreme Court of India Justice KS Puttaswamy (Retd)... vs Union Of India And Ors. on 24 August, 2017.

256 Naik, A. R. (2025). Phone Tapping in India: Understanding Its Legal and Constitutional Dimensions. *Available at SSRN 5140629*.

operations lawful without any judicial review.[257] Informational privacy, and the right to be forgotten, in particular, which has been more and more established in India, such as in Jorawar Singh Mundy v. Union of India, (2021)[258], also applies to the digital record-keeping requirements of BNSS. The requirement of section 173(3) of audio-video recording of survivor statements amounts to a permanent digital record of the statement of a victim.[259] No such provision regarding the retention of these records, their access rights, or deletion is present in the BNSS, which is not very comfortable in relation to the right to privacy and the new data protection principles of the Digital Personal Data Protection Act, 2023 (DPDP Act).

The data protection and privacy law, the DPDP Act, which became presidential law in August 2023 and is being gradually implemented, obligates all data fiduciaries who process personal data of Indian citizens with the intention to limit its purpose, minimize it, and keep it limited.[260] Whether the police forces and investigating agencies are considered as data fiduciaries under the DPDP Act and, as such, fall under its protective regime when handling digital evidence is an issue that the legislature has not resolved in either the BNSS or the DPDP Act itself. The difference is substantial, as digital evidence in criminal proceedings is, practically, personal information; that is, it contains messages, location information, financial data, and biometrics of the

257 Arun, P. (2021). In pursuit of personal data: A survey on state surveillance and democracy in India. In *Companion to Indian Democracy* (pp. 234-255). Routledge India.

258 *Jorawar Singh Mundy v. Union of India*, 2021 SCC OnLine Del 2306 (Delhi High Court, India).

259 Penugondla, A., & Deep, V. A. (2024). Efficacy of Enhanced Punishment in Reducing the Offence against Women in India. *Jus Corpus LJ*, *5*, 443.

260 Dhir, M., & Verma, S. (2024). *AI for good: India and beyond: Detailed analysis of AI & laws, policies, ethical frameworks and judgements*. Notion Press.

accused individuals, witnesses, and, very often, completely innocent third parties.

4. Judicial Architecture: Key Case Law on Digital Evidence and Surveillance

The legal system of dealing with digital evidence in India has been largely created by the courts, which have occupied the loopholes left open by the legislature. The following table 2 gives the major decisions that characterize this framework and their individual relevance to the digital provisions in the BNSS.

Table 2: Key Judicial Decisions on Digital Evidence, Surveillance, and Privacy in India (and Comparative Jurisprudence)

Case Citation	Year	Court	Legal Significance for Digital Evidence / Surveillance under BNSS
Justice K.S. Puttaswamy (Retd.) v. Union of India, (2017) 10 SCC 1	2017	Supreme Court of India (9-Judge Bench)	Unanimously recognized the right to privacy as a fundamental right under Article 21; established proportionality, legality, and necessity as tests for state surveillance; and constitutionally foundational for evaluating BNSS surveillance provisions

Case Citation	Year	Court	Legal Significance for Digital Evidence / Surveillance under BNSS
Anwar P.V. v. P.K. Basheer, (2014) 10 SCC 473[261]	2014	Supreme Court of India	Resolved the S. 65B certificate controversy; held that oral secondary evidence of electronic records is inadmissible; certificate mandatory for admissibility; directly applicable to S. 530 BNSS / S. 63 BSA proceedings
Arjun Panditrao Khotkar v. Kailash Kushanrao Gorantyal, (2020) 7 SCC 1[262]	2020	Supreme Court of India (Constitution Bench)	Clarified that S. 65B certificate may be filed at any stage before judgment; dispelled uncertainty created by Tomaso Bruno; shapes practice under BSA S. 63, which governs electronic records in BNSS proceedings

Case Citation	**Year**	**Court**	**Legal Significance for Digital Evidence / Surveillance under BNSS**
Selvi v. State of Karnataka, (2010) 7 SCC 263[263]	2010	Supreme Court of India	Held that narco-analysis, brain mapping, and polygraph tests administered without consent violate Art. 20(3) and Art. 21; sets constitutional limits on forensic investigation under S. 176 BNSS; direct relevance to compelled digital device access
Ritesh Sinha v. State of Uttar Pradesh, (2019)[264]	2019	Supreme Court of India	Held that a Magistrate can direct accused to provide voice samples; bridges gap between Selvi's non-self-incrimination protection and investigative necessity; applicable to orders compelling device passcode disclosure

Case Citation	Year	Court	Legal Significance for Digital Evidence / Surveillance under BNSS
State (NCT of Delhi) v. Navjot Sandhu, (2005)[265]	2005	Supreme Court of India	Permitted secondary evidence of mobile call data records (CDRs) despite absence of S. 65B certificate in certain circumstances; partially qualified by Anwar; illustrates evolving judicial treatment of telecom metadata as investigative evidence
Shafhi Mohammad v. State of Himachal Pradesh, (2018)[266]	2018	Supreme Court of India	Held that S. 65B certificate cannot be insisted upon when the party seeking to rely on electronic evidence was not in possession of the device; balanced certificate requirement against investigative realities; shapes BNSS forensic evidence practice

Case Citation	Year	Court	Legal Significance for Digital Evidence / Surveillance under BNSS
Gobind v. State of Madhya Pradesh, (1975)[267]	1975	Supreme Court of India	Early recognition of privacy as implied fundamental right; developed 'compelling state interest' test later refined in Puttaswamy; underpins the constitutional scrutiny applicable to BNSS surveillance authorisations

The Electronic Evidence Certification Trilogy

The history of the Supreme Court involvement in the admissibility of electronic evidence can be described as one of gradual evolution, as the trial courts and the practitioners have struggled to resolve the problems posed by the certification requirement of the Indian Evidence Act (since repealed and replaced by Section 63 of the BSA) of the Section. The Court in Anwar P.V. v. P.K. Basheer (2014) left no doubts that the electronic records could not be evidenced by oral secondary evidence and that the certificate of Section 65B is a strict requirement of admissibility when the party who wanted to rely on the

261 *Anvar P.V.* (2014)

262 *Arjun Panditrao* (2020)

263 *Selvi v. State of Karnataka*, (2010) 7 SCC 263 (India).

264 *Ritesh Sinha v. State of Uttar Pradesh*, (2019) 8 SCC 1 (India).

265 *State (NCT of Delhi) v. Navjot Sandhu*, (2005) 11 SCC 600 (India).

266 *Shafhi Mohammad v. State of Himachal Pradesh*, (2018) 2 SCC 801 (India).

267 *Gobind v. State of Madhya Pradesh*, (1975) 2 SCC 148 (India).

record was in a position to receive it.[268] This ruling ended a long line of contradictory High Court jurisdiction, but caused real-life challenges in instances where the police officers attempted to introduce call data records, CCTV photos and digital communications materials without having acquired certificates during the time the evidence was gathered.

Such challenges resulted in the second part of the trilogy. In Shafhi Mohammad v. State of H.P. (2018), a two-judge court overturned the position of Anwar P.V. and ruled that the certificate requirement could not be enforced upon when the party that relied on electronic evidence did not have control of the device or system that the evidence was obtained.[269] Though this was a pragmatically sensitive adjustment, jurisprudentially it was dubious, and the case was sent to a constitution bench. In Arjun Panditrao Khotkar v. Kailash Kushanrao Gorantyal (2020) the primacy of the Anwar P.V. position was reinstated by the constitution bench, but it was also stated that the certificate could be filed at any time before judgment, even after the electronic record had been marked as an exhibit.

The implications of the study on the BNSS practice are practical. Section 530 BNSS, which interprets Section 63 BSA, maintains the certification system.[270] A proper certificate should be secured by the person in charge of the system generating a record in order to enable the investigators collecting digital evidence, such as audio-video

268 Ghatak, C. (2018). Leaving My Legacy Online-Weighing the Viability of Recognising Digital Wills in India. *Nirma ULJ*, 7, 87.

269 Kavlekar, P. C. (2022). A Critique on Admissibility and Mode of Proof of Third-Party Electronic Records. *CMR Univ. J. Contemp. Legal Aff.*, *4*, 78.

270 Mohan, M. K. (2024). Comparison between Chapter 37 of CrPC (1973) and Chapter 39 of BNSS (2023). *Issue 6 Int'l JL Mgmt. & Human.*, 7, 1165.

recordings under Section 173(3), to access the evidence.[271] The lack of a national standardized procedure for this process, and the chronic under-training of investigating officers in digital evidence processes recorded in the Crime in India reports compiled by NCRB (National Crime Records Bureau), is a significant operational threat to the integrity of the evidence of BNSS proceedings.

Compelled Access to Digital Devices: The Selvi–Ritesh Sinha Axis

Whether an accused individual can be forced to decrypt a digital device, or to give the password or biometric credential that would allow them to gain access to it, is a question that borders on the right against self-incrimination in Article 20(3) and the investigative requirements of digital forensics. According to the decision of the Supreme Court in Selvi v. State of Karnataka (2010), the mandatory application of such methods as narco-analysis and brain mapping is contrary to Article 20(3), which safeguards against forcing a person to be a witness against himself.[272] The Court determined that the protection of Article 20(3) applies not only to the formal court proceedings but also to police investigation and that the term testimonial compulsion refers to all procedures that force an unwilling individual to provide information.

The Court, in Ritesh Sinha v. State of U.P. (2019) 9 years later, determined that a Magistrate may order an accused to provide a voice sample, making a distinction between testimonial evidence (to which Article 20(3)) applies) and a physical evidence, whose probative value is not determined by the content contained therein but rather by its

271 KAUR, G., & DHAWAN, A. (2024). *Laws of electronic evidence and digital forensics*. PHI Learning Pvt. Ltd..

272 Bhattacharya, S. (2017). Selvi vs. State of Karnataka: a critical analysis. *State of Karnataka: A Critical Analysis*.

physical nature.[273] The Court recognized that the digital frontier had presented a grey zone; it specifically stated that the forced unlocking of a phone and the forced delivery of a fingerprint to unlock a biometrically secured device presented unique constitutional issues that it was not adjudicating on and needed legislative action. The BNSS has failed to offer such an intervention; the issue of forced access to devices is still unadjudicated, as of 2024, a constitutional issue of urgent practical significance, because practically any serious criminal investigation now includes taking control of mobile devices.

5. Forensic Science Infrastructure: The Capacity Gap

One of the best provisions in the statute in its ambition is section 176(3) of the BNSS. It requires a forensic expert to visit the scene of the crime and to gather forensic evidence in case of the investigation of the offences punishable by imprisonment of seven years or above.[274] This, once enforced, would be a radical change in the Indian system of investigation; it would be a change in the model that has historically dominated the activity of the Indian police, the model of the overwhelmingly testimonial, confessional model, to a model based on evidence and scientifically founded. The provision is coupled with the understanding that the state governments can establish forensic science capability in the mobile forensic units that can arrive at crime scenes.

273 Sinha, Y. S. (2020). The Unjustifiable Equivocation on the Constitutionality of Compelled Voice Sampling. *NLIU L. Rev.*, *10*, 497.

274 Puthalath, S., Sapna, S., & Kumar, P. (2025). Effective Police Investigation Under BNSS 2023: Existing Legal Framework and Challenges. In *Rethinking the Police for a Better Future: Navigating Policing Challenges with Accountability and Trust* (pp. 61-76). Cham: Springer Nature Switzerland.

The difference between this legislative ideal and the working reality of the Indian forensic science complex is, to say the least, staggering. The Crime in India 2022 report by the National Crime Records Bureau recorded the presence of about 30 central and state forensic science laboratories (FSLs) in India, which have a cumulative examining capacity that is structurally overwhelmed by the number of cases.[275] Many cases were awaiting examination at FSL. The number of FSL facilities per population is very low, about five laboratories per 10 crore people in the country, compared to other countries in the world.[276] There are numerous district-level police departments with no certified digital forensic examiner and the mobile forensic teams that were the envisioned system in Section 176(3) are present in very few states.[277]

This general capacity shortage is complicated by the special issue of digital forensics. According to the NCRB data of 2022, cases of cybercrime registered under the IT Act have increased by 24.4 percent in the period between 2020 and 2022 and registered 52,974 cases of cybercrime cases in 2022 alone.[278] The available quantity of specialized

275 JJ, A. R., & HEMAVATHY, M. INFRASTRUCTURE DEFICITS IN INDIA'S FORENSIC LABS: CHALLENGES AND REFORMS FOR CRIMINAL JUSTICE DELIVERY.

276 Badiye, A., Sulke, P., Bhandarkar, M., & Kapoor, N. (2023). Forensic Science Laboratories in India. In *Textbook of Forensic Science* (pp. 67-98). Singapore: Springer Nature Singapore.

277 Tshishonga, M. (2022). *An exploration of the operational functioning of the South African Police Service Crime Information Management and Analysis Centre* (Doctoral dissertation, University of South Africa (South Africa)).

278 Manral, M. S., & Sinha, J. (2023, December 4). *24% rise in cybercrime in 2022, 11% surge in economic offences: NCRB report. The Indian Express.* https://indianexpress.com/article/india/rise-cybercrime-2022-economic-offences-ncrb-report-9053882/

cyber forensic labs that can extract and examine evidence on mobile devices, cloud accounts, encrypted applications, and social media platforms is completely insufficient to this number of cases. Five years prior to the enactment of the BNSS the Law Commission of India had in its 277th Report on the Need for a New Forensic Science Policy (2018) named the forensic capacity crisis as a structural hindrance to criminal justice and suggested a policy on forensic science nationally, a central system of funding, and the compulsory accreditation of forensic laboratories.[279] These are the recommendations that have not been put in place.

The clause of section 176(3) that its duty extends to the extent that it is possible is the equivalent of making a duty provision that is not mandatory into a wishful provision where the necessary infrastructure is not in existence. It is legally candid, since the legislature clearly understood the capacity limit, but it gives the police forces in states with insufficient forensic facilities an incentive to proceed with serious offence investigation without a forensic assistive background, and the as far as possible qualification can be taken advantage of by the prosecution to cover up the resulting gaps in evidence. This may result in the violation of the constitutional right to a fair trial and the right of the accused to question the reliability of the evidence presented against him or her.

279 NEXT IAS. (2026, April 9). *States told to clear forensic backlogs – India*. https://www.nextias.com/ca/current-affairs/09-04-2026/forensic-backlogs-india

6. A Comparative Lens: International Digital Evidence Frameworks

The comparative analysis of the experience of the other jurisdictions in the intersection of the digital investigation and protection of rights provides both educative exemplars and warning lessons. Table 3 below compares the key attributes of four key comparative frameworks with the current position of the BNSS.

Table 3: Comparative Framework — Digital Evidence Laws and Surveillance Oversight (2024)

Jurisdiction	Primary Legal Framework	Surveillance Oversight Mechanism	Applicable Lessons for BNSS Implementation
India (Post-BNSS)	BNSS 2023; BSA 2023; IT Act 2000; DPDP Act 2023; Telegraph Act 1885 (amended)	No independent oversight body; executive authorisation (MHA); no judicial warrant requirement for interception	Significant gap: Puttaswamy's proportionality test demands independent oversight; executive self-authorisation does not satisfy constitutional standard

Jurisdiction	**Primary Legal Framework**	**Surveillance Oversight Mechanism**	**Applicable Lessons for BNSS Implementation**
United States	Federal Rules of Evidence (Rule 901–902); Electronic Communications Privacy Act 1986; CLOUD Act 2018	FISA Court for national security surveillance; judicial warrant for content-level interception (Riley v. California, 2014)	Riley's requirement of judicial warrant before searching a seized mobile phone directly applicable to BNSS S. 94 device seizures
United Kingdom	Police and Criminal Evidence Act 1984 (PACE); Investigatory Powers Act 2016; Digital Economy Act 2017	Investigatory Powers Commissioner (IPC); Judicial oversight via IPC for targeted interception warrants	IPC model offers replicable architecture for independent digital surveillance oversight; could inform proposed Digital Oversight Authority under India's AI governance debate

Jurisdiction	Primary Legal Framework	Surveillance Oversight Mechanism	Applicable Lessons for BNSS Implementation
European Union	GDPR 2016/679; Law Enforcement Directive 2016/680; eEvidence Regulation 2023	Data Protection Authorities; CJEU judicial review; adequacy assessments	eEvidence Regulation's 'preservation and production orders' framework relevant to cross-border digital evidence challenges in BNSS investigations
Australia	Telecom-munications (Interception and Access) Act 1979; Surveillance Devices Act 2004; Assistance and Access Act 2018	Independent National Security Legislation Monitor (INSLM); Parliamentary Joint Committee on Intelligence and Security	INSLM model of independent review of surveillance laws directly instructive for institutional reform to complement BNSS digital provisions

There are a few comparative observations which are worthy of special notice. In the case of Riley v. California (2014)[280], the judgment of the United States Supreme Court was unanimous that police officers

280 *Riley v. California*, 573 U.S. 373 (2014).

should require a judicial warrant to search the digital contents of a cell phone acquired during the act of arrest. The unanimous court led by Chief Justice Roberts noted that the quantitative and qualitative disparities between what was contained in a mobile phone and the physical objects historically subject to warrantless search incident to arrest were so high that the traditional categorical rule did not apply.[281] The phone itself, he observed, 'could as easily be termed many-phones, ' a fact that the digital context fundamentally redefines the privacy calculus. This argument can be directly applied to the BNSS framework: the provisions on search and seizure in Section 94 specifically address the electronic devices, but there is no warranting requirement that is unique to access to the digital data stored in the electronic device.[282]

An example of a potentially instructive oversight model, provided by the Investigatory Powers Act 2016 (IPA) of the United Kingdom, albeit with controversial clauses about bulk data collection, which have been challenged in the European Court of Human Rights, is the Investigatory Powers Commissioner (IPC).[283] The IPC is a senior judicial officer who oversees the exercise of investigatory powers (such as interception warrants, equipment interference and bulk data retention) independently. The IPC issues annual reports and carries

281 Hunton Andrews Kurth LLP. (2014, June 26). *Supreme Court finds warrantless cell phone searches unconstitutional.* https://www.hunton.com/privacy-and-cybersecurity-law-blog/supreme-court-finds-warrantless-cell-phone-searches-unconstitutional

282 Malhotra, D., & Shrivastava, R. K. (2025). BYTES AND RIGHTS: UNPACKING SEARCH AND SEIZURE OF THE ELECTRONIC EVIDENCE UNDER INDIA'S LEGAL FRAMEWORK. *NFSU Journal of Forensic Justice*, *4*(1), 10-62995.

283 Shurson, J. (2023). *Rethinking Comity: Resolving Conflicts in Transnational Digital Investigations* (Doctoral dissertation, Queen Mary University of London).

out inspections of intelligence and law enforcement services, and can refer individuals to the Investigatory Powers Tribunal. This type of judicial independence is lacking in the Indian system, where the executive authorities under the Telegraph Act and the IT Act give telephone interception orders without any judicial review.

The Assistance and Access Act 2018 of Australia, which seeks to compel technology companies to offer law enforcement assistance in decrypting encrypted communication, has attracted a lot of controversy and even academic criticism due to the fact that it has proven how dangerous it is to legislate technical requirements of capability without attendant rights protection.[284] Civil liberties organizations and technology analysts have condemned the provisions of the Act, which allow notices of technical capability and technical assistance that may force a company to alter its products to make them easier to monitor, as causing systemic security vulnerabilities. This is a first-hand warning because India is deliberating on expanding its regulatory system to include end-to-end encrypted communications platforms, which is prompted by the IT (Intermediary Guidelines and Digital Media Ethics Code) Rules, 2021.[285]

7. Structural Gaps and a Proposed Reform Framework

The above discussion reveals a conglomerate of structural gaps within the BNSS coverage of digital evidence and surveillance, which, when

284 Farlow, H., & Edwards, B. M. (2022). Shining a light on 'going dark': A framework to guide the co-design and communication of decryption laws based on the passage of the telecommunications and other legislation (assistance and access) bill 2018. *Computer Law & Security Review*, *46*, 105726.

285 Grover, G., Rajwade, T., & Katira, D. (2021). The Ministry and the Trace: Subverting End-To-End Encryption. *NUJS L. Rev.*, *14*, 223.

combined, amounts to a major rights-protective negative. Such loopholes are not technical and procedural loopholes, but they get to the very root of whether the new criminal procedure code of India, with all its technological flair, sufficiently safeguards the constitutional rights of the citizens who find themselves in the digital era of the criminal justice system. These gaps are mapped in Table 4, and a proposal for a reform framework is made.

Table 4: Structural Gaps and Proposed Reform Framework for BNSS Digital Evidence and Surveillance Provisions

Reform Area	**Current Position under BNSS**	**Identified Gap / Risk**	**Recommended Reform**
Judicial Oversight of Surveillance	Executive authorisation only (MHA/ State Home Dept.)	No independent scrutiny; Puttaswamy proportionality test unsatisfied	Mandatory prior judicial warrant for device seizure and interception; Designated Digital Surveillance Judge
Electronic Evidence Certification (S. 530 BNSS / S. 63 BSA)	Certificate required; court may waive in limited cases	No standardised certificate format; inconsistent police training; chain-of-custody gaps	Uniform national e-evidence certification protocol; mandatory forensic training for investigating officers

Reform Area	Current Position under BNSS	Identified Gap / Risk	Recommended Reform
Forensic Mandate (S. 176(3) BNSS)	Mandatory for 7+ year offences; state govt. to develop capacity	Massive infrastructure deficit; 5 FSLs per 10 crore population nationally (NCRB 2022)	Time-bound national FSL capacity plan; accredited private forensic labs with judicial oversight; DPDP-compliant data handling
Compelled Device Access / Password Disclosure	No express provision; governed by Selvi and Ritesh Sinha	Operational uncertainty; risk of coerced compliance; self-incrimination concerns	Dedicated statutory provision with judicial authorisation, proportionality test, and legal aid guarantee for accused
Cross-Border Digital Evidence	Mutual Legal Assistance Treaties (MLATs); no express BNSS provision	MLAT timelines average 18–24 months; platform cooperation inconsistent; no preservation order mechanism	Statutory preservation order power; bilateral data-sharing agreements; alignment with Budapest Convention obligations

Reform Area	Current Position under BNSS	Identified Gap / Risk	Recommended Reform
AI and Algorithmic Policing	Not addressed in BNSS	No legal basis, accountability framework, or audit mechanism for predictive policing and facial recognition tools.	Statutory moratorium on facial recognition pending rights impact assessment; mandatory algorithmic audit before deployment; DPDP compliance

Judicial Oversight of Surveillance: The Constitutional Imperative

The most urgent reform in terms of the constitution is the establishment of independent judicial supervision of surveillance activities. Puttaswamy judgment did not state that the current executive authorization structure was invalid, but its proportionality criterion has provided a potent constitutional basis to be judicially reviewed. It is not the American FISA court, which in turn has been criticized as excessively deferential to the surveillance demands of the executive, but the UK Investigatory Powers Commissioner: a senior judicial figure with real investigative power, a mandate to inspect surveillance activities proactively, and may refer perceived violations to a specialist tribunal. Introducing a Designated Digital Surveillance Judge, with the power to grant an interception warrant over any set limit, and to examine a statistically significant portion of interception authorizations at the lower level, would be a constitutionally reasonable and practically practicable reform.

Standardizing Digital Chain of Custody

The integrity of the forensic process from seizure to presentation in court is crucial to the reliability of the digital evidence.[286] The fact that there is no statutory standard of chain-of-custody of digital evidence currently, and that the police practice of handling digital evidence has been documented to be inconsistent across states, constitutes a structural susceptibility to both accidental and intentional interference. A national digital evidence protocol, with statutory force as subordinate legislation to the BNSS, must specify: the cryptographic hash verification (SHA-256 or the equivalent) at the point of seizure and at each of the further stages of forensic processing; a digitally signed audit log registering each access to the evidentiary copy; the use of write-blocking hardware on the forensic examination; and the accreditation It is not a technologically challenging reform, as international standards like ISO/IEC 27037:2012 (Guidelines for Identification, Collection, Acquisition, and Preservation of Digital Evidence) include a ready template but it needs a legislative intent to make it a binding standard, not a best-practice guideline.

Resolving the Compelled Device Access Lacuna

The call of the Ritesh Sinha judgment of legislative intervention on the issue of forced access to devices should be responded to directly and principled in the BNSS framework. The provision must: (i) need that any order that requires an accused person to provide access to

286 Yeboah-Ofori, A., & Brown, A. D. (2020). Digital forensics investigation jurisprudence: issues of admissibility of digital evidence. *Journal of Forensic, Legal & Investigative Sciences*, *6*(1), 1-8.

a digital device be prior judicially approved; (ii) make a distinction between the forced provision of a physical biometric (fingerprint, facial recognition unlock) which, according to the logic of Ritesh Sinha, may be considered analogous to the forced provision of a physical sample, and the forced disclosure of knowledge.

Addressing Artificial Intelligence and Algorithmic Policing

The most obvious oddity of the BNSS in the digital framework is, perhaps, its complete silence regarding the use of artificial intelligence to investigate anything. Facial recognition technology has been implemented by the Indian police forces with more or less official recognition at least in 16 states as of 2023, based on the data collected by the Internet Freedom Foundation.[287] There are so-called predictive policing systems, an algorithmic tool that aims at predicting areas of high crime or a person at high risk of committing a crime, which have been tested in Andhra Pradesh, Telangana, and Delhi. These tools have documented risks of racial, caste, and gender-based discrimination; they are trained on historical crime data that recreates and augments the biases inherent in the historical crime data; and they produce outputs of the investigations, the algorithm of which is inaccessible to the subject of the investigation and the court at which the evidence is offered.

The BNSS does not provide a legal ground for such deployments, a framework of accountability for such deployments, or a system of questioning their outputs. The general powers of investigation contained in the BNSS or the IT Act do not satisfy the Puttaswamy standard of legality that requires a law that permits state action to be taken in relation to privacy. The least constitutionally defensible

287 *Internet Freedom Foundation.* https://internetfreedom.in/

is a statutory prohibition on the operational use of facial recognition technology in criminal investigations, pending the right impact assessment and the passage of special enabling legislation that includes requirements of judicial review. The wider AI governance legislation of algorithmic policing ought to be resolved with the proposed AI governance legislation, which is currently on the anvil of the Ministry of Electronics and Information Technology.[288]

8. Conclusion

Bharatiya Nagarik Suraksha Sanhita is another very real attempt to take the criminal procedure in India into the digital era. Its guidelines regarding the audio-video recording, forensic investigation, electronic evidence, and virtual proceedings are noteworthy innovations, and with the right approach and implementation, could become the key to enhancing the efficiency and the integrity of criminal justice in India. That is the ambition that should be recognized.

Law does not abstractly work. It works in the practicalities of police offices with poorly developed digital infrastructure, forensic labs with backlog, courts still working on the doctrinal frameworks needed to evaluate electronic evidence, and a surveillance system which has become technical in its capability without any increase in judicial responsibility. Under such circumstances, the technological provisions of the BNSS are both risky and promising but not properly tackled by the statute which is in its current form.

The Puttaswamy case provided the country with one of the most advanced privacy jurisprudences across the globe. Its tripartite requirement of legality, necessity, and proportionality is a truly rigorous

---

288 Ministry of Electronics and Information Technology. *IndiaAI: National program on artificial intelligence*. Government of India. https://indiaai.gov.in

constitutional criterion - one which the BNSS provisions in digital form are not always able to meet. There is no judicial control over surveillance, the issue on forced access of devices remains unresolved, the lack of forensic infrastructure is not a side effect, the silence of artificial intelligence policing, and the vacuity of digital record storage and security are not accidental flaws. They are the fundamental failures that need to be addressed by the legislators.

The reform agenda suggested in this chapter judicial surveillance, standardised digital chain of custody, principled legislation on forced access to devices, AI policing regulation and a national plan on forensic science capacity is not presented as a counsel of perfection. It is presented as a constitutional solemnity bare minimum with regard to a law that would aspire to regulate the criminal justice in a digital democracy. The citizens who will experience the practice of BNSS as accused persons, as victims, as witnesses and as members of a growing population of people the communications and movements of whom are more and more accessible to the investigators of the state, deserve no less.

Chapter 10

Data Protection, Privacy, and Surveillance Concerns Under Bnss: A Critical Analysis in Light of the Digital Personal Data Protection Act, 2023

Divyakshi Jain
Advocate, Meerut District Court, U.P.

Abstract

The Bharatiya Nagarik Suraksha Sanhita, 2023 (hereinafter referred to as "BNSS") was introduced to reform the existing criminal procedure and to update it according to the current technological standards so as to keep up with the demands of changing criminal and judicial requirements. Pursuant to which, several provisions relating to digital advancement including electronic summons, electronic identification of arrested persons, audio-video recording of searches, etc. However, these amendments have led to concerns being raised about lack of infrastructure and training for the above which could lead to potential state surveillance, non-consensual data collection and potential conflicts with the Digital Personal Data Protection Act, 2023 (hereinafter referred to as "DPDP") and subsequent amendments thereto.

The DPDP Act on the other hand was drafted in order to increase the efficiency of the criminal digital justice system while necessitating development of robust safeguards to balance security interests with individual privacy rights.

However, the Draft DPDP Rules introduced in 2025 paint a bothersome picture. Though aimed at establishing a robust data protection framework, the Rules fall short in important areas like enforcement and transparency, with particularly troubling provisions introduced under Rule 22, which has raised a question against the protection of privacy rights.

The concerns that arise from such unfettered digital powers being given to the police and judicial authorities includes expansion of State Power, exemptions for Security, vague Data Usage, Data Security Risks, Lack of Sensitive Data Specifics. There are various Legal and Privacy Implications. Therefore, this paper delves into the impact of the DPDP Act and BNSS and the introduced digital reforms on the right to privacy of individuals and the drawbacks of the same since the above amendments have led to concerns being raised about lack of infrastructure and training for the above which could lead to potential state surveillance, non-consensual data collection and potential conflicts with the Digital Personal Data Protection Act, 2023 (hereinafter referred to as "DPDP") and subsequent amendments thereto.

Introduction

The Bharatiya Nagarik Suraksha Sanhita, 2023[289] (hereinafter referred to as **"BNSS"**) was enacted to modernize India's criminal procedural framework by replacing the Code of Criminal Procedure, 1973[290]

289 Bharatiya Nagarik Suraksha Sanhita, 2023, No. 46 of 2023, India.

290 Code of Criminal Procedure 1973, No. 2 of 1974, India.

(hereinafter referred to as **"Cr.P.C."**) and aligning investigative and judicial processes with contemporary technological standards. It further seeks to modernize procedural law to address evolving criminal methodologies, especially cyber-enabled and technologically facilitated crimes. The statute thus introduced several digital reforms including summons[291], electronic identification of arrested persons[292], audio-video recording of searches[293], digital case diaries, and the use of electronic evidence systems. While these reforms were aimed to enhance efficiency, transparency and increase the resources of the stretched-thin judicial system, it has simultaneously expanded the technological footprint of the State within this judicial process.

However, digitization in criminal procedure inevitably raises concerns relating to:

- Surveillance expansion
- Data retention and sharing
- Biometric and digital profiling
- State access to personal information
- Interoperability of databases

Parallel to the same, the Digital Personal Data Protection Act, 2023[294] (hereinafter referred to as **"DPDP Act"**) was introduced to establish a comprehensive and robust framework for personal data and privacy protection in India, seeking to balance the State's interests in security and governance with the individual's fundamental right to privacy as recognized in *Justice K.S. Puttaswamy (Retd.) v. Union*

291 *BNSS, 2023,* Section 63.

292 *BNSS, 2023,* Section 54.

293 *BNSS, 2023,* Section 105.

294 Digital Personal Data Protection Act, 2023, No. 22 of 2023, India.

of India (hereinafter referred to as **"the Puttaswamy judgment"**[295]. However, concerns arise when digital policing powers under BNSS intersect with the exemptions and rule-making framework under the DPDP Act, particularly in light of the Draft DPDP Rules, 2025[296]. While the DPDP Act provides certain safeguards, it also grants broad exemptions to the State for purposes of sovereignty, integrity, public order, and security.

This dual development creates a constitutional tension:

Can enlarged digital powers given to the police coexist with effective data protection?

This paper will thus critically examine how the digital reforms introduced under BNSS affect the right to privacy, data protection safeguards, and surveillance architecture in India. It analyses issues relating to expansion of state power, security exemptions, vague data usage standards, data security risks, absence of sensitive data specificity, and limitations in enforcement under the DPDP regime. The paper argues that without robust procedural safeguards, infrastructure readiness, and accountability mechanisms, the BNSS may inadvertently enable intrusive surveillance practices that undermine constitutional privacy guarantees.

295 *Justice K.S. Puttaswamy v. Union of India*, (2017) 10 SCC 1 (India).

296 Draft Digital Personal Data Protection Rules, 2025.

Constitutional Foundations: Privacy as a Fundamental Right

In the Puttaswamy judgment[297], the Supreme Court of India unequivocally recognized privacy as a fundamental right under Article 21 of the Constitution[298]. The Court further clarified that privacy is broad and includes:

- **Bodily Privacy:** Protection against forced medical procedures and reproductive autonomy
- **Informational Privacy:** Protection of personal data, control over personal information and the basis for data protection laws
- **Decisional Privacy:** Personal choices regarding marriage, family, sexual orientation

The Court emphasized that any intrusion must satisfy the thresholds of legality, legitimate aim, proportionality and procedural safeguards to avoid infringement of the abovementioned right guaranteed under Article 14[299], 19[300] and 21[301] of the Constitution.

This means the State cannot violate the right to privacy arbitrarily. To summarize the above, the Court laid down that:

"The right to privacy is protected as an intrinsic part of the right to life and personal liberty under Article 21."[302]

---

297 *Puttaswamy v. Union of India*, 2017.

298 Constitution of India, art. 21.

299 Constitution of India, art. 14.

300 Constitution of India, art. 19.

301 Constitution of India, art. 21

302 *Puttaswamy v. Union of India*, 2017.

In *Puttaswamy*, the Court explicitly recognized informational privacy as a core component of the right to privacy. Informational privacy refers to an individual's right to control the collection, storage, processing, and dissemination of personal data. The Court acknowledged that in the digital age, personal data has become a powerful economic and political resource. Unregulated data collection by both the State and private entities poses serious risks to autonomy, dignity, and freedom.

By constitutionalizing informational privacy, the Court made it clear that data protection is not merely a regulatory convenience but a constitutional necessity. This recognition directly influenced legislative efforts aimed at creating a comprehensive data protection regime.

Following the *Puttaswamy* judgment, the Government constituted committees to frame a robust data protection framework. This eventually led to the enactment of the DPDP Act[303]. The Act derives its legitimacy from the constitutional mandate laid down in *Puttaswamy*.

The principles of legality, legitimate aim, proportionality and procedural safeguards now inform how data protection laws should be ideally structured, especially in matters involving government surveillance, data retention, and state access to personal data.

The Court linked privacy with dignity and individual autonomy. In the context of data protection, this means individuals must have control over their digital identity. Consent, purpose limitation, data minimization, and transparency: key principles of modern data protection law, flow directly from the constitutional value of autonomy.

303 *DPDP Act, 2023.*

For instance:

- Consent requirements reflect the individual's right to decide how their data is used.
- Purpose limitation ensures data collected for one reason is not misused for another.
- Data minimization prevents excessive or arbitrary collection.
- Right to correction and erasure reinforces control over personal information.

The *Puttaswamy* judgment was closely connected with the Aadhaar litigation. It clarified that large-scale data collection by the State must meet strict constitutional standards. Even where welfare objectives are involved, data collection must not be excessive or disproportionate. The decision ensured that any expansion of digital governance must operate within constitutional privacy boundaries.

These principles form the constitutional benchmark against which the new technological reforms introduced by BNSS and DPDP must be evaluated.

Digital Innovations Under BNSS

BNSS has introduced several technology-centric provisions such as:

1. Electronic Registration of FIR and Complaints[304]

One of the most important digital reforms introduced by the BNSS is the recognition of electronic First Information Reports (e-FIRs). Section 173 of BNSS allows victims to register complaints and

304 *BNSS, 2023,* Section 173.

information relating to cognizable offences through electronic communication such as email or online portals.

Key Features

- Complaints can be filed electronically without visiting a police station.
- The complainant must sign the complaint within a prescribed period if it is submitted electronically.
- Police authorities are required to acknowledge such complaints.

Significance

This reform increases accessibility to justice, particularly for individuals who may face barriers in physically visiting police stations. It also promotes faster reporting of crimes, especially cyber offences, online fraud, and digital harassment.

2. Audio-Video Recording of Searches and Seizures[305]

Section 105 of BNSS introduces a significant requirement that searches and seizures conducted by investigating agencies may be recorded through audio-video electronic means.

Objectives

- To improve transparency and accountability in police investigations.
- To prevent allegations of fabrication of evidence or procedural irregularities.
- To ensure accurate documentation of investigative procedures.

305 *BNSS, 2023*, Section 105.

Implications

The use of audio-video recordings creates a reliable digital record that can later be examined by courts, reducing disputes regarding the legality or fairness of police actions.

3. Electronic Summons and Warrants[306]

Section 70 of BNSS allows summons, warrants, and other judicial processes to be served electronically, including through digital communication platforms.

Key Features

- Electronic service of summons through email or electronic messaging systems.
- Digital acknowledgement of receipt.
- Faster communication between courts, law enforcement agencies, and parties.

Benefits

This digital system significantly reduces delays caused by traditional physical service methods. It improves the efficiency of court proceedings and allows parties to receive legal notices quickly.

4. Use of Electronic Communication in Court Proceedings[307]

Section 530 of BNSS allows courts to use electronic modes of communication and digital documentation in criminal proceedings.

306 *BNSS, 2023,* Section 70.

307 *BNSS, 2023,* Section 530.

Examples

- Electronic filing of documents
- Digital transmission of case records
- Use of electronic records as admissible evidence

This innovation aligns criminal procedure with modern judicial practices and the recognition of electronic evidence under the Information Technology Act, 2000[308].

5. Electronic Monitoring of Investigations

Another innovation under the BNSS is the creation of technology-based monitoring systems for investigations.

Key Provisions

- Supervisory officers can digitally track progress of investigations.
- Case management systems may be used to ensure timelines are followed.
- Digital records of investigative steps can be maintained.

Importance

This reform aims to reduce investigative delays and improve institutional accountability within police departments.

6. Electronic Identification of Arrested Persons[309]

Section 54 of BNSS enables authorities to collect electronic and biometric data of arrested individuals during investigations.

308 Information Technology Act, 2000, No. 21 of 2000, India.

309 *BNSS, 2023,* Section 54.

Types of Data

- Fingerprints
- Iris scans
- Photographs
- Other biometric identifiers

This provision assists law enforcement agencies in criminal identification, record management, and tracking repeat offenders.

These are just a few examples of the manner in which BNSS seeks to modernize criminal justice system by using technology, but are the police and the infrastructure ready for such a paradigm shift?

Expansion of State Power

As discussed above, several technological improvements have been introduced through BNSS which are intended to improve efficiency and transparency, however they also significantly expand the powers of the State in surveillance, investigation, and data collection. This expansion raises important constitutional and legal questions concerning civil liberties, privacy, and accountability within India's criminal justice framework.

1. Expansion of Surveillance Capabilities

One of the most significant consequences of technological integration under the BNSS is the enhanced ability of the State to monitor individuals and collect digital information. The recognition of electronic evidence, digital communication, and biometric data allows investigative agencies to access and analyze large volumes of personal information.

For example, Section 54 of BNSS permits the collection of biometric identifiers such as fingerprints, photographs, and iris scans of accused persons, which could be stored in centralized databases. While this assists in criminal identification and investigation, it also increases the State's capacity to maintain extensive digital records of individuals. Such databases, if not properly regulated, could potentially be used for broad surveillance purposes beyond specific criminal investigations.

2. Increased Investigative Authority of Law Enforcement

Technological reforms under the BNSS strengthen the investigative capacity of police authorities. The use of digital case management systems, electronic monitoring of investigations, and technological documentation of investigative steps provides law enforcement agencies with more structured and powerful tools.

Investigative agencies can now maintain digitally traceable records of suspects, evidence, and procedural steps, enabling faster information sharing between departments and jurisdictions. This expansion of investigative capability increases the operational power of the State in criminal proceedings.

However, while such systems improve efficiency, they also create the possibility of overreach or misuse if adequate oversight mechanisms are not established. Digital records, once created, can be accessed or shared widely, raising concerns about the potential misuse of sensitive personal data.[310]

310 Karapetyan, M. (2024, October 28), *Ethics of data sharing and digital privacy*, Viterbi Conversations in Ethics, https://vce.usc.edu/volume-7-issue-2/ethics-of-data-sharing-and-digital-privacy/

3. Expansion of Data Collection and Storage by the State

Another major effect of technological reforms under BNSS is the large-scale collection and storage of personal data by government authorities which is evidenced by no procedure being provided for the disposal of the data collected under the above discussed provisions. Electronic FIR systems, digital investigation records, and biometric identification processes create a vast amount of data that may be stored in government databases.

Such data may include:

- Personal identification details
- Digital communications and electronic records
- Biometric information
- Criminal investigation records

The expansion of state-controlled data infrastructure increases the State's informational power. While such information can assist in effective policing and crime prevention, it also creates risks of data breaches, misuse, and unauthorized surveillance.

These concerns are particularly relevant in the context of India's evolving data protection regime under the DPDP Act, which seeks to regulate the processing of personal data and ensure safeguards against misuse.

4. Enhanced Control over Criminal Procedure and Evidence

Technological integration also expands the State's procedural control over criminal investigations and trials. The use of audio-video recordings during searches and seizures[311], digital documentation of investigative processes[312], and electronic transmission of court documents[313] strengthens the evidentiary framework available to prosecution authorities.

This can enhance the reliability of evidence and reduce disputes about procedural irregularities. However, it also places greater evidentiary power in the hands of investigative agencies, which may affect the balance between prosecution and defense if safeguards regarding authenticity and tampering of digital evidence are not strictly enforced.

Furthermore, technological evidence often requires specialized expertise to challenge or verify, which may disadvantage accused persons who lack the resources to obtain digital forensic assistance.

5. Potential for Digital Policing and Predictive Enforcement

The digitization of criminal records and investigative processes creates the possibility of data-driven policing models, including predictive analysis and automated surveillance systems. When large databases of criminal records, biometric identifiers, and digital evidence are

311 *BNSS, 2023,* Section 105.

312 *BNSS, 2023,* Section 173.

313 *BNSS, 2023,* Section 230.

integrated, authorities may use analytical technologies to identify patterns or predict potential criminal behavior.[314]

While such systems may improve crime prevention strategies, they also raise concerns regarding profiling, algorithmic bias, and disproportionate targeting of certain communities. Without proper regulation, predictive policing technologies may lead to discriminatory enforcement practices.

6. Reduced Procedural Barriers for State Action

Digital systems reduce many of the logistical barriers that previously limited the speed and scope of state action. Electronic summons, digital investigation records, and automated case tracking systems enable authorities to initiate and conduct proceedings more rapidly.

While this contributes to procedural efficiency, it also means that the State can exercise its coercive powers more quickly and extensively than before. In the absence of adequate checks and balances, this could potentially weaken procedural safeguards designed to protect the rights of accused persons.

Such power, if unchecked, may undermine proportionality.

Exemptions Under the DPDP Act

The above developments intersect directly with India's data protection framework under the DPDP Act. While the DPDP Act establishes safeguards for the processing of personal data, it also contains several broad exemptions for the State, particularly in areas related to law enforcement, sovereignty, and public order.

314 Singla, Dr. P., *The Impact of Technology on Criminal Investigations and Evidence*, Internation Journal of Creative Research Thoughts (2025) Volume 13, Issue 3.

In the context of the BNSS's digital innovations— such as biometric data collection, electronic investigation records, and digital evidence management— the exemptions under the DPDP Act become especially significant because they determine the extent to which State authorities are bound by data protection obligations.

1. Exemption for Sovereignty, Security, and Public Order

Section 17 of the DPDP Act provides one of the most significant exemptions and allows the Central Government to exempt any government agency from the application of the Act if such exemption is necessary in the interests of:

- Sovereignty and integrity of India
- Security of the State
- Friendly relations with foreign states
- Maintenance of public order
- Prevention or investigation of offences[315]

This exemption has direct relevance to investigative powers exercised under the BNSS. When law enforcement agencies collect personal or biometric data during criminal investigations, the government may exempt such processing from many of the obligations imposed by the DPDP Act. As a result, authorities engaged in criminal investigations may not always be required to comply with certain protections normally available to individuals, such as consent requirements or limitations on data processing.

315 *DPDP, 2023*, Section 17.

While such exemptions may be justified in the context of national security or serious criminal investigations, they also raise concerns about potential overreach and insufficient oversight.

2. Exemption for Law Enforcement and Criminal Investigations

The DPDP Act also provides exemptions where personal data is processed for the prevention, detection, investigation, or prosecution of offences.[316]

This exemption is particularly relevant to the digital investigative mechanisms introduced by the BNSS. Investigative agencies may process personal data without adhering to several standard data protection principles when such processing is necessary for criminal law enforcement.

These powers significantly strengthen the operational capacity of law enforcement agencies. However, they also create a large zone of state-controlled data processing that remains outside the full scope of data protection regulation.

3. Exemption from Consent Requirements

Under normal circumstances, the DPDP Act requires that personal data be processed only with the consent of the data principal. However, when data is processed for law enforcement or governmental functions authorized by law, consent may not be required.

In the context of BNSS investigations, individuals whose data is collected, whether suspects, witnesses, or other persons involved in investigations, may not have the ability to refuse such data collection.

---

316 *DPDP, 2023,* Section 17.

This significantly enhances the State's capacity to obtain personal information without procedural barriers, thereby expanding the investigative authority of law enforcement agencies.

4. Exemption from Certain Data Principal Rights

The DPDP Act grants individuals several rights, including:

- The right to access personal data[317]
- The right to correction and erasure[318]
- The right to grievance redressal[319]

However, when data is processed under the exemptions relating to law enforcement or national security, these rights may be restricted.

For example, a person whose personal data is stored in a law enforcement database may not be able to demand access to that data or request its deletion if doing so would interfere with an ongoing investigation.

Such restrictions reflect the tension between individual privacy rights and the State's interest in effective law enforcement.

5. Exemption for Judicial and Regulatory Functions

The DPDP Act also provides exemptions for data processing carried out for judicial or quasi-judicial functions.[320] This means that courts and other adjudicatory bodies handling criminal proceedings may process personal data without being bound by all the provisions of the Act.

---

317 *DPDP, 2023,* Section 11.

318 *DPDP, 2023,* Section 12.

319 *DPDP, 2023,* Section 13.

320 *DPDP, 2023,* Section 17(1)(b).

Since the BNSS encourages digital case management systems and electronic documentation, courts will increasingly handle large volumes of personal data during criminal trials. The exemption ensures that judicial processes are not hindered by rigid compliance requirements.

However, this also means that the data protection obligations applicable to private entities are not always equally applicable to state institutions.

The exemptions provided under the DPDP Act play a crucial role in determining the scope of data protection in India, particularly in the context of technologically enhanced criminal procedures under the BNSS. While these exemptions enable law enforcement agencies to perform their functions effectively, they also expand the State's capacity to collect and process personal data with limited regulatory constraints. Ensuring that these powers are exercised responsibly and in accordance with constitutional principles remains essential for maintaining the balance between national security, effective policing, and the protection of individual privacy.

Draft DPDP Rules, 2025 and Rule 22 Concerns

The Draft Rules of 2025 attempt to operationalize the DPDP Act but reportedly introduce concerning provisions under Rule 22[321] relating to:

- Expanded governmental access
- Reduced transparency thresholds
- Limited reporting obligations Concerns include:

321 *Draft DPDP Rules, 2025, r. 22.*

- Weak enforcement mechanisms
- Absence of independent oversight
- Insufficient clarity on data retention timelines
- No clear audit standards for law enforcement

This regulatory gap intensifies risks when combined with BNSS digital mechanisms.

What does it mean for personal data?

Under the Rules, one of the primary grounds to demand data is "in the interest of sovereignty and integrity of India or security of the State,"[322] as outlined in the Seventh Schedule. This ground is disturbingly vague, allowing for potential misuse or arbitrary decisions without clear, enforceable limits.

Additional grounds for requesting data include "performing functions under existing laws, fulfilling obligations under any law in force, actions by persons authorised under applicable laws, and conducting assessments to designate certain entities as Significant Data Fiduciaries"[323]. Such broad and ambiguous grounds give government authorities almost unlimited power to access personal data whenever they wish.

This is while keeping in mind that there is no requirement for a formal, written request by the authorities, who are themselves government agents or functionaries. This thus creates a system where government-appointed agents can demand sensitive personal information without impunity, all the while bypassing the need for

322 *DPDP, 2023,* Section 17.

323 *DPDP, 2023,* Section 2(i).

individual consent and raising significant concerns about privacy and misuse of power.

Secondly, Rule 22 also permits the government to withhold any and all information if its disclosure is deemed to jeopardise national security or sovereignty. The phrasing – "*prejudicially affect the sovereignty and integrity of India or security of the State*" – is unnervingly broad and could potentially be invoked without clear, enforceable limits.

In the past, such vague language has been used to render the state's actions hard to challenge, and this case may be no different.[324]

Rule 22 also does not provide any safeguards in situations where the government requests information, which grants broad and unfettered power without clear limitations, exceptions or oversight to the government. This provision thus bypasses the safeguards established by the Supreme Court in *PUCL v. Union of India*[325], which held that intercepting communications violates the constitutional right to life and personal liberty unless done through a legally established procedure. The judgment mandated specific safeguards, including oversight by a review committee and a requirement for requests to detail the intended use of the information.[326] But Rule 22 undermines these protections, allowing government authorities unchecked access to personal data.

The other, bigger problem with Rule 22 is that it does not have a requirement for an independent review mechanism to check the legitimacy or necessity of the government's demands for data to ensure that they are reasonable, justified or proportionate. This leaves room

324 *Indian Dental Association v. Union of India*, 2004 (1) KAR LJ 282 (India).

325 *People's Union for Civil Liberties v. Union of India*, (1997) 1 SCC 301 (India).

326 *PUCL v. UOI*, 1997.

for arbitrary use. In fact, without proper oversight, the rule has the potential to enable covert surveillance programs that bypass checks and balances and can lead to excessive data collection and the monitoring of ordinary citizens by the government.

Finally, there is no mechanism to challenge such requests, and data fiduciaries and intermediaries may not have an effective way to challenge such data requests from the government, potentially resulting in a surveillance state without public awareness or recourse.

We have often seen how overbroad directions for censorship have been made and required to be kept confidential under Section 69 of the IT Act, 2000[327]. Such an opaque framework has prevented social media users from challenging the takedown of their content before court and is at the heart of the judicial challenge in the Karnataka high court where X has challenged the Union government[328]. The lack of transparency and the over-collection of data allows for the broad, unchecked use of data and for its potential misuse by prosecuting agencies.

For example, in the case of FIRs where police often lack the information needed to identify suspects, the data collected by the government could be wrongfully used to implicate individuals. This eliminates the need for the police to seek out information, as they already have access to it through the government's data collection, which could be used to target individuals unjustly.

327 *ITA, 2000,* Section 69.

328 *X Corp v. Union of India on 24 September, 2025,* Karnataka High Court (India).

What does this mean for our privacy?

The A.P. Shah Report[329] stressed on the need for a transparent process that includes the disclosure of surveillance to those who have been placed under it. Access to information under Section 95 of the BNSS[330] is subject to judicial oversight, as a court order must be issued before accessing information.

In a similar vein, the guidelines issued by the Supreme Court in *PUCL v. Union of India*[331] included oversight by a review committee and required interception requests to specify the intended use of the information.

Complicating matters is the fact that the broad definition of a data fiduciary[332] means it could apply to anyone, including journalists. For journalists acting as data fiduciaries, Rule 22 has profound implications, particularly in terms of their ability to safeguard sensitive information, such as the identities of sources.

This raises serious questions about the future of privacy in India. As it stands, Rule 22 opens the door for unchecked government surveillance, with minimal accountability or transparency.

The first step for the same is ensuring that the requests conform with the standards laid down in the *Puttaswamy*[333] judgment, which held that while the right to privacy is not absolute, any state intrusion must meet a three-fold requirement. This includes legality, which

329 Government of India, Planning Commission. (2012). *Report of the Group of Experts on Privacy (Chairperson: Justice A.P. Shah).*

330 *BNSS, 2023, Section 95.*

331 *PUCL v. Union of India, 1997.*

332 *DPDP, 2023,* Section 2(i).

333 *Puttaswamy v. Union of India,* 2017.

necessitates the existence of a law authorising the intrusion; a legitimate state aims to justify the need for such intrusion; and proportionality, ensuring a rational connection between the law's objectives and the means adopted, thereby preventing disproportionate impacts on individual rights.

Additionally, the process should allow for a clear appeal mechanism and be subject to independent oversight. At any rate, the provision as it stands now does not bode well for privacy in India.

Legal and Privacy Implications

1. Fundamental Right Concerns

One of the central legal concerns arising due to these reforms relates to the right to privacy as a fundamental right under the Constitution of India. In the landmark decision of *Justice K.S. Puttaswamy v. Union of India*[334], the Supreme Court of India unequivocally recognized privacy as an intrinsic part of the right to life and personal liberty guaranteed under Article 21 of the Constitution[335]. The Court held that any state action that interferes with privacy must satisfy the principles of legality, necessity, and proportionality. The digital reforms under the BNSS involve extensive collection and processing of personal data during criminal investigations, which may potentially infringe upon these privacy protections if not accompanied by adequate safeguards.

Another important legal question arises from the expanded powers granted to law enforcement agencies. The ability to collect

334 *Puttaswamy v. Union of India*, 2017.

335 Constitution of India, art. 21.

biometric information[336], maintain digital records of investigations[337], and electronically monitor procedural steps[338] significantly increases the State's capacity to gather and analyze personal data. While such powers may be necessary for effective law enforcement, they may also create risks of excessive surveillance and disproportionate state intrusion into individual lives. Without clear limitations on the scope and duration of data collection, these mechanisms may conflict with the constitutional requirement that restrictions on fundamental rights must be reasonable and proportionate.

The lack of detailed procedural safeguards governing the handling of digital evidence also raises constitutional concerns. For instance, while the BNSS encourages audio-video recording of searches and seizures to enhance transparency, it does not comprehensively regulate the storage, access, and deletion of such recordings. If such digital records are not adequately protected, they may be misused or disclosed without authorization, thereby violating the privacy and dignity of individuals involved in investigations.

The interaction between the BNSS and the DPDP Act further complicates the legal landscape. Although the DPDP Act establishes a framework for the protection of personal data, it provides broad exemptions for government agencies involved in law enforcement and national security functions. Consequently, investigative bodies operating under the BNSS may not always be bound by the full set of data protection obligations. This raises questions regarding whether individuals whose data is collected during criminal investigations have adequate legal remedies in cases of misuse or unauthorized disclosure.

336 *BNSS* 2023, Section 176.

337 *BNSS* 2023, Section 105.

338 *BNSS* 2023, Section 185.

Another issue relates to due process and informational autonomy. Digital investigative mechanisms may involve the collection of personal data from individuals who are not necessarily accused of any offence, such as witnesses or persons associated with a suspect. The absence of clear procedural requirements for obtaining consent, notifying individuals, or limiting the use of such data may create tensions with constitutional principles protecting personal liberty and procedural fairness.

Additionally, the accumulation of digital investigation records could lead to long-term profiling or surveillance if proper data retention limits are not established. The indefinite storage of biometric or investigative data may expose individuals to potential misuse by authorities or unauthorized actors, thereby raising concerns regarding the protection of dignity and autonomy under Article 21. The BNSS reforms also facilitate the integration of broader digital policing technologies within the criminal justice framework. Such technologies include automated facial recognition systems, interoperable national databases, predictive analytics, and large-scale metadata analysis. Although these tools may enhance investigative efficiency and crime prevention, they also raise serious surveillance and privacy concerns.[339] So these digital reforms must pass the proportionality test.

The key questions that thus arise are:

- Is mass biometric capture proportionate?
- Are blanket exemptions constitutionally valid?
- Is judicial oversight robust enough?

339 *Tracing the Rise of Predictive Policing in India,* Software Freedom Law Center, https://sflc.in/tracing-the-rise-of-predictive-policing-in-india/.

2. DPBI Limitations

While the above technological developments aim to enhance efficiency and transparency in the criminal justice system, they also raise concerns regarding the adequacy of institutional oversight mechanisms responsible for protecting personal data. In this context, the role of the Data Protection Board of India (hereinafter referred to as **"DPBI"**), established under the DPDP Act[340], becomes particularly relevant. However, the Board faces several structural and legal limitations in effectively overseeing the data processing activities arising from these digital reforms.

One of the primary limitations stems from the restricted jurisdiction of the DPBI over government agencies engaged in law enforcement activities. The DPDP Act provides broad exemptions allowing the Central Government to exempt certain government bodies from the application of the Act in the interests of national security, public order, or the prevention and investigation of offences. As a result, investigative authorities operating under the BNSS may not always be fully subject to the data protection obligations enforced by the Board. This significantly reduces the DPBI's ability to supervise how personal data is collected and used during criminal investigations. Another limitation arises from the nature of the Board's powers, which are primarily remedial rather than regulatory. The DPBI largely functions as an adjudicatory body responsible for addressing complaints and imposing penalties for violations of the DPDP Act. It does not possess broad supervisory authority comparable to independent data protection regulators in some other jurisdictions. Consequently, the Board may have limited capacity to proactively monitor or audit government data processing practices associated with BNSS-related investigations.

340 *DPDP Act, 2023,* Section 18.

The lack of strong independence and institutional autonomy may also affect the Board's effectiveness. Since the establishment, composition, and functioning of the DPBI are determined by the Central Government under the DPDP Act, concerns have been raised regarding the extent to which the Board can independently scrutinize government data practices. When data processing is conducted by state agencies engaged in law enforcement, the Board's ability to challenge or regulate such practices may be constrained by these structural dependencies.

Furthermore, the DPDP Act focuses primarily on personal data protection within a general regulatory framework, while the BNSS introduces sector-specific digital procedures related to criminal investigations. The DPBI may therefore lack the specialized mandate or technical expertise necessary to oversee complex law enforcement technologies such as biometric databases, digital evidence systems, or surveillance tools used during criminal investigations.

The Board's effectiveness may also be limited by procedural barriers for individuals seeking remedies. Persons whose personal data is collected during criminal investigations may not always be aware of how their information is being used or stored. Without adequate transparency mechanisms, affected individuals may find it difficult to file complaints or challenge potential misuse of their data before the Board.

These limitations become particularly significant when considered in light of the constitutional recognition of privacy as a fundamental right. If oversight bodies such as the DPBI lack sufficient authority or independence, the protection of privacy rights in the context of expanding digital surveillance powers may be weakened.

In conclusion, while the establishment of the DPBI represents an important step toward building a comprehensive data protection framework in India, its current structure and jurisdiction present several limitations in effectively overseeing the digital investigative mechanisms introduced under the BNSS. Addressing these challenges may require clearer statutory mandates, stronger institutional independence, and enhanced oversight mechanisms to ensure that technological advancements in criminal procedure remain consistent with constitutional principles of privacy, accountability, and rule of law.

Infrastructure and Training Gaps

1. Rural Connectivity Deficits

One of the major challenges in implementing digital criminal procedures is the uneven digital infrastructure across India, particularly in rural and remote areas. Many police stations and judicial institutions in rural regions still face unreliable internet connectivity, inadequate digital equipment, and limited access to secure data management systems.[341] Since many of the BNSS reforms depend on digital communication and electronic record-keeping, the lack of reliable connectivity may hinder the smooth execution of these processes.

341 India, T. O. (2025, February 5). Inadequate basic infra hits functioning of village offices. *The Times of India*. https://timesofindia.indiatimes.com/city/thiruvananthapuram/inadequate-basic-infra-hits-functioning-of-village-offices/articleshow/117959139.cms

2. Inconsistent Digital Literacy Among Officials

Another significant challenge is the variation in digital literacy and technical proficiency among law enforcement and judicial personnel. The effective use of digital investigation tools requires officers to be trained in handling electronic evidence, operating digital documentation systems, and maintaining cybersecurity standards.

However, in many jurisdictions, particularly at the district and sub-district levels, police officers and administrative staff may not have received adequate training in digital technologies. This lack of technical familiarity may lead to improper handling of digital evidence, errors in electronic documentation, or failure to follow prescribed technological procedures. Such gaps can compromise both the efficiency and the legal reliability of digital investigative processes.

3. Lack of Uniform Encryption and Cybersecurity Standards

The increased use of digital systems in criminal investigations raises important concerns regarding data security and encryption standards. Sensitive information such as biometric identifiers, investigation records, and audio-video recordings must be securely stored and transmitted to prevent unauthorized access or tampering.

However, there is currently no universally implemented encryption protocol across all law enforcement and judicial institutions handling digital criminal procedure.[342] The absence of standardized cybersecurity measures may expose digital records to risks such as hacking, data breaches, or manipulation of electronic evidence. Weak cybersecurity

342 E-Committee, Supreme Court of India (2021), *Digital Courts Vision & Roadmap E-Courts Project Phase III* p. 72.

infrastructure can therefore undermine the reliability and integrity of digital investigative processes.

These concerns also intersect with broader data protection issues addressed in the DPDP Act, which emphasizes the importance of safeguarding personal data processed by institutions.

4. Limited Digital Forensic Capabilities

The increasing reliance on digital evidence in criminal investigations requires specialized digital forensic expertise to properly collect, analyze, and authenticate electronic data. Digital forensics plays a crucial role in ensuring that electronic evidence presented in court is reliable, untampered, and admissible.

However, India currently faces a shortage of well-equipped forensic laboratories and trained digital forensic experts, particularly at the state and district levels.[343] Many investigative agencies must rely on a limited number of centralized forensic laboratories, leading to delays in evidence analysis and case processing. Additionally, the lack of trained personnel capable of handling digital evidence may increase the risk of procedural errors or evidentiary challenges during trial.

Conclusion

Both the technological reforms brought in by BNSS and the DPDP act are laws brought in with good intentions. But as they say the path to hell is paved with good intentions and unless effective mechanisms are provided to curb the current inadequacies to implement them then this law will do more harm than good. We urgently need to deal with

343 Deloitte (2025), Indian digital forensic market report, https://www.deloitte.com/in/en/services/consulting/services/risk-regulatory-forensic/indian-digital-forensic-market-report.html.

the implementation issues discussed above so that both the actual intentions behind these laws can be realized. The first step that needs to be taken is a complete overhaul of Rule 22 of draft DPDP rules before they are brought into effect because as can be seen from the current trend, data is the currency of the future and its protection has to take precedence.

Thus, to achieve the above, the following recommendations are proposed:

1. Explicit retention limits under BNSS
2. Mandatory judicial warrants for biometric collection
3. Independent audit of digital infrastructure
4. Clear prohibition of secondary data usage
5. Strengthening DPBI independence
6. Transparency reports from police agencies
7. Encryption standards uniform nationwide
8. Citizen notification rights post-investigation
9. Explicit safeguards for sensitive data
10. Harmonization clause between BNSS and DPDP.

Thus, if the government is not able to provide proper safeguards and without any oversight wherein the data of individuals is unsafely handled then this will be the worst consequence these laws can have and it would be better to not bring them into effect in such a way.

Chapter 11

Digital Due Process Under the Bnss: Reassessing State Surveillance Powers in the Context of Evolving Privacy and Data Protection Norms

Neha Sharma
Research Scholar, School of Law, Shoolini University, Solan, H.P.

Shubham Sharma
Research Scholar, Yogananda School of AI, Computers and Data Science, Shoolini University, Solan, H.P.

Prof. Nandan Sharma
Associate Dean, School of Law, Shoolini University, Solan

Abstract

The notification of the Bharatiya Nagarik Suraksha Sanhita, 2023 (BNSS) in the Gazette marks a significant development in the reform of India's criminal procedural framework, reflecting a shift from colonial-era structures toward a technology-integrated system of governance. The incorporation of technology-enabled mechanisms such as electronic First Information Reports (e-FIRs) and videography in criminal investigations is intended to enhance efficiency and transparency within investigative procedures. However, these developments also raise important concerns regarding whether adequate procedural safeguards exist to balance state access to digital evidence with the protection of the right to privacy.

This chapter engages with the evolving concept of digital due process, which involves extending constitutional guarantees of fairness, legality, and proportionality into the domain of electronic surveillance and data extraction. It critically examines the compatibility of the BNSS with the right to privacy as recognized by the Supreme Court of India in Justice K.S. Puttaswamy (Retd.) v. Union of India (2017), particularly in light of the tests of legality, necessity, and proportionality applicable to restrictions on fundamental rights. The analysis focuses on Section 94 of the BNSS, which permits the compulsory production of digital evidence and electronic communications. It argues that, in the absence of clear procedural thresholds and judicial oversight, this provision risks enabling overly broad searches and undermining digital due process.

These concerns are further intensified by the interaction between Section 94 and the Digital Personal Data Protection Act, 2023. Specifically, the exemptions granted to law enforcement under Section 17 of the DPDP Act create a structural tension between consent-based data protection principles and expanded surveillance objectives.

The chapter also considers institutional challenges related to digital forensic capabilities, which may affect evidentiary reliability, procedural fairness, and accountability (Committee of Experts, 2018). Finally, it proposes a contextual model of digital due process designed to balance investigative efficiency with constitutional protections in an increasingly digital criminal justice system.

1. Introduction

The Bharatiya Nagarik Suraksha Sanhita, 2023 (BNSS) is an important legislative reform in the criminal justice system in India, replacing the Code of Criminal Procedure, 1973, and indicating an endeavour to reform procedural laws in conformity with changing technological realities. The BNSS has incorporated several innovations in procedural laws with the objective of ensuring greater efficiency and transparency in criminal investigation, such as the use of electronic First Information Reports, mandatory audio-visual recording, and digital evidence in procedural mechanisms. This is part of a wider shift in governance, as reflected in the concept of digital governance, in which state agencies increasingly depend on technology to achieve greater efficiency in governance.

The shift in procedural laws, as reflected in the introduction of digital investigation, raises several critical issues with regard to state intrusion into individual privacy, as opposed to conventional investigation techniques, which were restricted by spatial limitations. The use of smartphones, computers, and cloud services has given rise to digital platforms as repositories of highly sensitive personal information, which can be accessed through digital investigation techniques. The shift to digital investigation techniques has, therefore, given rise to greater possibilities for state intrusion into individual privacy.

Such developments can be evaluated through the framework of the constitutional provisions of the right to privacy as recognized in the judgment of Justice K.S. Puttaswamy (Retd.) v. Union of India[344]. The Supreme Court recognized that the right to privacy is indeed a

344 (2017) 10 S.C.C. 1.

fundamental right under Article 21[345] of the Constitution and that any restriction on this right must satisfy the principles of legality, necessity, and proportionality. The framework of such principles is crucial in evaluating state action in such matters. However, the application of such principles to digital investigations under the newly enacted provisions of law is still in its infancy.

One of the important aspects of the BNSS in this context is Section 94 of the BNSS that permits the compulsory production of documents and electronic records for the purpose of investigation, inquiry, or trial. While such provisions were also available under the CrPC, 1973, their applicability in the digital sphere is much wider. The lack of clear guidelines on the procedural limits of such access is of concern to the extent to which such access might be overly broad.

This issue is compounded by the interplay between criminal procedure and data protection law. The DPDP Act of 2023 sets up a framework of data protection through the principles of consent and lawfulness of processing. However, it also grants sweeping exemptions to state agencies for their activities in preventing and investigating crimes. The interplay of such provisions is likely to undermine the efficacy of the right to privacy.

This chapter seeks to examine the extent to which the BNSS meets the requirements of digital due process in the regulation of state access to electronic data. The research questions that guide this chapter are:

---

345 B. C. Rodrigues, Commonwealth Human Rights Initiative, The Right to Information in the Ugandan Context 1–6 (Dec. 2003). Also see: Deepak Kumar, The Right to Privacy Under Article 21: Implications of the DPDP Act, 2023 for Data Protection in India, 6(8) Int'l J. Leading Rsch. Publ'n (IJLRP) 1 (2025)

i. To what extent does the BNSS extend the powers of surveillance in the context of digital investigations?

ii. Are the procedural protections provided under the BNSS consistent with the constitutional standards of privacy set out in the Puttaswamy case?

iii. How does the relationship between the BNSS and the DPDP Act shape the regime of personal data protection?

This chapter follows a doctrinal and analytical methodology. The work will be evaluated in light of established doctrines of constitutional law, principles of legal interpretation, and pertinent academic literature. The analysis will contend that although the BNSS marks a significant advancement in the modernization of investigative processes, it does not adequately incorporate the safeguards required to regulate digital surveillance in a manner consistent with constitutional principles and data protection law.

The structure of the chapter is as follows: Section 2 will conceptualise the idea of digital due process and its relationship to constitutional law. Section 3 will examine the expansion of the regime of surveillance powers created under the BNSS, with a particular focus on the powers created under Section 94. Section 4 will evaluate the expansion of the regime of surveillance powers under the BNSS against the constitutional standards of privacy and proportionality. Section 5 will examine the relationship between the BNSS and the DPDP Act, which will highlight the tension between the two statutes. Section 6 will highlight the structural problems with the current regime of personal data protection. Section 7 will propose a contextual approach to the idea of digital due process and make some concluding observations.

2. Digitalization of Criminal Procedure and Emergence of Digital Due Process

The transformation of criminal procedure in India must be understood in relation to the larger context of digitalization of governance, wherein technological systems increasingly play a mediating role in state activities and decision-making. In the last decade or so, criminal investigation practices have increasingly shifted from physical evidence to the collection, storage, and analysis of data in electronic form. The Bharatiya Nagarik Suraksha Sanhita, 2023 (BNSS) is a part of this transformation, wherein digitalization is formally incorporated into criminal procedure to redefine the nature and scope of criminal investigation. In other words, digitalization is formally incorporated into criminal procedure in India to redefine the nature and scope of criminal investigation. Under the previous Code of Criminal Procedure, 1973 (CrPC), criminal investigation practices were limited by physical realities. Searches were limited to specific locations, documentary evidence was physical in nature, and investigation itself was limited by physical realities. Although amendments to the CrPC and developments in case law have increasingly acknowledged the value of electronic evidence, such developments are merely ancillary to the main framework. The BNSS represents a significant departure from earlier procedural developments by formally recognizing digital data as a primary form of evidence, thereby expanding both the scope and depth of criminal investigations. This shift is not merely procedural but also carries substantial implications for individual rights. Digital data differs fundamentally from physical evidence due to its expansive, enduring, and deeply intrusive nature. A single digital device may contain years of communications, financial transactions, browsing histories, and location data, offering detailed insights into an individual's personal and social life. As Solove (2006) observes, digital data enables the creation of behavioural patterns and personal profiles that extend beyond isolated facts, thereby intensifying privacy concerns associated with state access. Consequently, digital searches are not simply extensions of traditional investigative methods but are qualitatively distinct from them[346].

The emergence of digital due process can be understood as a response to these developments. In India, the concept of due process evolved through judicial interpretation of Article 21, which Justice V.R. Krishna Iyer described as a "Procedural Magna Carta." This evolution was particularly evident in Maneka Gandhi v. Union of India (1978), where the Supreme Court held that any procedure affecting life and personal liberty must be "just, fair and reasonable." This judgment established that procedural rules must satisfy substantive standards of fairness rather than merely comply with formal legality.

This constitutional foundation was further strengthened in Justice K.S. Puttaswamy (Retd.) v. Union of India (2017), where the Supreme Court recognized privacy as a fundamental right and laid down a framework for evaluating state intrusion into privacy. According to this framework, any restriction on privacy must satisfy three requirements: legality, necessity, and proportionality. These principles now form the core standard for assessing state surveillance and data collection practices.

On this jurisprudential basis, digital due process may be understood as the extension of constitutional safeguards into the domain of electronic data and surveillance. It requires that state access to digital information be governed not only by statutory authority but also by safeguards ensuring that such access is justified, limited, and proportionate to the objectives of investigation. Digital due

346 Daniel J. Solove, A Taxonomy of Privacy, 154 U. Pa. L. Rev. 477 (2006).

process recognizes the unique features of digital data—its volume, interconnectedness, and sensitivity—which necessitate stronger procedural protections than those applicable to traditional forms of evidence.

A human-centric approach to digital due process highlights the imbalance between expanding state capabilities and individual vulnerabilities in the digital environment. Individuals often lack awareness, control, or meaningful participation in decisions concerning access to their personal data during investigations, thereby reinforcing the need for stronger procedural safeguards. Further, there is a high possibility of obtaining data that is not relevant to the crime, including data that is extremely personal in nature. In this context, it is not only the right to privacy, but also the right to informational liberty and dignity, which is a fundamental component of liberty, as propounded by Puttaswamy (2017). The concept of digital due process, therefore, underscores the need to rebalance the procedural framework in light of technological advancements. Although the BNSS introduces a range of features to address the need for modernization of criminal procedure, it is imperative to assess if this is matched with adequate protection against the potential for state surveillance. This issue will be examined further in the following section through a detailed analysis of state surveillance under the BNSS, particularly in the context of digital search and seizure.

3. Expansion of Surveillance Powers Under the BNSS

The adoption of digital investigation in criminal procedure through the Bharatiya Nagarik Suraksha Sanhita, 2023, is further characterized by the substantial enlargement of investigatory powers. This development may be partly justified by the evolving nature of crime and evidence, but it also represents a broader shift in the balance between state authority and individual rights. In this context, the BNSS enables greater access to electronic records and digital devices, thereby extending investigative reach into areas that were previously less accessible under traditional criminal procedure.

This expansion must be understood not only as a technological development but also in terms of its substantive implications for surveillance. Digital investigations enable access to vast amounts of data from multiple sources, including personal devices and communication networks. Unlike traditional searches, which are confined to specific locations and items, digital surveillance can reveal a comprehensive picture of an individual's private life. Consequently, this expansion raises significant concerns regarding the absence of clearly defined boundaries and limitations.

3.1 Nature and Scope of Digital Surveillance

While the BNSS does not expressly refer to "digital surveillance," it is evident that it incorporates several provisions that permit access to digital data and may therefore be interpreted as forms of 'surveillance.' The provisions that have been highlighted as enabling digital surveillance are the right to demand the production of documents and records, the acknowledgment of electronic evidence, and the procedures that facilitate the collection of digital information[347]. The scope of digital surveillance can thus extend to accessing information on personal devices, accessing information stored in the cloud, and accessing digital communications.

347 Digital Personal Data Protection Act, No. 22 of 2023, Acts of Parliament, 2023.

One of the characteristics of digital surveillance is that it can access large volumes of information. A single act of accessing information can thus access large volumes of data that may contain both relevant and irrelevant information. The large volumes of information accessed can thus lead to over-collection of information. Over-collection is where the scope of information accessed is beyond what is necessary to investigate. According to (Solove, 2006), the aggregation of information can thus lead to the creation of detailed information about individuals.

Another characteristic of digital surveillance is that it is not limited to accessing information within one domain. Physical searches can only access information within one domain at any given time. The characteristic of digital surveillance is that it can access information in multiple domains at the same time. For instance, accessing information on a smartphone can access information in multiple domains such as communication information, financial information, information on internet usage, and information on geographical location.

3.2 Section 94: Digital Search and Seizure

Section 94 of the BNSS is another significant provision that needs to be taken into account while assessing the expansion of digital surveillance powers. This section allows for the production of documents or other things necessary for the purposes of investigation, inquiry, or trial by a court or police officer. Although this provision was also present in the CrPC, its implications in digital India are more significant.

While assessing this provision in relation to digital data, it is pertinent to understand that the term "documents or other things" could also refer to digital gadgets and access to digital accounts. When complying with this provision, access to large amounts of personal information could be granted, including information that is not relevant to the offense. However, this provision does not specifically require that only relevant information be accessed and that the scope of this access be limited. Therefore, issues regarding procedural safeguards arise.

For instance, in traditional circumstances, access to documents would only be granted for identified items. However, in digital India, access to digital data would be granted in integrated form, and separating relevant information from irrelevant information would be impossible without access to digital data. As such, access to large amounts of information could be granted, and investigative authorities could intrude into areas of personal lives that are irrelevant to the offense.[348]

Moreover, it is unclear that there is any prior judicial scrutiny that is appropriate to the sensitivity or quantity of the information. While such oversight may exist in some cases, the lack of clear statutory requirements makes it unclear when such powers might be exercised. From the point of view of digital due process, this is important because it is possible that even lawful action might produce disproportionate results.

3.3 Implications for Digital Due Process

The expansion of the surveillance powers under the BNSS, and specifically the provisions introduced in Section 94, underscore the need to address the issue of the adaptation of procedural law in the digital sphere and the need to bolster the related due process requirements. Digital searching is notable for its intensity and magnitude, which differ significantly from conventional investigative

348 Daniel J. Solove, A Taxonomy of Privacy, 154 U. Pa. L. Rev. 477 (2006)

methods. Therefore, the simple extension of the traditional provisions in the digital sphere may not be considered adequate in meeting the requirements of constitutional due process. From the point of view of digital due process, the core concern is the lack of clear guidelines in terms of the thresholds that the state is expected to follow in accessing the data. The lack of clear requirements in terms of the need to be satisfied, the principle of proportionality, and the principle of limiting the scope of the search may underscore the risk of excessive and intrusive searches.

The relevance of this concern is further compounded in the light of the constitutional provisions that recognize the right to privacy as a fundamental right and underscore the need for the state's interference in this sphere to be justified and narrowly tailored.[349]

Further, the greater reliance on digital evidence may underscore the need to address the related concerns in terms of the handling and management of the related data. The need for the adaptation of the data-based governance model is underscored in the Srikrishna Committee Report (2018)[350] and the need to bolster the related requirements in terms of the prevention of the misuse of the related data and the need for accountability in the handling of the related evidentiary processes[351] Overall, these developments appear to indicate that although the BNSS is a significant step forward in terms of modernising criminal procedure, there are still certain aspects that do not adequately address the issue of digital surveillance. The following

349 Deepak Kumar, The Right to Privacy Under Article 21: Implications of the DPDP Act, 2023 for Data Protection in India, 6(8) Int'l J. Leading Rsch. Publ'n (IJLRP) 1 (2025).

350 Justice B. N. Srikrishna Comm., Government of India, A Free and Fair Digital Economy: Protecting Privacy, Empowering Indians (2018).

351 *Ibid.*

section will explore these issues from a constitutional perspective, specifically in relation to the requirements of legality, necessity, and proportionality as laid down in Supreme Court decisions.

4. Constitutional Framework: Right to Privacy and Proportionality

The constitutional validity of surveillance powers granted in the Bharatiya Nagarik Suraksha Sanhita, 2023 (BNSS) must be tested in light of the framework of the Right to Privacy as laid down in Article 21 of the Constitution. The judgment in Justice K.S. Puttaswamy (Retd.) v. Union of India (2017) was a landmark decision in constitutional law in India, which recognised a fundamental right to privacy. It was held that individual autonomy, dignity, and self-determination are all integral aspects of personal liberty. Significantly, a framework for adjudicating such a right was laid down, wherein a limitation on privacy must satisfy the tests of legality, necessity, and proportionality.

This framework has developed upon previous decisions, especially the case of Maneka Gandhi v. Union of India[352], which emphasized that any process that touches upon the aspects of life and personal liberty must be "just, fair and reasonable." This framework of decisions ensures that the assessment of procedural law does not remain confined to the parameters of legality but must also be tested on the grounds of fairness and reasonableness. This requirement assumes considerable significance while assessing the case of digital surveillance, as it touches upon the very intrusive nature of accessing electronic data[353].

352 (1978) 1 S.C.C. 248

353 *Ibid.*

4.1 The Requirement of Legality

The first requirement of the framework developed by the Puttaswamy case is the requirement of legality, which asserts that any restriction on the right to privacy must be based on a legal requirement. With regard to the BNSS, the legal requirement of accessing the documents and electronic data is provided under various provisions, especially Section 94[354]. This requirement of legality is formally satisfied as the requirement of accessing data is provided for under the law. However, the requirement of legality is not merely the presence of a legal provision. It must also be sufficiently clear, accessible, and precise in its definition of the scope and limitations of the powers of the state. A law that does not provide for a clear definition of the powers of the state may be deemed to be failing on the grounds of legality, as it does not provide adequate protection against the arbitrary exercise of powers. In respect to BNSS, the lack of explicit instructions regarding the extent of access to electronic information and the circumstances under which these powers can be exercised might be considered inadequate.

4.2 The Requirement of Necessity

Secondly, there must be a legitimate state interest justifying the restriction on the right to privacy, and the restriction must be necessary to achieve that objective. In the context of criminal investigations, the prevention and detection of crime clearly constitute legitimate state interests. Access to digital data may therefore be necessary for effective investigations, particularly where offences leave behind digital footprints.

354 Bharatiya Nagarik Suraksha Sanhita, No. 46 of 2023, Acts of Parliament, 2023

However, the requirement of necessity also demands that intrusive measures be properly justified. It is not sufficient to merely assert that access to digital data is useful for investigations. Instead, it must be demonstrated that accessing such data is required for achieving a specific and legitimate investigative objective.

The absence of explicit justification requirements under Section 94 suggests that access to digital data may be employed as a routine investigative tool rather than as a measure of last resort grounded in necessity.

4.3 The Requirement of Proportionality

The requirement of proportionality is a central component of the constitutional test. It requires that the measures adopted by the state must be proportionate to the objective sought to be achieved. In the context of criminal investigations, this requirement assumes particular importance due to the sensitive and expansive nature of digital data.

When this framework is applied to Section 94, certain concerns emerge. As discussed earlier, the provision permits compelled disclosure of electronic data but does not clearly define the limits or scope of such access. This raises the possibility that investigative authorities may obtain large volumes of information, including data unrelated to the alleged offence.

Accordingly, questions arise regarding whether such access meets the requirement of proportionality, particularly when less intrusive investigative methods—such as targeted data requests—may be available.

In addition, the framework of proportionality requires the presence of procedural limitations to ensure the potential for abuse is minimized.

This may include the presence of judicial oversight or limitations on data retention. In this sense, the absence of procedural limitations of this nature within the legislative framework serves to undermine the proportionality of this measure, even in the presence of a legitimate investigative concern.

4.4 Digital Surveillance and the Intensification of Privacy Concerns

In applying the Puttaswamy framework to digital surveillance, there is a qualitative difference between physical and digital intrusions. As highlighted earlier, there is an expansive nature of digital data, which can be used to reconstruct detailed personal profiles (Solove, 2006). In this sense, access to this information is not only a concern for informational privacy, but also for broader issues of control and dignity (*Justice K.S. Puttaswamy (Retd.) v. Union of India*, 2017).

In this sense, the Supreme Court highlighted in Puttaswamy that informational privacy is concerned with the control individuals have over the dissemination and use of their information. In the context of digital surveillance, this control is diminished, especially as individuals may have limited knowledge or control over the access of this information by state agencies (Kumar, 2025).

4.5 Evaluating the BNSS through the Lens of Digital Due Process

From the lens of digital due process, it is apparent that the constitutional framework points to a lack of balancing between the expansion of surveillance powers and the incorporation of adequate protective measures. Although the BNSS establishes a foundation for access to digital data, it does not necessarily ensure that access is necessary and proportionate and subject to adequate oversight.

This is more pertinent in view of the increased importance placed on digital evidence in criminal proceedings. As the scope of state access to digital data increases, it is more pertinent to ensure that adequate procedural limitations are established. The constitutional framework established in the Puttaswamy case is therefore not only relevant for assessing existing provisions but also for establishing more stringent provisions in digital due process.

The following section seeks to build on this discussion and assess the interface between the BNSS and the Digital Personal Data Protection Act, 2023, and how this leads to tensions between surveillance powers and data protection principles.

5. Data Protection Framework and the Legislative Paradox

An analysis of the extension of surveillance powers as provided by the Bharatiya Nagarik Suraksha Sanhita, 2023 (BNSS) must be understood in the context of the development of data protection law. The Digital Personal Data Protection Act, 2023 (DPDP Act) marks the beginning of a new regime of data protection law, which emphasizes the principles of consent, purpose, and accountability. It has the potential to provide greater control of personal data to the individual. It has the potential to provide greater control of personal data to the individual, as well as impose obligations on entities processing personal data. However, when viewed from the perspective of the development of criminal procedural law, specifically the BNSS, there exists a structural tension. On the one hand, the DPDP Act provides a framework of data protection based on the rights of the individual. On the other hand, it provides wide exemptions to the state agencies undertaking law enforcement activities. In other words, there exists a legislative paradox, where the data protection regime provides wide scope for the use of personal data by the state, albeit with certain constraints (Kumar, 2025)(Digital Personal Data Protection Act, 2023).

5.1 Consent and the Structure of Data Protection under the DPDP Act

The DPDP Act, therefore, operates on the premise of the processing of personal data based on the premise of consent, except in certain circumstances. Data principals, as defined, have certain rights with respect to the personal data processed, including the right of access, correction, and erasure of the data, as per the conditions stipulated (Digital Personal Data Protection Act, 2023). Thus, the DPDP Act has moved towards the premise of recognizing the informational autonomy of the individual as a fundamental aspect of liberty, as enshrined in the constitution, as per the ruling of Puttaswamy (2017).

In the normal course of events, the requirement of consent ensures the non-arbitrary collection of data. It ensures the individual has control over the processing of data, thereby restricting the ability of both the private sector as well as the state from accessing personal data. However, the effectiveness of the DPDP Act, as well as the ability of the legislation to provide the required data protection, largely depends on the exemptions provided.

5.2 Section 17 and State Exemptions

Section 17 of the DPDP Act provides certain exemptions with respect to the processing of personal data by the state, including the prevention, detection, investigation, and prosecution of offenses[355].

355 Digital Personal Data Protection Act, No. 22 of 2023, Acts of Parliament, 2023.

These exemptions, as provided, are with respect to the processing of personal data, thereby allowing the state agencies to process personal data without the requirement of adhering to the other key aspects of the DPDP Act, including the requirement of obtaining the consent of the data principal. Thus, the exemptions provide a wide latitude of powers to the state, thereby affecting the balance of powers.

Moreover, the relationship between Section 17 of the DPDP Act and other provisions such as Section 94 of the BNSS is of great significance. While the BNSS allows for the compulsory production of digital data, the DPDP Act seems to negate many of the checks and balances that might control access to such data. The ultimate outcome of such provisions might be to allow access to PD on a large scale without any such constraints.

5.3 The Legislative Paradox: Protection and Expansion

Such a combination of the two approaches leads to a structural paradox. While the DPDP Act aims to strengthen data protection through greater focus on consent, accountability, and rights, the Act permits exceptions for state agencies performing their investigative duties. The latter renders these provisions meaningless precisely when the extent of access to data is the greatest.

Thus, legislative paradoxes may be described as instances when a legislative system supports, but also negates, some value at the same time. In this case, although the DPDP Act recognizes and affirms the value of data protection, its numerous exceptions allow state agencies to circumvent provisions that protect personal data. When combined with the enhanced power of monitoring granted to the BNSS, such a framework creates a context within which the value of protecting personal data becomes dependent on circumstances.

In terms of constitutional considerations, it means that the new legal framework has raised questions about its internal consistency. According to the Puttaswamy judgment, the value in question must be actual rather than symbolic. Nevertheless, from this point of view, the DPDP Act and BNSS represent a legal framework whose value of data protection is conditional and symbolic[356].

5.4 Implications for Digital Due Process

The dual nature of legislative regulation of the problem in question has important consequences for understanding the concept of digital due process as elaborated upon above. As can be seen from the interaction between the BNSS and DPDP Act examined herein, not all of the elements of the digital due process are always met in practice.

In particular, the lack of limitations on the use of exemptions provided for by Section 17 greatly impairs the ability to implement data protection principles in connection with criminal investigations. This, in turn, has serious implications for state powers versus individual rights as access to the information is controlled by regulations which are practically not applicable.

What is more, the provisions regulating exemptions in the legislation allow investigators to exercise substantial power but offer no mechanisms of control over their actions in this respect. From the point of view of digital due process, this issue becomes quite relevant as it gives rise to the risk of overreach on the part of state institutions.

356 Justice K.S. Puttaswamy (Retd.) v. Union of India, (2017) 10 S.C.C. 1

From the discussion presented in this section, it can be inferred that neither criminal procedural nor data protection laws can solve the existing problems alone. There is a need for a combination of both approaches in order to reconcile the needs of investigation with constitutional privacy. The following section will continue to explore the issues identified in this one.

6. Structural Deficits in Digital Due Process

As shown above, the problems arising from the Bharatiya Nagarik Suraksha Sanhita, 2023, vis-à-vis digital surveillance are not confined only to specific clauses but instead reveal a more substantial deficit within the scheme of procedural safeguards employed. The aforementioned problems are overbreadth, questions of judicial review, conflicts with data protection legislation, and institutional deficits. All of the above imply that the existing scheme fails to live up to constitutional norms of digital due process.

6.1 Overbreadth of Surveillance Powers

Firstly, the issue of overbreadth of the powers provided by the BNSS and their application to digital data will be discussed. It is important that, according to Section 94, the order regarding disclosure of documents and electronic records is formulated in vague terms and lacks any particularity at all. When applied to the issue of digital data, such broadness of powers presents special problems since a single device may provide considerable information about an individual not connected with the crime.

In turn, such lack of particularity presents a problem when considered from a constitutional perspective because it fails the test of the legitimacy established by Puttaswamy (2017). The absence of particularity may lead to the abuse of powers in that excessive data irrelevant to a legitimate purpose is being collected.

6.2 Limited Judicial Oversight and Procedural Safeguards

Secondly, the second important factor is the minimal use of judicial review in regulating digital surveillance. While some kinds of investigations may need to have the authorization of a judge, the law does not require judicial review in the regulation of digital surveillance based on the kind of data being accessed. This is especially highlighted in Section 94, where the law does not require the provision of a warrant or judicial order indicating the nature of data being collected.

The judiciary's role in reviewing and controlling any form of exercise of governmental powers is essential. It provides the much-needed procedural safeguards to prevent any arbitrary exercise of governmental powers. As observed by the Supreme Court in Justice K.S. Puttaswamy (Retd.) v. Union of India (2017), Maneka Gandhi v. Union of India (1978) and other cases, there should be procedural fairness when considering Article 21.

6.3 The Legislative Paradox and Normative Inconsistency

The relationship between the BNSS and the DPDP Act, 2023 has given rise to several new issues. First, as observed earlier, the broad exemptions granted under Section 17 of the DPDP Act enable state authorities to deal with personal data without taking into account the procedural mechanisms that are supposed to be in place, which includes obtaining consent or providing notification.

It creates a discrepancy within the law itself. While the data protection system is designed to give people more control over their personal information, the criminal procedure system enables state authorities to obtain such information without too many restrictions.

6.4 The Practicality Gap: Institutional and Forensic Limitations

Another aspect that is important to consider in this context is the problem of what can be called a 'practicality gap,' in which there is a discrepancy between the purpose and scope of the relevant provisions and their implementation.

The need to utilize digital evidence also requires substantial institutional capacity to address problems associated with digital forensics and evidence management.

As highlighted earlier[357], despite the increase in data-driven governance, it is crucial to ensure that the required technical and organizational support is present in order to facilitate this process. The absence of such a structure might lead to improper management of digital evidence, affecting the integrity of the latter, and ultimately, its admissibility in court proceedings.

Another issue is related to inconsistencies in evidence management across different jurisdictions and institutions. This, in turn, complicates matters regarding procedural limitations and restrictions associated with digital evidence. The gap between legal provisions and practical implementation also raises concerns relating to fairness and accountability within the criminal justice system.

---

357 Justice B. N. Srikrishna Comm., Government of India, A Free and Fair Digital Economy: Protecting Privacy, Empowering Indians (2018)

6.5 Implications for Informational Privacy and Individual Autonomy

The net effect of the whole process is thus the erosion of the capacity of ensuring informational privacy and individual autonomy.

According to Justice K.S. Puttaswamy (Retd.) v. Union of India, 2017, although privacy does not essentially mean secrecy, it is the individual's power of controlling the distribution and use of his own personal information. The presence of the practice of digital surveillance and its capacity of providing access to vast personal information could undermine this power.

This is made all the more alarming especially if the individual is not aware of the extent to which the data has been accessed or utilized. This discrepancy between the power of the state and that of the individual, then, calls for procedural reforms.

6.6 Reassessing the Framework of Digital Due Process

On the basis of the foregoing observations concerning the structural problems, it may be reasonably assumed that the existing system of law fails to comply with the standards of digital due process. Despite the reformative measures taken by BNSS, the protection devices have not been incorporated into the framework, having regard for the special nature of digital information and its risks regarding access to it.

It follows, hence, that the task does not consist merely of identifying the shortcomings of the legal system, but instead lies in providing an all-around approach to addressing the situation. The following sections of the chapter will attempt to tackle this problem, formulating a digital due process framework with the objectives of effective criminal investigation and protection of individual rights in mind.

7. A Contextual Digital Due Process Framework for Bnss Surveillance (Revised with Layers)

However, the examination presented in the preceding sections shows that although the scope of surveillance powers has expanded under the BNSS, 2023, this development has not been matched by a corresponding strengthening of procedural safeguards. This is reflected in the absence of clear threshold requirements, limited judicial oversight, and normative inconsistencies with the Digital Personal Data Protection Act, 2023.

To restore balance between state authority and individual rights, it is therefore necessary to develop a more comprehensive framework that effectively operationalizes constitutional protections within the context of digital investigations.

A Contextual Digital Due Process Framework is proposed in this section, based on constitutional requirements of legality, necessity, and proportionality as articulated in Justice K.S. Puttaswamy (Retd.) v. Union of India (2017). It is termed 'contextual' because it is adapted to the unique relationship between criminal procedure law, data protection law, and institutional realities in India.

The framework is based on a layered approach to due process, recognizing that protections must be in place across different stages of the investigation—from initiation of surveillance to post-surveillance. These layers are depicted in Figure 1.

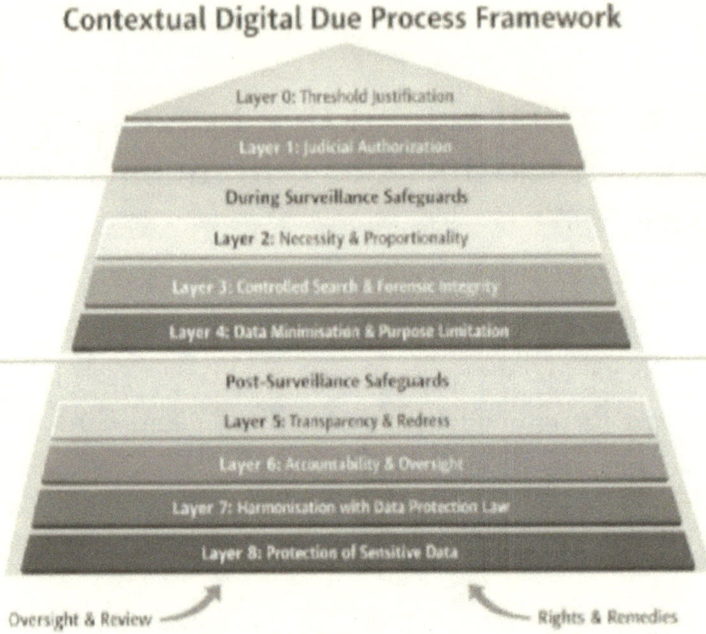

Figure 1: Layered structure of the BNSS framework on digital surveillance, encompassing pre-surveillance justification, procedural checks, and post-surveillance checks.

As depicted in Figure 1 above, the BNSS framework comprises nine interrelated layers (Layer 0 to Layer 8), each of which addresses a unique gap in the current legal regime. These nine layers collectively guarantee that the legal basis for surveillance is not just legally permissible but also substantively limited and subject to review.

7.1 Layer 0: Threshold Justification Requirement

The first layer provides a foundation for the BNSS framework. It necessitates a justification requirement for accessing digital data. The investigating agencies must establish the relevance of the data sought to be accessed in relation to a specific offense. This requirement will prevent the agencies from accessing data for exploratory purposes.

This layer directly addresses the concern that the provisions of Section 94 may be invoked for the purpose of accessing data for exploratory and informational purposes[358]. This requirement will implement the necessity requirement under the Puttaswamy ruling, where digital intrusion will be justified from the outset.

7.2 Layer 1: Judicial Authorisation

The second layer of the BNSS framework introduces judicial authorisation as a check on arbitrary surveillance. Ex-ante judicial authorisation is necessary to prevent arbitrary and exploratory data access. Digital intrusion is a serious invasion of the right to privacy. Prior judicial authorisation will guarantee that data access is subject to judicial review.

7.3 Layer 2: Necessity and Proportionality Assessment

This layer of the BNSS framework necessitates a proportionality assessment to guarantee that the extent of data access is proportionate to the purpose of the investigation. The investigating agencies must demonstrate that the data sought to be accessed is necessary for the purpose of the investigation.

- The data sought is necessary
- Less intrusive alternatives are unavailable

358 Bharatiya Nagarik Suraksha Sanhita, No. 46 of 2023, Acts of Parliament, 2023.

In the digital environment, the requirement of the fifth layer assumes particular importance, as there must be checks against the uncontrolled or mass transfer of data, which might take place owing to the interconnected nature of digital data.

7.4 Layer 3: Controlled Digital Search and Forensic Integrity

The sixth layer regulates the process of data handling, ensuring the reliability of digital evidence. It includes:

- Standardised forensic protocols
- Secure data extraction protocols
- Maintenance of the chain of custody

This addresses the practicality gap created above, specifically the digital forensic infrastructure, which might prove inadequate.[359]

7.5 Layer 4: Data Minimisation and Purpose Limitation

The fifth layer includes the essential data protection principles. It ensures:

- Only relevant data is collected
- Irrelevant data is excluded or deleted

This addresses the risk of data over-collection, thereby ensuring the narrow focus of surveillance, as required by the principle of proportionality (Digital Personal Data Protection Act, 2023).

---

359 Justice B. N. Srikrishna Comm., Government of India, A Free and Fair Digital Economy: Protecting Privacy, Empowering Indians (2018).

7.6 Layer 5: Post-Surveillance Transparency and Individual Rights

The sixth layer introduces the aspect of transparency. In the interest of national security, the individual has the right to know:

- Of data access
- To challenge data misuse

This addresses the practicality gap created above, specifically the issue of the balance between the state and the individual.

7.7 Layer 6: Accountability and Oversight Mechanisms

The sixth layer introduces the aspect of accountability. It ensures:

- Audit trails
- Periodic reviews
- Internal and external oversight

Such mechanisms would ensure that the provisions are implemented and that the misuse of the powers of surveillance is recognized and addressed.

7.8 Layer 7: Harmonisation with Data Protection Law

The seventh layer addresses the legislative paradox in relation to BNSS and DPDP Act, as discussed in this study. This layer proposes that exemptions granted in Section 17 of the DPDP Act be narrowly construed in conformity with constitutional principles (Digital Personal Data Protection Act, 2023).

The constitutional principles will ensure that data protection principles continue to guide the exercise of power in surveillance, rather than being completely replaced by exemptions granted to law enforcement agencies.

7.9 Layer 8: Protection of Sensitive Digital Data

The final layer acknowledges that some forms of digital data, such as personal communications, financial information, and health-related data, warrant additional protection due to their sensitive nature.

Access to such data will be restricted by higher standards and additional safeguards.

The protection of informational privacy and dignity, as established in Puttaswamy (2017), will be further strengthened in this layer.

7.10 Integrating the Layers: Towards Digital Due Process

The eight layers, as discussed in this study, will form a structured and coherent framework for digital surveillance in BNSS. This approach will result in moving away from the broad discretionary powers of the statute to the multi-level protections that will come into effect at every step in the investigation.

Integration of constitutional principles with procedural and institutional protections will achieve the right balance between state power and individual rights. The suggested approach will neither hinder the attainment of valid goals in criminal procedure set out in this paper but will allow doing so within the framework of the rule of law and digital due process.

8. Conclusion

The transition from the Code of Criminal Procedure, 1973 to the Bharatiya Nagarik Suraksha Sanhita, 2023 (BNSS) can be regarded as an important step in developing the criminal justice system in India. Introduction of digital elements such as electronic FIRs, electronic evidence, and audio/video recording of proceedings in the criminal procedure indicates a desire of the Indian government to make it technologically up-to-date.

However, as has been demonstrated in this chapter, the introduction of digitalisation raises many issues regarding the protection of individual rights. Expansion of state powers relating to surveillance and collecting electronic data is an important issue since violation of individual rights through this tool is more invasive than using traditional tools. Moreover, the provision in the BNSS (Section 94) concerning access to electronic data is too extensive since it does not comply with the principles of legality, necessity, and proportionality.

In this regard, the abovementioned judgment delivered by the Indian Supreme Court (Justice K.S. Puttaswamy (Retd.) v. Union of India, 2017) will serve as a landmark to assess such a situation. These principles imply that any intervention by the state into private life of its citizens should be justified, limited in scope, and monitored. Even though BNSS complies with the formality requirement of legality, it fails to satisfy the substantivity requirement of necessity and proportionality.

There is one more paradox in this situation. The new legislation regarding the criminal procedure is inconsistent with the existing laws. In particular, DPDP Act, whose main purpose is to provide protection to the citizen in relation to collection and processing of personal data creates exceptions that undermine the rights of individuals. This indicates that the privacy rights become ineffective. Finally, this chapter has shown that the digitalisation of the procedural criminal law raises a number of issues pertaining to the 'practicality gap'. For example, lack of forensic capability, variation in data handling techniques, and failure to develop standardised protocols may have negative impacts on the validity of evidence and procedural processes involved.

Thus, this chapter has proposed to adopt the Contextual Digital Due Process Framework as a possible solution. It includes various levels of protection, namely justification for exercising surveillance powers, judicial authorization, data minimisation, transparency, and accountability. All these measures attempt to implement constitutional principles within the digital investigation framework. More importantly, adoption of this approach implies that surveillance powers must have a sufficient degree of protections.

The overall implication of the discussion presented in this chapter is that digitisation of the criminal procedure law should be consistent with the development of procedural protections. Although efficiency and technological progress are highly desirable, they cannot be a goal at the expense of constitutional principles. If the final aim of reforming the criminal procedural law is to create a fairer system, it needs the protection of individual rights corresponding to expanding state powers. Moving forward, it is necessary to develop a framework of digital surveillance involving collaboration among judiciary, legislature and regulatory agencies. The role of the judiciary in interpreting criminal procedure acts as well as in revising the BNSS legislation will be vital in this respect. Also, building capacities of regulatory agencies dealing with digital forensics and data governance will be essential.

In conclusion, it should be stated that although digitisation of the criminal justice system opens up many opportunities, there are also numerous threats. The key challenge in this context is to make sure that this process does not undermine fundamental principles of the criminal justice system in relation to justice, accountability, and dignity. Thus, digital due process becomes an important issue.

Chapter 12

Videography of Crime Scenes and Statements Under the Bharatiya Nagarik Suraksha Sanhita, 2023: Transparency, Accountability, or an Architecture of Surveillance?

Dr. Caesar Roy
Assistant Professor of Law, Surendranath Law College, Kolkata.

Abstract

The Bharatiya Nagarik Suraksha Sanhita, 2023 (BNSS) signals a profound shift in India's criminal procedural imagination by formally embedding digital technologies within everyday police work. One of its most significant innovations is the recognition of videography in crime scene investigation and the recording of statements. This article offers a doctrinal and normative engagement with this development, moving beyond a purely technical reading of the law to examine its human, constitutional, and social consequences. It asks whether videography genuinely strengthens transparency, procedural fairness, and evidentiary reliability, or whether it simultaneously constructs a new architecture of surveillance that quietly reshapes the relationship between the citizen and the state. Drawing upon constitutional jurisprudence, comparative legal experiences, and interdisciplinary scholarship, the article argues that videography is not inherently liberating or inherently oppressive. Its democratic value depends on the ethical culture of policing, the presence of regulatory safeguards, and the quality of judicial oversight. The article concludes that BNSS represents a meaningful step towards modernization, but its promise will only be realised if technology is governed by constitutional morality, human dignity, and rights-based data protection norms.

1. Introduction

Criminal procedure has always evolved alongside the tools available to the state—from handwritten case diaries to forensic laboratories and digital databases. Each technological shift reshapes how truth is produced, recorded, and judged. Yet this relationship has never been comfortable. Technologies that promise efficiency and accuracy simultaneously expand state power, often in ways that are difficult to reverse. This enduring tension between technology and justice is now most visible in the videographic documentation of crime scenes and statements.[360]

India's enactment of the Bharatiya Nagarik Suraksha Sanhita, 2023 (BNSS) marks a decisive move toward institutionalising such technology within routine investigative practice.

By embedding videography into everyday procedures, the BNSS shifts Indian criminal process from a predominantly text-based system to an audio-visual one. Crime scenes, searches, seizures, and statements are no longer merely written narratives prepared by officials but visual records that claim to capture events as they unfold. This transformation

360 Smith, J. (2021). *Evidence and technology in criminal investigations.* Oxford University Press

is not merely procedural but philosophical: it alters how facts are constructed, how credibility is assessed, and how power operates within the criminal process.[361] While framed as part of a citizen-centric, efficient, and transparent reform agenda, this normalization of videography also raises constitutional concerns, particularly regarding privacy and protection against self-incrimination.

At a human level, videography promises protection against fabrication and abuse for citizens, and professional accountability and institutional protection for the police. At the same time, constant recording risks generating fear, silence, and self-censorship, especially among marginalised communities already distrustful of state institutions.[362]

This article examines videography under the BNSS through a critical lens, asking whether it functions primarily as an instrument of transparency or as an expansion of surveillance. It addresses four core questions: (i) the legal rationale for videography under the BNSS; (ii) its role in enhancing transparency and accountability; (iii) the surveillance and privacy risks it creates; and (iv) how Indian law can reconcile these competing imperatives. The analysis is doctrinal, comparative, and normative, grounded in constitutional values rather than technological determinism.

361 Galanter, M. (1989). *Law and society in modern India* (pp. 221–225). Oxford University Press

362 Baxi, U. (1987). The crisis of the Indian legal system. *Journal of the Indian Law Institute, 35*(1), 1–15

2. Evolution of Videography in Indian Criminal Procedure

A. Pre-BNSS Position

Prior to the BNSS, Indian criminal procedure relied primarily on written documentation. Although photography and videography were occasionally used, their deployment was discretionary, uneven, and guided more by judicial encouragement than statutory mandate, particularly in contexts such as searches, seizures, and post-mortem examinations.[363] The absence of a clear legal framework resulted in inconsistent practices across jurisdictions, with usage dependent on local infrastructure and individual initiative. Investigative integrity thus rested largely on the credibility of officials and witnesses, generating uncertainty, inconsistency, and frequent procedural disputes, and often leaving courts to resolve competing narratives without objective audiovisual evidence.[364]

B. Legislative Intent behind BNSS

The BNSS attempts to resolve this inconsistency by institutionalising technology as part of ordinary procedure. Videography is presented as a symbol of modern governance—objective, reliable, and transparent. Legislative materials reveal a desire to reduce arbitrariness in investigation and to rebuild public trust in policing institutions.[365]

---

363 Jones, A., & Patel, R. (2020). Video recording standards in criminal procedure: A comparative study. *Journal of Criminal Law & Criminology, 110*(3), 563–598

364 *State of Punjab v. Baldev Singh*, (1999) 6 SCC 172 (India)

365 Ministry of Home Affairs. (2023). *Statement of Objects and Reasons, Bharatiya Nagarik Suraksha Sanhita Bill, 2023*. Government of India

However, law does not operate in abstraction. When technology is embedded in coercive state functions, it does not merely record reality; it reorganises power. What appears as neutrality often carries hidden hierarchies of control, access, and interpretation. The same camera that documents abuse can also normalise constant observation.[366]

3. Videography as an Instrument of Transparency

A. Crime Scene Documentation and Evidentiary Accuracy

Crime scenes are inherently fragile. Physical conditions, spatial relationships, and temporal factors can be altered, intentionally or inadvertently. Videography offers a dynamic method of preserving the scene in situ, capturing details that may elude written descriptions or still photographs.[367]

From a judicial perspective, this enhances evidentiary reliability. Judges are no longer entirely dependent on retrospective narratives prepared by investigating officers. Visual records allow courts to independently assess the quality and integrity of investigation. This strengthens procedural fairness and aligns with the constitutional commitment to due process.[368]

366 Lyon, D. (2001). *Surveillance society: Monitoring everyday life* (pp. 54–60). Open University Press

367 Brown, T. (2019). Forensic documentation and evidentiary reliability. *International Journal of Law and Forensic Science, 5*(2), 77–94

368 *Maneka Gandhi v. Union of India*, (1978) 1 SCC 248 (India)

B. Recording of Statements and Protection against Coercion

One of the most significant promises of videography lies in the recording of custodial statements. Interrogations have long been vulnerable to coercion, inducement, and abuse, making recorded statements a potential safeguard against forced confessions and ill-treatment.[369] The constitutional importance of voluntariness in custodial questioning has been firmly recognised in Indian jurisprudence, particularly through the protection against compelled self-incrimination under Article 20(3) and the right to dignity under Article 21 of the Constitution.[370] Videography provides objective evidence of the conditions and voluntariness of statements, protecting the accused from coercion while shielding investigators from unfounded allegations. In doing so, it introduces a shared regime of visibility that constrains both state power and individual vulnerability, restructuring the custodial relationship through accountability and transparency.[371]

C. Enhancing Institutional Accountability

Transparency is a cornerstone of democratic policing. Videographic records facilitate internal audits, judicial review, and public confidence.[372] When investigative steps are recorded, deviations from procedure become visible and contestable. This visibility can incentivize professional conduct and adherence to legal norms.

---

369 Lee, M., & Chen, K. (2022). Interrogation recordings and rights protection. *Law Review, 58*(4), 301–325

370 *Nandini Satpathy v. P. L. Dani*, (1978) 2 SCC 424 (India)

371 Iyer, V. R. K. (1985). Human rights and the Indian prison system. *Journal of the Indian Law Institute, 27*(1), 1–13

372 Davis, P. (2020). Judicial perspectives on recorded evidence. *Judicature, 103*(1), 12–20

4. Surveillance Concerns and the Right to Privacy

A. Videography and the Expansion of the State Gaze

Although videography is often justified as a mechanism to curb abuse of power and enhance transparency, it simultaneously enlarges the scope of the State's surveillance capacity. The act of recording crime scenes, arrests, searches, and statements rarely confines itself to the accused or the alleged offence alone. Such recordings inevitably capture bystanders, neighbouring households, private interiors, family members, and personal spaces that bear no relation to the criminal investigation. This expansion of visual documentation transforms investigative tools into instruments of continuous observation, thereby normalising a culture of routine surveillance within the criminal justice process.[373]

The concern is not merely speculative. Surveillance scholarship demonstrates that the accumulation of audiovisual data enables the construction of behavioural profiles, facilitates predictive policing models, and allows retrospective scrutiny that extends far beyond the original investigative purpose.[374] Once stored, such data acquires an autonomous institutional value detached from the context of its collection. Videography, therefore, risks shifting its normative function, from accountability and evidentiary integrity – towardssystemic control and governance through visibility.[375] This transformation reflects a subtle but significant shift in the relationship between the

373 Baxi, U. (1982). *The crisis of the Indian legal system.* Vikas Publishing

374 Lyon (2001)

375 Foucault, M. (1995). *Discipline and punish: The birth of the prison.* Vintage Books

citizen and the State, where visibility becomes an obligation rather than a safeguard.

B. Constitutional Dimensions of Privacy

The constitutional recognition of privacy as a fundamental right within Indian jurisprudence imposes substantive limits on the State's surveillance practices. Privacy, as articulated by the Supreme Court, is not confined to spatial secrecy but encompasses informational autonomy, bodily integrity, and decisional freedom.[376] Videographic recording directly implicates all three dimensions: it captures bodily presence, generates permanent informational records, and influences individual decision-making through psychological pressure and perceived coercion.

In custodial contexts, videography raises particularly acute concerns. The recording of statements, interrogations, and interactions within police control environments challenges the authenticity of consent and voluntariness.[377] The presence of a camera may create performative compliance rather than genuine participation, thereby undermining the fairness of the process it seeks to protect. While statutory frameworks such as the BharatiyaNagarik Suraksha Sanhita (BNSS) provide formal legal authorization for videographic procedures, constitutional legitimacy demands more than legality alone.[378]

Any intrusion into privacy must satisfy the tripartite test of legality, necessity, and proportionality.[379] Routine videography, especially in minor offences, non-custodial investigations, or low-risk procedural

376 *K.S. Puttaswamy v. Union of India*, (2017) 10 SCC 1 (India)

377 BharatiyaNagarik Suraksha Sanhita, 2023 (India)

378 BharatiyaNagarik Suraksha Sanhita, 2023 (India)

379 K.S. Puttaswamy v. Union of India, (2017) 10 SCC 1 (India)

contexts, fails to automatically meet this threshold. Proportionality requires a calibrated approach that distinguishes between serious offences warranting enhanced documentation and routine policing activities where recording becomes excessive and intrusive. Without such differentiation, videography risks constitutional overreach under the guise of procedural reform.[380]

C. Data Retention, Secondary Use, and Digital Governance

Perhaps the most structurally consequential dimension of videographic policing lies not in the act of recording itself, but in the governance of recorded data. Videography transforms transient investigative encounters into permanent digital artefacts. Questions of ownership, custodianship, access, duration of storage, and permissible secondary use therefore assume constitutional significance. In the absence of a clearly articulated regulatory architecture, videographic records risk evolving into enduring digital archives of personal life, detached from their original investigative purpose.[381]

Data collection in criminal procedure acquires coercive power not merely through capture, but through retention, aggregation, circulation, and repurposing. Recordings initially generated for evidentiary use may later be redeployed for training, intelligence databases, behavioural analytics, profiling systems, or predictive policing models, often without the knowledge or consent of the individuals recorded. This phenomenon of function creep transforms limited procedural documentation into broad-spectrum data surveillance. What begins

---

380 *Modern Dental College & Research Centre v. State of Madhya Pradesh*, (2016) 7 SCC 353 (India)

381 Foucault, M. (1995). *Discipline and punish: The birth of the prison*. Vintage Books

as investigative necessity gradually evolves into systemic governance through information accumulation.[382]

Without statutory limits, videographic policing risks converting temporary investigative justification into permanent institutional memory. The absence of deletion protocols, purpose-limitation safeguards, independent oversight mechanisms, and clear destruction timelines allows data to acquire autonomous institutional value, severed from the legal context of its collection. Videography thus ceases to operate merely as evidentiary preservation and begins to function as an infrastructure of continuous visibility.[383]

Constitutionally, this raises profound concerns for informational privacy and personal liberty. The recognition of privacy as a fundamental right imposes positive obligations on the State not merely to justify collection, but to regulate storage, access, and secondary use. Informational autonomy requires that personal data remain purpose-bound, proportionate, and temporally limited. Without such containment, videographic systems become structurally incompatible with constitutional guarantees of dignity and autonomy.[384]

Effective governance of videographic data therefore demands a comprehensive regulatory framework. Such a framework must include clearly defined rules on chain of custody, encryption standards, authorised access hierarchies, audit trails, inter-agency data sharing restrictions, and time-bound deletion of non-evidentiary material. Storage limitation must operate as a legal norm, not an administrative

382 Lyon, D. (2001). *Surveillance society: Monitoring everyday life*. Open University Press

383 Zuboff, S. (2019). *The age of surveillance capitalism*. PublicAffairs

384 *K.S. Puttaswamy v. Union of India*, (2017) 10 SCC 1 (India)

discretion. Access control must be institutionally structured, not informally negotiated.[385]

Equally critical is the prohibition of secondary use without judicial or statutory authorization. Data collected for criminal investigation cannot be repurposed for surveillance analytics, intelligence profiling, research databases, or administrative monitoring without violating purpose-limitation principles. Regulatory design must ensure that videographic records remain legally bounded instruments of justice rather than administratively mobile data commodities.[386]

Absent such governance, videography does not merely record crime – it permanently records lives. Without strict boundaries on retention and reuse, the technology risks converting procedural reform into digital surveillance infrastructure. Investigative recording thereby shifts from being a rights-protective safeguard to a mechanism of long-term population visibility.[387]

Accordingly, videographic reform under the BNSS must be embedded within enforceable data governance norms that constitutionally discipline technological power. Recording must remain context-specific, necessity-driven, purpose-limited, and temporally bounded. Only through such regulatory containment can videography function as an evidentiary safeguard rather than an architecture of surveillance.[388]

---

385 European Union. (2016). *General Data Protection Regulation* (Regulation (EU) 2016/679, arts. 5, 25, 32)

386 European Data Protection Board. (2019). *Guidelines on processing of personal data through video devices* (EDPB Guidelines 3/2019)

387 Marx, G. T. (2010). Surveillance studies. In K. D. Haggerty & M. Samatas (Eds.), *Surveillance and democracy* (pp. 23–45). Routledge

388 Srikrishna, B. N. (2018). *A free and fair digital economy: Protecting privacy, empowering Indians* (Committee of Experts Report). Government of India

5. Comparative Perspectives

A. United States: Body-Worn Cameras and Police Reform

The adoption of body-worn cameras (BWCs) by law enforcement in the United States illustrates both the promise and the limitations of technological interventions in policing. Empirical research indicates that BWCs can reduce citizen complaints, incidents of excessive use of force, and disputes over factual events during investigations.[389] However, these outcomes are heavily contingent upon the design and implementation of institutional policies. Critical factors include mandatory activation of cameras during enforcement activities, clear access and disclosure protocols, secure storage of recordings, and strict retention schedules consistent with evidentiary and privacy considerations.[390]

Legal frameworks such as the Police Body-Worn Camera Act in various states codify these practices, ensuring both accountability and procedural uniformity. For instance, the law often specifies that footage cannot be selectively withheld to favor law enforcement narratives and that recordings must be retained for periods proportionate to the severity of the incident captured.[391] Yet, American debates reveal an important lesson: technology alone is insufficient to reform policing. Without independent oversight, robust disciplinary mechanisms,

389 White, M. D., & Ariel, A. (2018). The impact of body-worn cameras on police–citizen encounters: Evidence from the United States. *Journal of Criminal Law & Criminology, 67*, 103–136

390 White, M. D., & Ariel, A. (2018). The impact of body-worn cameras on police–citizen encounters: Evidence from the United States. *Journal of Criminal Law & Criminology, 67*, 103–136

391 Police Body-Worn Camera Act, §§ 5–7 (Various U.S. states, 2015–2022)

and community engagement, BWCs risk legitimizing questionable practices by providing a controlled narrative rather than an objective truth.[392]

The United States experience underscores the tension between transparency and discretion. Courts and legislatures continue to grapple with reconciling evidentiary utility, individual privacy, and public accountability – abalance that remains dynamic and context-specific.[393]

B. European Union: Privacy-Centric Regulation

European jurisdictions approach recording and surveillance through a privacy-centric, rights-based lens. The General Data Protection Regulation (GDPR) provides the overarching legal framework, emphasizing principles such as purpose limitation, data minimization, accuracy, storage limitation, and accountability.[394] Law enforcement agencies may record and store personal data, including video footage, but only when strictly necessary for legitimate investigative purposes and subject to independent supervision.[395]

The European Data Protection Board (EDPB) guidelines further clarify that any processing of personal data, including videography at crime scenes—must comply with proportionality and necessity tests, and individuals retain enforceable rights of access, rectification, and

392 Ariel, B., Farrar, W. A., & Sutherland, A. (2017). Police body-worn cameras: A systematic review. *Criminal Justice and Behavior, 29*, 1–25

393 Ariel, B., Farrar, W. A., & Sutherland, A. (2017). Police body-worn cameras: A systematic review. *Criminal Justice and Behavior, 29*, 1–25

394 Regulation (EU) 2016/679, General Data Protection Regulation, arts. 5–6

395 European Data Protection Board. (2020). *Guidelines on processing personal data by law enforcement* (EDPB Doc. 2020/04, paras. 12–18)

objection where feasible.[396] Similarly, national frameworks such as Germany's *Bundesdatenschutzgesetz* and France's *Loi Informatique et Libertés* impose additional constraints on the use of recording devices by police, mandating prior authorization, periodic audits, and procedural safeguards against misuse.[397]

This model illustrates that transparency and privacy are not inherently opposed. Instead, they can coexist when technology deployment is embedded within a robust, rights-oriented regulatory ecosystem. European experience demonstrates that procedural rigor, coupled with independent oversight, can prevent the instrumentalization of surveillance technologies for state overreach.[398]

6. Reconciling Transparency and Surveillance Under the Bnss

A. Role of Judicial Interpretation

Judicial interpretation constitutes the primary normative filter through which the transparency–surveillance tension under the BharatiyaNagarik Suraksha Sanhita, 2023 (BNSS) must be reconciled. The mere statutory mandate of videography does not, by itself, guarantee rights protection; rather, it is the courts that transform technological mechanisms into constitutionally compatible practices. Through evolving jurisprudence on admissibility, proportionality,

396 European Data Protection Board. (2020). *Guidelines on processing personal data by law enforcement* (EDPB Doc. 2020/04, paras. 12–18)

397 Bundesdatenschutzgesetz [BDSG], §§ 26–27 (Germany); Loi n° 78-17 du 6 janvier 1978 (France).

398 Buttarelli, G. (2020). Data protection in Europe: From principles to practice. *International Review of Law, Computers & Technology, 42*, 67–82

redaction, and controlled access, the judiciary performs a crucial mediating function between investigative necessity and civil liberty.

Indian constitutional jurisprudence has consistently recognised that procedural innovations in criminal justice must operate within the substantive boundaries of Article 21 of the Constitution, which protects not merely life and liberty, but dignified existence and personal autonomy.[399] In *Justice K.S. Puttaswamy v. Union of India*,[400] the Supreme Court clarified that privacy is not extinguished by state interest but must be balanced through structured proportionality, legality, necessity, and least intrusive means. Applied to BNSS videography mandates, this doctrine requires that recording practices must not become routine instruments of data accumulation, but remain context-specific, necessity-driven, and purpose-limited.

Judicial guidelines on selective recording, restricted dissemination, judicial custody of sensitive footage, and anonymisation of non-accused individuals are therefore indispensable. Courts must also regulate evidentiary use by ensuring that videographic material is not treated as infallible proof but is subjected to the same standards of authenticity, relevance, and probative value as other forms of evidence.[401] Without such interpretive discipline, videography risks evolving into an architecture of technological authority rather than a mechanism of accountability.

Further, proportionality analysis must inform decisions regarding mandatory recording in sensitive spaces such as private premises, hospitals, and custodial environments. Judicial oversight becomes essential in ensuring that transparency does not dissolve the private

399 Constitution of India, art. 21

400 (2017) 10 SCC 1 (India)

401 *State of Rajasthan v. Kashi Ram*, (2006) 12 SCC 254 (India)

sphere altogether, thereby preserving the constitutional boundary between legitimate investigation and impermissible surveillance.[402]

B. Training and Institutional Culture

Technological reform cannot succeed in isolation from institutional culture. Videography, like any procedural innovation, reflects the values and norms of the institutions that deploy it. If policing culture is grounded in control and domination, videography will merely digitise coercion. If it is grounded in legality and service, videography can become a tool of trust-building and legitimacy.

Police training under the BNSS must therefore move beyond technical instruction and incorporate constitutional ethics, human dignity, and rights-based investigation models. Recording must be internalised as a mechanism of mutual accountability, protecting both citizens and officers, rather than as an instrument of authority display.[403] Ethical policing frameworks emphasise that transparency technologies are sustainable only when embedded within cultures of restraint and legality.

Institutional norms should also recognise that videography produces psychological and behavioural effects on both investigators and the public. The presence of recording devices alters power dynamics, communication patterns, and compliance behaviour. Training must therefore sensitise officers to the symbolic power of surveillance and the responsibility it entails.[404] Ultimately, the

402 *Maneka Gandhi v. Union of India*, (1978) 1 SCC 248 (India)

403 Iyer, V. R. K. (1985). Human rights and the Indian prison system. *Journal of the Indian Law Institute, 27*(1), 7–12

404 Foucault, M. (1977). *Discipline and punish: The birth of the prison* (pp. 195–228). Pantheon Books

legitimacy of BNSS videography will not be determined by statutory text alone, but by institutional practice. Where videography is aligned with constitutional morality, it can enhance trust, accountability, and procedural fairness. Where it is aligned with coercive governance, it will entrench surveillance structures and deepen public alienation. Reconciliation between transparency and surveillance thus requires not only legal safeguards, but cultural transformation within enforcement institutions themselves.[405]

7. Conclusion

Videography under the Bharatiya Nagarik Suraksha Sanhita, 2023 (BNSS) represents not merely a procedural reform but a conceptual reordering of Indian criminal process. It redefines how truth is institutionally produced, preserved, and legitimised within the justice system. Visual recording technologies introduce a new grammar of legality, where evidentiary credibility is increasingly mediated by digital documentation rather than testimonial hierarchy. This transformation holds the promise of enhancing procedural fairness, improving evidentiary accuracy, and reducing arbitrariness in investigation. Simultaneously, it introduces structural risks of normalising observation, expanding data extraction, and converting criminal procedure into a continuous information-generating system.

This article has sought to demonstrate that videography cannot be evaluated through an efficiency lens alone. Its legitimacy must be assessed through constitutional values, democratic accountability, and rights-based governance. Indian constitutional theory has long emphasised that procedural law is not merely instrumental but normative, it

405 Cherukuri, S. (2007). *Women in prison: An insight into captivity and crime* (pp. 3–11). Foundation Books

shapes power relations between the State and the individual.[406] When investigative technologies become structurally embedded, they reshape the citizen–State relationship itself. Videography thus functions not simply as a tool of transparency, but as a form of institutional power that must remain normatively constrained.

The BNSS creates a statutory architecture for visual documentation, but statutory recognition is only the first layer of legitimacy. Democratic sustainability requires legal containment through clear regulatory design: purpose limitation, minimal intrusion, restricted access, independent oversight, and time-bound data erasure. Without such regulatory structuring, videographic systems risk transforming from evidentiary safeguards into permanent infrastructures of observation.[407] Criminal procedure then shifts from being rights-protective to data-centric, where governance is exercised through information accumulation rather than legal accountability.

Equally critical is the ethical dimension of institutional practice. Legal systems do not operate through norms alone but through the daily conduct of officials. Recording technologies amplify asymmetries of power unless embedded within cultures of restraint, dignity, and professional responsibility.[408] Where policing institutions internalise constitutional values, videography may function as a shield for citizens and officers alike. Where coercive institutional logics dominate, the same technology may deepen structural inequality and social mistrust.

---

406 Austin, G. (1966). *The Indian constitution: Cornerstone of a nation* (pp. 164–179). Oxford University Press

407 Mehta, P. B. (2012). The rise of judicial sovereignty. *Journal of Indian Law and Society, 18*, 5–19

408 Skolnick, J. (1966). *Justice without trial: Law enforcement in democratic society* (pp. 42–61). Wiley

At a structural level, videography under the BNSS forces a deeper confrontation with the meaning of transparency in democratic governance. Visibility is not inherently emancipatory. When unregulated, it becomes a mechanism of control rather than accountability. Surveillance, when proceduralised, ceases to appear exceptional and becomes administratively routine.[409] The task of constitutional governance, therefore, is not to reject technological reform but to discipline it through law, ethics, and institutional design.

Indian criminal justice thus stands at a normative threshold. Videography may evolve into a rights-affirming mechanism that strengthens due process, public confidence, and procedural integrity. Alternatively, it may harden into a surveillance infrastructure that subtly reconfigures liberty through digital means. The trajectory will not be determined by cameras or codes, but by constitutional interpretation, regulatory imagination, and democratic vigilance. True reform lies not in technological expansion, but in constitutional containment, where innovation remains subordinate to dignity, power remains answerable to rights, and law retains mastery over machines.[410]

---

409 Shoshana Zuboff, *The Age of Surveillance Capitalism* 93–115 (PublicAffairs 2019)

410 Sathe, S. P. (2002). *Judicial activism in India* (pp. 286–299). Oxford University Press

Chapter 13

The Ghost in the Machine: Why Mandatory Videography under Section 105 BNSS Might Be a Digital Trap

Vibhor Tiwari
Founder Chairman, Lawerness. Advocate,
High Court of Uttarakhand at Nainital and
Assistant Professor (Guest) Dr Rajendra Prasad Law Institute,
Kumaun University, Nainital

Abstract

With the adoption of the Bharatiya Nagarik Suraksha Sanhita (BNSS), India's criminal justice system experienced a significant change, shifting from a British era reliance on oral testimony to a digital procedural regime involving videography and electronic evidence. An important feature of this change is Section 105, which mandates that search and seizure operations are to be audio-video recorded to ensure accountability and transparency. This research paper will argue on the fact that in the era of sophisticated deepfakes and generative AI, the legislative mandate has unintentionally produced a "Ghost in the Machine" i.e. to say a presumption of digital infallibility that disregards the shortcomings of electronic records. This research paper will critically analyise the constitutional and evidentiary gaps this provision creates. This research paper will also argue that in an era of generative AI and deepfakes one cannot assume a video is the absolute truth. The paper will further explore how this digital bias might unfairly shift the burden of proof on the accused and will highlight the lack of forensic infrastructure to verify these recordings. The study aims to demonstrate how the digital witness could jeopardise the very justice it was intended to uphold in the absence of stringent techno-legal protections.

1. Introduction

Bhartiya Nagrik Suraksha Sanhita (BNSS) has evolved the criminal procedure into a critical new phase. We have made a change from the colonial legacy of the Code of Criminal Procedure, 1973, by modernising the justice delivery system by incorporating technology into its core process.[411] One of the most interesting new ideas is section 105, which makes it mandatory to record search and seizure operations on audio and video. The idea behind this change is that it will make things more open, accountable, and reliable as evidence. Prima facie, this reform seems to be based on a broader institutional belief that technology can be used to correct human fallibility.[412] So, in this framework, the camera is seen as an objective observer, or an uncorrupted witness that can capture the truth in its most pure

411 LawStreet Journal. (2024, July 30). A new dawn in India's criminal justice system: Replacing colonial shackles with indigenous legal reforms. LawStreet Journal. https://lawstreet.co/vantage-points/a-new-dawn-in-indias-criminal-justice-system-replacing-colonial-shackles-with-indigenous-legal-reforms

412 Bhatt & Joshi Associates. (2025, October 22). The evolution of criminal justice: Understanding India's historic legal transformation. Bhatt & Joshi Associates. https://bhattandjoshiassociates.com/the-evolution-of-criminal-justice-understanding-indias-historic-legal-transformation/

form. With the rise of generative AI and deepfake technologies, the reliability of visual evidence is now in doubt, which calls for immediate investigation.[413]

This reform embodies a prevailing institutional conviction that the technology can rectify human fallibility. In this context, the camera is seen as an unbiased observer i.e. an uncorruptible witness that can record the truth in its most pure form. This assumption, however, needs to be looked at right away. With generative AI and deepfake technologies changing the digital world quickly, visual evidence is no longer always reliable. What used to be the most convincing type of proof is now more likely to be changed, made up, or twisted.

This paper contends that Section 105 BNSS, despite its good intentions, may engender a perilous evidentiary fallacy i.e. a "Ghost in the Machine" where digital recordings are granted an unquestioned assumption of authenticity. Such a presumption not only overlooks the technological vulnerabilities found inherent in electronic evidence but also has deeper constitutional implications. It may try to subtly shift the burden of proof onto the accused, destroy the safeguards of due process, and create an uneven playing field in criminal trials where the ability to challenge digital evidence is limited by access to expertise and resources.[414]

---

413 Sandoval, MP., de Almeida Vau, M., Solaas, J. et al. (2024, November 17). Threat of deepfakes to the criminal justice system: A systematic review. Crime Science. https://link.springer.com/article/10.1186/s40163-024-00239-1

414 Radina Stoykova (2021). Digital evidence: Unaddressed threats to fairness and the presumption of innocence. Computer Law & Security Review, 41. https://www.sciencedirect.com/science/article/pii/S0267364921000480

So, the problem isn't with technology itself, but with how it is used without rules or questions in the legal system. The law seems to have accepted digital tools without also putting in place the forensic, institutional, and doctrinal protections needed to make sure they are safe. In doing so, it risks replacing the uncertainties of human testimony with the false certainty of digital representation. In this context, this paper aims to critically analyze the techno-legal ramifications of mandatory videography pursuant to Section 105 BNSS. It questions the idea that digital information is always right, looks at its effects on the Constitution and evidence, and stresses the need for a more careful and measured approach. In a time when seeing isn't the same as believing, the justice system needs to protect itself from the seductive but possibly dangerous power of the digital image.

2. Literature Review

2.1 Videography in search & seizure under BNSS, 2023: Method vs. implication (Lamiya Sultana, Swami Vivekananda University)[415]

The research paper examines the implementation of compulsory videography in search and seizure operations pursuant to Section 105 of the Bharatiya Nagarik Suraksha Sanhita (BNSS), 2023, emphasizing it as a reform intended to improve transparency, accountability, and evidentiary integrity in criminal investigations. It argues that videography can help stop wrongdoing and make prosecutions stronger, but putting it into practice is hard because of things like not having the right equipment, police officers not getting enough

415 Sultana, L. (n.d.). Videography in search & seizure under BNSS, 2023: Method vs. implication. Indian Journal of Integrated Research in Law, V(VI), 167–175.

training, technology not being good enough, privacy issues, and the fact that there aren't clear rules for when digital evidence can be used in court. The paper uses case studies and qualitative research to show both the benefits of properly recorded evidence, like faster trials and fewer disputes, and the risks of poor implementation, like acquittals and mistakes in the process. It concludes that the reform may not work without a complete system that includes standard equipment, proper training, clear legal guidelines, and privacy protections. It also stresses the need for coordinated efforts to close the gap between what lawmakers want and what actually happens.

2.2 Role of Forensic Evidence under BNSS 2023: Enhancing Credibility in Criminal Investigation (Samridhi Mittal)[416]

The research paper examines the enhanced role of forensic evidence under the Bharatiya Nagarik Suraksha Sanhita (BNSS), 2023, emphasizing its importance in improving the credibility, reliability, and scientific rigor of criminal investigations in India. It talks about important changes like making it mandatory to collect forensic evidence in serious crimes, filming crime scenes, giving police more power to collect samples, recognizing digital and electronic evidence, and strict rules for keeping evidence safe to stop tampering. The paper talks about how these steps cut down on the need for subjective testimony, make things more open, speed up expert testimony, and make evidence more useful in court. The study shows that forensic evidence is very important for fair trials, finding the truth, and getting

416 Mittal, S. (2025). Role of forensic evidence under BNSS 2023: Enhancing credibility in criminal investigations. International Journal of Law Management & Humanities, 8(3), 547–553. https://doij.org/10.10000/IJLMH.119699

justice faster. It also shows that the criminal justice system needs better infrastructure, training, and quality control to make sure that mistakes are kept to a minimum and that the full potential of scientific investigation is realized.

2.3 Audio-Video Electronic means and Electronic Communication under the BNSS (Dr. John Varghese, kerala Judicial Academy)[417]

The research paper investigates the integration of "audio-video electronic means" and electronic communication within the Bharatiya Nagarik Suraksha Sanhita (BNSS), 2023, to modernize investigations and trials in the criminal justice system. It says that the BNSS takes a technology-driven, citizen-centered approach by letting people use things like mobile phones, video conferencing tools, and digital platforms to gather evidence, conduct searches and seizures, record statements and confessions, and even bring accused people to court. The law gives a wide and all-encompassing definition of electronic communication, accepts digital records as valid evidence, and stresses the need to replace old-fashioned manual methods with more efficient electronic recording systems. It also shows how important mobile apps like e-Sakshya and NyayShruti are for making sure that evidence is real, time-stamped, and has a clear chain of custody. The paper does, however, bring up some practical and legal issues, such as how unclear provisions can be (for example, the use of the word "preferably"), the risk of duplication between written and electronic records, infrastructure limitations, data security issues, and the need

417 Varghese, Dr. John, Audio-Video Electronic Means and Electronic Communication Under the BNSS (December 13, 2024). Judicial Vision December 2024 (forthcoming), Available at SSRN: https://ssrn.com/abstract=5055971 or http://dx.doi.org/10.2139/ssrn.5055971

for clear rules and training. Overall, it concludes that while BNSS marks a significant technological shift in criminal procedure, its success depends on proper implementation, clarity in legal interpretation, and robust digital infrastructure.

2.4 Flaws in the Bharatiya Nagarik Suraksha Sanhita, 2023 (BNSS): A Critical Study (Md. Imran Wahab, IPS, Inspector General of Police, West Bengal)[418]

The research paper critically examines the Bharatiya Nagarik Suraksha Sanhita (BNSS), 2023, emphasizing various structural, procedural, and practical deficiencies that could impede its effective implementation, notwithstanding its objective to modernize India's criminal justice system. It points out problems like unclear rules for community service, vague rules for private arrests, unclear rules for electronic FIRs, too much police discretion in preliminary inquiries, and no clear rules for canceling bail or protecting witnesses. The paper also talks about problems with operations, such as not having enough forensic infrastructure, having to use personal devices for videography, and having timelines for investigations that are too short. It also makes people worry about possible violations of basic rights, unfair sentences, a lack of alternative ways to settle disputes, and the exclusion of marginalized groups like LGBTQ+ people. The study finds that BNSS is an important reform, but its success depends on filling in these gaps with clearer rules, better infrastructure, and stronger protections to make sure the justice system is fair, efficient, and accountable.

418 Wahab, M. I. (2024). Flaws in the Bharatiya Nagarik Suraksha Sanhita, 2023 (BNSS): A Critical Study. International Journal for Multidisciplinary Research (IJFMR), 6(5), 1–8. https://doi.org/10.36948/ijfmr.2024.v06i05.28425

3. Hypothesis

The compulsory videography requirement as mentioned under Section 105 of the BNSS which is intended to enhance transparency and accountability may inadvertently create a presumption of digital infallibility that might undermine the due process and fair trial rights in the absence of adequate safeguards against manipulation through emerging technologies such as generative AI and deepfakes.

4. Research Objective

The main goal of this study is to critically look at the audio and video recording requirement in Section 105 of the Bharatiya Nagarik Suraksha Sanhita (BNSS) in light of new technologies like generative AI and deepfakes. This is to find out if digitalization really makes things more open and accountable or if it accidentally undermines due process and fair trial rights by making people think that digital information is always correct. The following sub-objectives will help us reach our main objective:

1. To assess how the current laws and evidence rules, especially the Bharatiya Sakshya Adhiniyam, deal with the acceptability, reliability, and authentication of electronic evidence in the context of mandatory videography.
2. To analyze the impact of deepfake technology and AI-generated content on the credibility of video evidence and the risks associated with treating such evidence as inherently trustworthy.
3. To see if using video evidence in Section 105 BNSS might shift the burden of proof to the accused and change the rules of due process and a fair trial.

4. To find out if India's forensic and institutional infrastructure is good enough to find manipulation in digital evidence and make sure it stays safe.
5. To suggest techno-legal protections and changes that can lower the risks that come with digital evidence while still keeping the goals of openness and responsibility in criminal procedure.

5. Research Question

This research paper will focus into and would try to address the following research questions -:

1. Does the mandatory videography requirement in Section 105 of the BNSS lead to unintended consequences by assuming that digital evidence is always correct in criminal cases?
2. How do emerging technologies such as generative AI and deepfakes challenge the reliability and authenticity of video evidence within the existing evidentiary framework?
3. How much does using video evidence in Section 105 BNSS affect the principles of due process and a fair trial, especially when it comes to the burden of proof on the accused?
4. Are the current laws in the Bharatiya Sakshya Adhiniyam enough to deal with problems of authentication, admissibility, and possible manipulation of digital evidence?
5. What legal and technological protections and policy changes can be made to make sure that using video improves openness without compromising justice?

6. Methodology

The research methodology that will be used in this study will be doctrinal in nature. This means that the research will primarily rely on primary and secondary sources of data such as statutory provisions, judicial precedents, legal commentaries, and scholarly articles. The study will seek to critically analyze the legal framework surrounding Section 105 of the Bharatiya Nagarik Suraksha Sanhita (BNSS) along with the evidentiary principles under the Bharatiya Sakshya Adhiniyam, particularly in the context of electronic and digital evidence. The study will focus on looking at the basic ideas behind due process, fair trial, and the burden of proof. It will also look at how technology studies can help us understand these ideas, especially when it comes to generative AI and deepfake technologies. It will try to find and study the differences between what the law meant by mandatory videography and the problems that come up because the digital world is always changing. But there are some limits to the research. It is limited by the lack of empirical data and the fact that the law on BNSS and AI-generated evidence is still new. No empirical or field-based study has been conducted due to time constraints, resulting in an analysis that is predominantly theoretical. Also, because technology changes so quickly, some observations may need to be re-evaluated as new information comes to light.

7. Analysis

The change in India's criminal procedure, especially the mandatory videography requirement in Section 105 of the Bharatiya Nagarik Suraksha Sanhita (BNSS), seems like a step forward for openness and accountability at first. Search and seizure operations, which used to rely heavily on oral testimonies and written records, are now being documented through audio-video recordings.[419] At first glance, this seems to reduce arbitrariness and strengthen evidentiary reliability. However, beneath this surface-level advancement lies a deeper and more complex concern. In an age where technology is no longer neutral, but actively capable of manipulation through tools such as generative artificial intelligence and deepfakes, a fundamental question arises *Can we still assume that what we see is the truth?*

The idea of the "Ghost in the Machine" comes into play here. The law may have unintentionally created a new type of bias by trying to get rid of human bias. This new type of bias is called "digital bias," and it means that video evidence is assumed to be true without checking its authenticity.[420] This research endeavors to investigate the tension between technological advancement and legal protections. It wants to find out if using video evidence under Section 105 BNSS really makes justice stronger or if it opens up new weaknesses that could hurt due process, shift burdens unfairly, and make it look like the truth instead of the truth.

---

419 Aashayein Legal Education Centre. (n.d.). Recording of search and seizure through audio-video electronic means under Section 105 of the BNSS. ALEC. https://www.alec.co.in/show-blog-page/recording-of-search-and-seizure-through-audio-video-electronic-means-under-section-105-of-the-bnss

420 Maras, M.-H., & Alexandrou, A. (2019). Determining authenticity of video evidence in the age of artificial intelligence and in the wake of deepfake videos. International Journal of Evidence & Proof, 23(3), 255–262. https://doi.org/10.1177/1365712718807226

7.1 The Unintended Consequences of Mandatory Videography under BNSS

The introduction of the compulsory videography operates within the broader legal and evidentiary framework of India, and like any reform, it brings with it certain unintended consequences. One of the main concern is that people think video evidence is real. Investigators and courts may start to see recorded footage as definitive evidence, which would mean they don't have to look into things more closely.[421]

The illusion of objectivity is a big problem in this area. Video recordings give the impression of being neutral, unlike oral testimony, which is inherently subjective and can be challenged through cross-examination. However, this neutrality is deceptive. A camera only records what it sees, and even that recording can be changed, edited, or shown in a certain way. So, what looks like a full account might actually be a carefully chosen version of events.[422]

Another serious concern is the risk of manipulation through emerging technologies. With the advancement of deepfake technology, it has become possible to change videos in ways that are nearly indistinguishable from reality. One can make or change facial expressions, voices, and even whole sequences. In this case, it becomes very hard to treat video evidence as always reliable.

---

421 Maras, M.-H., & Alexandrou, A. (2019). Determining authenticity of video evidence in the age of artificial intelligence and in the wake of deepfake videos. International Journal of Evidence & Proof, 23(3), 255–262. https://doi.org/10.1177/1365712718807226

422 Resnick, B. (2019). The science of why video evidence can mess with our brain. Scientific American. https://www.scientificamerican.com/article/the-science-of-why-video-evidence-can-mess-with-our-brain/

There is also a worry about the change in the burden of proof. In the past, it was up to the prosecution to prove guilt beyond a reasonable doubt. But when a video recording is used as evidence, the person who is accused may have to prove that the recording has been changed or is not reliable. This not only places an additional burden on the defence but also raises serious concerns regarding fairness and access to justice, especially considering the high cost and technical expertise required to challenge digital evidence.

Another unintended consequence is the absence of standard protocols and safeguards. Section 105 requires videography, but it doesn't fully cover things like how to store, handle, authenticate, and verify these recordings. Without clear rules, there is a chance of mistakes, tampering, and misuse.[423] So, even though the goal of mandatory videography is to make things more open, the lack of proper protections could lead to a system where what looks true is more important than what is true.

7.2 The Problem of Digital Truth: Deepfakes and the Crisis of Authenticity

To understand the gravity of the issue, it is important to recognize how the concept of truth itself is evolving in the digital age. In the past, visual evidence was thought to be one of the most reliable types of proof because it showed what was really happening. However, with the advent of generative AI, this assumption is no longer valid. Deepfake technology makes it possible to make videos that look very real and show things that never happened. Unlike traditional forms

423 Live Law. (2025, January 19). Recording of search and seizure through audio-video electronic means under Section 105 of the BNSS. https://www.livelaw.in/articles/recording-of-search-and-seizure-electronic-mode-section-105-bnss-281366

of tampering, which often leave visible traces, modern AI-generated manipulations are subtle, seamless, and increasingly difficult to detect.[424] This makes it hard to tell the difference between truth and what has been created.

To make this easier to understand, imagine a situation where a search operation is filmed and the video shows the police finding evidence of a crime at the home of the person being accused or a drug being recovered in NDPS matters from a vehicle. If a video like this is shown in court, it has a lot of power to convince the court. But what if that video has been changed? What if some parts have been added, taken out, or changed? The problem is that neither the court nor the defendant may be able to easily detect this kind of manipulation.

This brings us to a more serious philosophical and legal question: What is the truth in the digital age? The law has historically depended on notions like authenticity, reliability, and admissibility for evidence. But these ideas are now under a lot of scrutiny. A video may be acceptable and look real, but it may still not be reliable.[425]

Also, this issue has a psychological side to it. People tend to believe what they see. Visual evidence has a strong effect on the brain, and it often beats out logical doubt. This means that even if a video is questioned, its first impression may still have an effect on how the court thinks. So, the problem isn't just with technology; it's also with how we think and how our institutions work.

---

424 Tariq, S., Malik, A., & Batool, U. (2025). Generative artificial intelligence and the evolving challenge of deepfake detection: A systematic analysis. Journal of Cybersecurity and Privacy, 14(1), 17. https://doi.org/10.3390/jcp14010017

425 Doan, T. N., Le, T. H., & Nguyen, T. D. (2025). DeepFake video detection: Insights into model generalisation — A systematic review. AI and Society. https://doi.org/10.1016/j.aiopen.2025.100175

7.3 Due Process, Fair Trial, and the Need for Techno-Legal Safeguards

The issues mentioned above have a direct effect on the constitutional rights to due process and a fair trial. A fair trial necessitates that the accused be afforded a substantive opportunity to contest the evidence presented against them. But when it comes to digital evidence, this chance might be limited by real-world problems and the other practical constraints.[426] The absence of forensic infrastructure is one of the most significant concerns. To find manipulation in digital recordings, one needs special tools, knowledge and resources. In a system with limited infrastructure and resources, it is very hard to know whether the accused can effectively contest video evidence.[427] Another problem is that there aren't clear legal standards for authentication. The evidentiary framework and the laws in question acknowledges electronic evidence but fails to comprehensively address the complexities arising from AI-generated content. Therefore what we need is a stricter standards that go beyond just basic certification and make sure that the content is true. There is also a strong need to build up the capacity of institutions. Judges, lawyers, and investigators need to know what digital evidence can't do and what new technologies can do that could be dangerous. Without this kind of awareness, people may rely too much on technology.

426 Scanlon, M., & Farina, J. (2021). Digital evidence: Unaddressed threats to fairness and the presumption of innocence. Computer Law & Security Review, 43, 105614. https://doi.org/10.1016/j.clsr.2021.105614

427 Oriwoh, E., & Conrad, M. (2015). Digital forensics investigation jurisprudence: Issues of admissibility of digital evidence. Herald Open Access. https://www.heraldopenaccess.us/openaccess/digital-forensics-investigation-jurisprudence-issues-of-admissibility-of-digital-evidence

Finding the problem is just the first step, the next step is to create a framework that really try to solve it. If video evidence is going to be useful in court without causing unfairness, the legal system needs to come up with strong techno-legal protections with some urgency.

This means that video evidence must be verified by forensic experts before it can be used in court. This is not just a formality; it is a real authentication process that includes checking metadata, hash values, and looking for signs of AI-generated manipulation. It also means setting up standard procedures for recording, storing, and transferring footage so that there is never any doubt about the chain of custody and how it can be used.

In addition to that, there is a clear need for independent oversight mechanisms like an organization ot bodies or processes that are not directly involved in the case and can look at digital evidence with the same level of objectivity that the justice system is supposed to have.

An equally important change is how courts deal with digital evidence at the level of presumption. If a legal system thinks that video recordings are always reliable just because they are in digital form, it is not being strict, it is being gullible. Judges must be trained and have the right beliefs to look at this kind of evidence with the same level of critical scrutiny they would use on any other kind of proof.[428] None of this means that technology is bad. The solution is not to avoid digital tools, but to use them honestly by recognizing what they can do, knowing what they can't do, and building the ability to tell the difference in the institution. Technology, used well and

428 Legal Service India. (2025). Digital fortresses and physical integrity: Evidence protection under the new criminal laws. https://www.legalserviceindia.com/Legal-Articles/digital-fortresses-and-physical-integrity-evidence-protection-under-the-new-criminal-laws/

questioned properly, can genuinely strengthen the justice system. Used uncritically, it becomes one more thing the system has to be protected from.

8. Conclusion & Recommendations

When Section 105 of the Bharatiya Nagarik Suraksha Sanhita went into effect, it changed the way India's criminal justice system thinks about evidence. For a long time, courts relied a lot on human testimony, even though it was often full of flaws, contradictions, and lies. The change to requiring videography was meant to fix that. The idea was simple: let the camera be the witness. A witness who will be honest, fair, and not easily bribed. But the assumption is now getting harder to defend. We live in a time when AI can make up faces, voices, and whole conversations that never happened. Deepfake technology has come so far that even trained eyes have a hard time telling the difference between what's real and what's fake. In light of that, it's not only stupid to treat video footage as self evident truth, but it is also dangerous. It's very likely that courts will start to trust digital recordings too much without asking the hard questions about where the footage came from, who handled it, and whether it has been authenticated at all.

This is why the "Ghost in the Machine" problem is so serious. We have traded one type of fallibility or biasness i.e. human fallibility, for another type that seems more authoritative but is just as weak. The accused pays the price when the system stops questioning its proof. Most people who are accused of a crime don't have access to digital forensics experts. They can't hire someone to look at their own metadata or use deepfake detection software. The prosecution can, with the help of state resources. That's not a fair fight, and a justice system that doesn't do anything about that is wrong. The infrastructure isn't ready yet either. Forensic labs in many parts of the country still don't have the tools they need to reliably verify complicated digital evidence. There aren't any clear, standard rules for how to record, store, move, or check video recordings. That space is very big, which means there is a lot of room for mistakes and manipulation.

So what does that mean for Section 105? The idea behind it is good. It's a good idea to make search and seizure operations more open and follow a set procedure. The goal isn't the problem but the rea problem is how we get there. If the supporting framework isn't built at the same time as the reform, it could quietly weaken justice. With that in mind, a few things need to happen urgently.

Before a court can use a video recording as evidence, it must go through proper forensic verification. This should include checking the metadata, confirming the hash value, and looking for signs of AI manipulation. In addition, there need to be clear, consistent rules about how this footage is recorded, handled, and stored so that the chain of custody is not a gray area. The state also needs to put a lot of money into digital forensic labs and the people who work there. This is not just for the prosecution, but also to make sure the defense can get the same level of scrutiny. A trial in which only one party can authenticate the evidence and the other can't is not a genuine trial. Judges, lawyers, and prosecutors also need to be trained correctly. It's not a technical luxury to know the limits of digital evidence but it's necessary to do the job right when that evidence is in front of us in the court. Courts should not automatically trust video. The same level of scrutiny that is used to judge a witness's testimony should be used to judge digital recordings, or even with more gravity.

The law must also catch up on the legislative front. The Bharatiya Sakshya Adhiniyam should be updated to specifically address AI-generated content and the increasing sophistication of digital manipulation, as it does not currently account for either. The more important point is that technology is a tool, not a judge. The future of criminal justice doesn't belong to the person who can make the most convincing video but it belongs to a system that is strict enough to question what it's being shown. If the law stops doing that, it doesn't just put the wrong person in jail. It risks becoming an unintentional part of the very trick it was made to stop.

Chapter 14

Anchoring Criminal Justice with Forensic Science: Navigating the BNSS Regime in Indian Waters

Divya Sharma
Senior Associate in the Corporate Legal and Advisory Division, Hero FinCorp Limited.

Abstract

Forensic Science means pursuing truth by using scientific methods to evaluate and examine evidence. This paper attempts to trace the historical development of forensic science in India. In India, historically the traces of forensic science can be found in the Kautilya's Arthashashtra which led to the introduction of toxicology to identify the type of poison (visha) given to the victim. Forensic science though cannot be considered as an impeccable source of examining evidence. This paper tries to highlight the nitty-gritties of forensic science through the lens of India Judicial system by evaluating case laws and its impacts on the criminal justice system. The Bharatiya Nagarik Suraksha Sanhita ("BNSS") 2023 has introduced the concept of having a forensic expert on the crime scene for certain offences. To embrace the technology of forensic sciences, every police officer must undergo effective training sessions for effectively implementing the provisions of BNSS. The paper demonstrates that to provide criminal justice, constitutional rights cannot be undermined. Forensic science is built on the pillar known as consent of the people proposed to be accused by the investigating officers. The consent is a double-edged sword, if granted will make forensics a striking tool for solving mysteries or if withheld it may render it as a toothless tiger. This paper concludes by providing solutions to implement the notions of the BNSS, such as building enough infrastructure, training and awareness sessions for all the court officers including investigating officers to utilize forensic science emphatically in delivering justice.

Introduction

Since the inception of humankind, crime has also been a part of society. However, the ways to identify the accused have been transformed magnanimously. During ancient times, the Sovereign used to have sole authority and power to identify accused person and allocate punishment for the crime as per its sole discretion. The Sovereign rule is based on the concept of power rather than proof. Later, clergy and experts became part of the King's court to develop reason for the decision of the Sovereign. Consequently, the criminal justice system witnessed the shift from rule to institutionalized mechanism wherein courts and persons of expertise will then rely on testimonies and reason to determine culpability.

The Administration of justice has been on a cruise passing from king's decision to an eye for an eye to relying on evidence and witnesses. The criminal justice system has continuously been evolving by different societal notions.

Evidence constitutes verifiable facts, data, observations or artifacts that substantiate or corroborate or refute a specific hypothesis or question at enquiry. It provides for documentary foundation ensuring that conclusions are not derived from conjectures but from reason, indisputable facts and proofs.

One of the specialized domains of evidence is that of forensic science, it involves taking into account all the physical, biological, chemical and digital traces that are methodically accumulated, preserved and analyzed to establish factual precision. Forensic evidence ranges from fingerprint analysis, DNA profiling, ballistic profiling, toxicology and others. These have been proved to be a linchpin at the hands of the investigators and judicial officers to establish link between circumstantial inference and rigorously demonstrated facts in the pursuit of truth.

Consequently, forensic science has transformed inconspicuously, that underpins the administration of justice framework drastically. By application of scientific instruments to determine culpability, forensic science ensures that the punishment of a crime is not dependent on any person in authority or on presumptions but on scientific proofs.

Traces of Forensic Science in India

In India, forensic science is not a new concept and thus the traces of the same can be dated back to Kautilya's "*Arthashashtra*". Around 4th century BC, Kautilya composed "*Arthashasthra*" which is one of the most comprehensive code on administration of justice, statecraft, governance and law in ancient India. The *Arthashastra* contains several references to criminal investigations, toxicology and forensic sciences. These references reveal that earlier *danda niti* (scientific way of punishment) was based upon scientific observations and systematic ways. Kautilya's code "*Arthashashtra*" lays down the foundation of forensic science in the *danda-niti* and early development of forensic science in Indian intellectual history[429].

During ancient times, one of the major political threats was poisoning of king and the army. Kautilya had also discussed at length different types of poison and their effects in Book XIV of *Arthshashtra*[430] while describing secret weapons of warfare. In this section Kautilya laid down description of various types of poison made out of animals, plants, fumes, minerals and others which could prove deadly to the enemies. Although, the text provides for such strategic methods in warfare, it also illustrates countermeasures such as preventive measures and remedies against poisoning. This signifies awareness during ancient times about toxicology as both proactive and protective science.

Another aspect of toxicology can be witnessed from the procedure wherein King's food and drink were required to be examined before its consumption. Special officers were designated to conduct testing of poison and to observe early signs of contamination. Kautilya also illustrates that there are visual indicators such as change in smell, color or texture when substances are exposed to heat. These pragmatic instructions smack modern techniques of toxicology wherein chemical reactions are used to detect poison.

The *Arthashashtra* also highlights usage of expert physicians and individuals by the royal courts capable of identifying poison and its

---

429 Sharma, B. R. (2020). *Forensic science in criminal investigation & trials* (6th ed.). LexisNexis.

430 Shamasastry, R., Translated version of Kautilya's Arthashashtra, 584- 606. https://ia800402.us.archive.org/34/items/Arthasastra_English_Translation/Arthashastra_of_Chanakya_English.pdf.

corresponding antidotes. This signifies early institutionalization of toxicology.

In developing forensic Science in India, Judiciary has played a pivotal role.

Forensic Science Under Judicial Lens

The forensic science has been deliberated upon by the judicial system of India in great depth. The judicial precedents in both pre and post independence era indicates inclination towards objectivity and authenticity in proving disputed facts.

I. Application of forensic science in pre-independence period: One of the first case to recognize forensic science in criminal investigation during British empire is the murder case wherein fingerprint was used for identifying accused person and for granting conviction.[431] The case is commonly referred as " *The Bengal Fingerprint cases*", the facts of the case were the manager of tea plantation in Jalpaiguri, Bengal was found dead with his throat slit in his bed, his room was ransacked and theft of rupees. The primary suspects were his plantation servants, cook at house on whose clothes blood stains were also found, woman with whom he had illicit affair and some others. The case was resolved by examining victim's calender book wherein faint fingerprint was

431 Sarkar, Abhishek,(2025, January 21), Origins of Fingerprint Classification in Bengal https://www.researchgate.net/profile/Abhishek-Sarkar-10/ publication/348778064_Origins_of_Fingerprint_Classification_in_Bengal/links/6010048e92851c13fe3a26a0/Origins-of-Fingerprint-Classification-in-Bengal?_tp=eyJjb250ZXh0Ijp7ImZpcnN0UGFnZSI6InB1YmxpY2F0aW9uIiwicGFnZSI6InB1YmxpY2F0aW9uIn19&_cf_chl_tk=9fdFyeVmgr7khljy2aubCsw4sLMAEJwteMAW_X84Xy4-1773503674-1.0.1.1-PQovxpHHu72IuLNqT_kXCQCmVUPrm03Op4nWcZVVSXQ.

detected. It was later discovered that one person named Kangali Charan who was sent to jail by the victim earlier on account of theft and he wanted to take revenge and was released earlier from jail just before the crime was committed. Although he was tried for murder and theft, he was convicted only for the theft and the same was upheld by the Supreme Court in the pre-constitutional era.

The next famous case is *Ram Prasad and ors. Vs. Emperor*[432] *(the Kakori Conspiracy case)* where train robbery was committed by members of revolutionary organization. This conspiracy was intended to seize government funds and property being transported by train in order to finance activities against the British government. The British government initiated detailed investigations and arrested several persons including Ram Prasad Bismil and Ashfaqulla Khan. The Court convicted the accused persons after relying on the evidence of handwriting analysis and ballistic examination among other evidence. In this case, prosecution relies on handwriting analysis of documents recovered from accused and the letters and coded communication done by the revolutionaries. Experts examined the documents based on handwriting habits, letter formation, space and stroke patterns which helped in corroborating the planning of conspiracy and connection between other revolutionary activities. Further, analysis of arms and ammunition in possession of accused person and the spent cartridges seized from the scene of crime led to the reinforcement of the story of the prosecution and confirmed the participation of accused person in the conspiracy. Although the scientific method of examining handwriting and ballistic analysis was still in their nascent stage of development, but court relied upon the testimonies of the experts while convicting the accused persons.

432 AIR1927Oudh369a, MANU/OU/0100/1927

There are other similar cases like *Meerut conspiracy case*[433] and *Bhagat Singh Trial case*[434], which are classic examples wherein growth in reliance on proto-forensic methods were witnessed in criminal investigations. In the Meerut Conspiracy case, the British authorities examined various pamphlets, letters, printing styles to establish link between the accused persons and coordinated conspiracy.

Similarly in the proceedings against acts of Bhagat Singh, colonial investigators employed forensic techniques of ballistic and explosive analysis. In addition to the cartridges and bullets comparison, chemical analysis was deployed to understand the chemical composition of the bomb and the devised used.

From the above, the investigative practices and reliance on forensic science in the trials of pre-independence era provide an insight into the then prevailing methods of scientific examination in criminal investigations.

II. development of forensic evidence in the post-independence era. One of the historical cases is *Alavandar Murder case*[435]*(Trunk Murder case)*, wherein C. Alavandar, 42-year-old businessman went missing from Madras. The mystery turned into macabre when in August, 1952 a wooden trunk was discovered in the third-class compartment of the Indo-Ceylon Express at the Manamadurai railway station. Upon opening the trunk, headless body of a man wrapped in blood-soaked cloth was found. After few days dismembered head washed ashore at beach in Madras. During investigation it was discovered that the victim was harassing wife of Prabhakar Menon to reveal her past intimacy with him. The plan was hatched and wife lured Alavandar

433 *K.N. Joglekar vs. Emperor*, AIR1931All504

434 *Bhagat Singh vs Emperor*, (1931)33BOMLR950

435 https://crimemagazine.com/alavandar-murder-case

and murder was committed. Forensic science played an important in identifying bodyless structure and connecting head to the torso. Then investigating team found blood traces at Menon's home to confirm the scene of crime. Also, the wooden trunk was identified to be purchased by Menon and thus accordingly, convicted for the crime. This case displayed medico-legal expertise and showcased transition from testimonial evidence to scientific rigor in criminal investigations. Then in *Khatri & Ors. v. State of Bihar & Ors.*[436] (Bhagalpur blindings case) wherein police blinded several undertrial prisoners forcibly by pouring acid into their eyes in order to punish them extrajudicially. In this case also, ophthalmic assessments and medical records proved police brutality and played key role is establishing culpability.

India then moved from rudimentary methods to towards more modernized techniques of forensic science which can be illustrated in the next section. To elaborate further, following are some of the famous cases which needs to be discussed to understand the focal length of modern forensic science in India.

In the case of Santosh Kumar Singh vs. State Through CBI[437] (Priyadarshini mattoo case) wherein the accused has been convicted for harassment and rape. The accused then killed her by strangulating her with a helmet visor and by hitting her head with a motorcycle helmet. However, the investigating agency analyzed the semen samples, fingerprint recovered from the crime scene, strangulation marks and autopsy report led to the conclusive conviction of the accused person.

The next case for discussion is that of *Amrit Singh vs State of Punjab*[438], wherein minor was raped and murdered by accused person.

436 (1981) 1 SCC 627

437 (2010) 9 SCC 747

438 2006 (12) SCC 79

Although circumstantial evidence and last evidence seen was against accused but conclusive proof was not there. The prosecution wanted to compare the hair samples recovered from the hands of the victim but since accused denied providing samples, the court drew the adverse inference against the accused. This is a classic case wherein one of the shortcomings of forensic science was highlighted and that consent of accused is required to run forensic examinations.

The next case is historical for evaluating digital forensic evidence which is *Suhas Katti V. State of Tamil Nadu*[439] and first case for the conviction under the Information Technology Act read together with sections 469 and509 of the Indian Penal Code. In this case, accused after being rejected for marriage, harassed the victim by posting obscene and objectionable messages about her on Yahoo groups and also created fake email accounts in her name and published her phone number. During investigation, digital logs of electronic records, email content, IP address tracing, server logs which linked the acts to the accused.

The next major case is that of *Aarushi Murder case*[440] which highlights the necessity of examining crime scene for forensic science to establish culpability. This case also highlights how errors in forensic evidence can devastate criminal investigation and judicial system. Brief facts of the case are during the month of May, 2008, Aarushi, a 14-year old girl was found dead in her bedroom with her throat slit and in the same flats her parents were sleeping. Initially Hemraj, their household help, was suspected of committing murder but his body was also recovered on the terrace of the same building after two days. The most glaring issue in this case was non-preservation of crime

439 Case no. C No. 4680 of 2004 dated 5/11/2004

440 *Dr. (Smt.) Nupur Talwar vs State Of U.P. And Anr.* Criminal Appeal No. - 294 of 2014 dated 12.10.2017

scene, presence of neighbors, media to contaminate the scene and the parts of the house were cleaned as well. All this led to destruction of vital evidence such as DNA, fingerprint, hair and other important evidence. The postmortem reports of the deceased persons could not yield any conclusive evidence against the accused persons. Instead, the conviction was based on conjectures, parent's behaviors, and without any forensic evidence conclusively. The trial court in 2013 convicted the parents' basis the circumstantial evidence, however, Allahabad High Court acquitted the Parents and criticized the investigations and highlighted the shortcomings in procuring forensic evidence from the crime scene.

The *Bilkis Bano case* which involved rape of Bilkis Bano by group of men alongwith homicide of multiple family members during 2002 riots happened in Gujarat. During the initial stage of the investigations, the case lost its strength however, reinvestigations were conducted and graves were exhumed by using forensic anthropology and pathology to examine skeletal remains in order to determine manner and cause of death. To establish biological relationships, DNA profiling was utilized which corroborated the survivor's testimony. It illustrates how reinvestigation combined with forensic re-examination can do the course correction and upheld the rule of law in sensitive cases.

Further cases such as *Nirbhaya case (Delhi Gang Rape Case), Sarika Shah rape* and murder case collectively exemplify the catalytic role of forensic science particularly in sexual offence, murder investigations and other heinous crimes wherein scrupulous collection of evidence leads to infallible conclusion in ascertaining the culpability of the perpetrators. In both the aforesaid cases, forensic pathology provided irrefutable and corroborative evidence which reinforced the narrative of the prosecution.

The illustrative cases explained hereinabove reflects how forensic science serves as an indispensable tool in modern criminal investigations and also highlighted the need for continued advancement in infrastructural facilities, expertise and ethical application while applying forensic science in investigations.

Forensic Science Under BNSS Regime

In 2023, the legislation passed the Bharatiya Nagarik Suraksha Sanhita with the intent to combine and modify the existing laws relation to the Procedural aspects of criminal justice system in India. The pivotal provision acknowledging the relevance of forensic science in criminal justice administration find enumeration under sub-clause (3) of Section 176, which provides as under:

"176. Procedure for investigation...

On receipt of every information relating to the commission of an offence which is made punishable for seven years or more, the officer in charge of a police station shall, from such date, as may be notified within a period of five years by the State Government in this regard, cause the forensic expert to visit the crime scene to collect forensic evidence in the offence and also cause videography of the process on mobile phone or any other electronic device:

Provided that where forensic facility is not available in respect of any such offence, the State Government shall, until the facility in respect of that matter is developed or made in the State, notify the utilisation of such facility of any other State."

As per sub-clause (3) of section 176 recognizes the role of forensic science in establishing chain of events and in identifying the culpability of the accused involved in commission of an offence. It emphasized that forensic experts should examine by visiting the crime scene, collect the samples and also record the process which has been mandated.

However, the section itself takes cognizance of the fact that forensic evidence is dependent on the following:

1. **Quality and quantity of Forensic Expert:** The qualified expert and number of such experts as may be required in proportion to the population of India is not very supportive even for the crimes which is punishable more than seven years.
2. **Specific Laboratories**: As on date India has around 136 laboratories[441] which is again too less and may not be sufficient for the corresponding population.
3. **Preservation of crime scene**: In India, preservation of the crime scene is another big challenge in order to collect correct and error-free forensic evidence. As in the above section, it has been explained preservation of the crime scene is the foremost requirement to rely on such evidence by the prosecution.
4. **Infrastructural facilities:** Training of all the court officials including police officials are required to make most of this provision is prosecuting the actual perpetrators of laws.

---

441 As per data published Ministry of Home Affairs on Forensic Labs posted on 18th December, 2024 by Press Information Bureasu, Delhi available at : https://www.pib.gov.in/PressReleasePage.aspx?PRID=2085688&reg=3&lang=2 following are the numbers of laboratories as reproduced below:
"Presently, there are 7 Central Forensic Science Laboratories (CFSL) in the country under Directorate of Forensic Science Services. These CFSLs are located at Bhopal (Madhya Pradesh), Chandigarh, Kamrup (Assam), Hyderabad (Telangana), Pune (Maharashtra), Delhi and Kolkata (West Bengal). Further, as per the available information, there are 32 State Forensic Science Laboratories and 97 Regional Forensic Science Laboratories in the country."

The obtainment of forensic science is not error free as explained above, however the next hurdle for trial of forensic science is the Constitutional right as provided under Article 20(3) of the Constitution of India which will be discussed in the next segment.

Constitutional Rights and Forensic Science

To ensure harmony between state authority and individual freedoms, fundamental rights have been enshrined in the Constitution of India. Rights such as equality before law, freedom of speech, movement and right to life with dignity, acts as bulwarks against arbitrariness in the system. From the lens of administration of criminal justice, Article 20 becomes very important. Article 20 provides protection to individuals against ex-post facto laws, double jeopardy and the most important is sub-clause (3) of Article 20, which provides for the right against self-incrimination. In today's world nexus between this right and Forensic Science must be examined critically so that scientific methods of Forensic Science do not transgress the spirit of Article 20(3). This section will illustrate the jurisprudence evolved through judicial precedents paving way for Forensic Science by drawing the *Laxman Rekha* between testimonial compulsion and collection of physical evidence. Thus, the confluence of constitutional rights and Forensic Science underscores the need for a judicial balance where the fundamental rights are not eclipsed in the pursuit of truth.The issue relating to constitutional rights of the accused and use of scientific evidence has been discussed at length by Hon'ble Supreme Court in the case of *State of Bombay Vs. Kathi Kalu Oghad and Ors.*[442] In this case, the respondent along with other persons were convicted for murder under section 302 of the Indian Penal Code and trial court relied on the handwritten chit in addition to other evidence. The

442 AIR1961SC1808

sample of handwriting of accused was taken while he was in police custody and responded raised objection to its admissibility stating it is a violation of Article 20(3)[443] of the Constitution of India. While the High Court acquitted on other grounds but did not accept objection to the admissibility of evidence. Hence, the appeal was filed before the Supreme Court and the main question which was raised is whether such handwriting samples collected while accused was in police custody will tantamount to witness against themselves as per Article 20(3) of the Constitution of India. The Court highlighted the difference between "furnishing evidence" or "to be a witness" and collecting handwriting, fingerprints etc. samples. The relevant extract of the judgment is mentioned below:

"11. *"To be a witness" may be equivalent to "furnishing evidence" in the sense of making oral or written statements, but not in the larger sense of the expression so as to include giving of thumb impression or impression of palm or foot or fingers or specimen writing or exposing a part of the body by an accused person for purpose of identification.*"[444]

Further, it is worthwhile to mention the observations made by the majority judgment which is reproduced below:

"18.... *(4) Giving thumb impressions or impressions of foot or palm or fingers or specimen writings or showing parts of the body by way of identification are not included in the expression 'to be a witness'*[445]..."

---

443 The Article 20(3) has been reproduced as follows:
"No person accused of any offence shall be compelled to be a witness against himself"

444 *State of Bombay Vs. Kathi Kalu Oghad and Ors.*, MANU/SC/0134/1961, Para 11.

445 *tate of Bombay Vs. Kathi Kalu Oghad and Ors.*, MANU/SC/0134/1961, Para 18.

In view of the above, it can be concluded that giving samples pertaining to identification of body does not violate Article 20(3) of the Constitution of India.

Further in the case of *Selvi and Ors. Vs. State of Karnataka*[446], 3 judge-bench of the Supreme Court drew distinction between testimonial compulsion and collection of physical evidence. In this case court held that administration of instruments such narco-analysis, polygraph tests and Brain Electrical Activation Profile for obtaining evidence violates Article 20(3) of the Constitution of India as it impairs the volition of the person. The court held that such use of such forcible instruments on a person is a violation of Article 20(3) as mentioned below:

"*Forcible interference with a person's mental processes is not provided for under any statute and it most certainly comes into conflict with the 'right against self-incrimination'.*"[447]

In the case of *Ritesh Sinha Vs. State of Uttar Pradesh & Ors.*[448] 3 judge-bench of the Supreme Court came up with the question whether compulsion to give voice sample violates Article 20 (3).

The Court upheld the view taken in *Kathi Kalu Oghad case* and expanded the scope of permissible investigating techniques by clarifying that modern scientific techniques such as voice spectrographs falls outside the ambit of Article 20(3) as it is not testimonial in nature.[449]

446 AIR2010SC1974

447 Selvi and Ors. vs. State of Karnataka, MANU/SC/0325/2010, Para 193.

448 AIR2019SC3592

449 Ritesh Sinha vs. State of Uttar Pradesh and Ors. MANU/SC/1023/2019, Para 9.

Similar view was taken in the latest case of *Rahul Agarwal Vs. State of West Bengal and Ors.*[450] and the relevant extract of the judgment is reproduced for ready reference:

"*...The said sampling is similar to voice sampling, as now possible by reason of the advancing technology. If it is the BNSS that is applicable, then there is a specific provision enabling such sampling. The reasoning was also that mere furnishing of a sample of the fingerprint, signature or handwriting would not incriminate the person as such. It would have to be compared with the material discovered on investigation, which alone could incriminate the person giving the sample, which would not fall under a testimonial compulsion, thus not falling foul of the Rule against self-incrimination.*"[451]

Additionally, in the era of cybercrime, the digital records of the person may still not be delved into without the person's consent as it might be considered as violation of right to privacy of an individual. Consequently, it has become imperative to rapidly evolve the Digital Forensic Science. The Legislature being futuristic through the enactment of the Digital Personal Data Protection Act, 2023, has consciously provided for exemptions by excluding processing of personal data undertaken for investigations from the purview of this Act. This calibrated approach strives to achieve balance between individual personal freedoms and effective investigations of offences thereby ensuring that the evolving Forensic Science is not unduly constrained by regulatory limitations.

450 AIR2025SC4928

451 Rahul Agarwal vs. The State of West Bengal and Ors.MANU/SC/1416/2025, Para 9.

Conclusion

After moving from history to judiciary to legislative evolution of forensic science, it can be concluded that every other arm of the constitution has been able to recognize the important role of forensic science in administration of criminal justice systems. It is now the turn of executive to take charge of implementing the provisions of BNSS.

Accordingly, it is imperative that all the concerned stakeholders including police officers and court officials are well equipped with the necessary knowledge and skills to implement Section 176 (3) of the BNSS. The provisions of BNSS such as mandating videography and forensic examination of crime scenes in certain offences represent a significant shift towards evidence grounded investigations. The true success of these provisions depends upon the capacity building and spreading awareness about procedural literacy among law enforcement agencies and authorities. All the law enforcement personnel shall be meticulously trained in the systematic and orderly collection, preservation and maintenance of the custody of scientific evidence, whereas judiciary must nurture forensic acumen in their officers to accurately determine its materiality. Interdisciplinary workshops, structured training programs and hands-on exposure to forensic technologies can inculcate institutional synergy and ensure uniformity in application of the legal provisions.

Additionally, there are central laboratories and state laboratories as explained above, so in order to have standardized procedure and to have uniformity across all the forensic laboratories across India, it is recommended to have an independent national regulator to regulate the conduct of all the forensic laboratories across all the states.

The dominance and extensive potential of AI (Artificial Intelligence) in the present times of makes it imperative to adopt measures wherein

AI driven forensic analysis can be used in investigations. India is facing challenges in respect of cybercrimes as well. Although, as on date there are legislations like Information Technology Act, 2000 and the Digital Personal Data Protection Act, 2023 however, amendments are still required to foster digital forensics field.

In the pursuit of truth, forensic science has the ability to transform suspicion into proof. Additionally, it is required to launch awareness camps for the citizens of India to understand preservation of crime scene is of utmost importance. The BNSS regime already seems to be sailing through Indian waters and after having forensic science on board as its compass, the ship of criminal justice system is moving towards propagating efficacy, equity, transparency and building public truth in the process of administration of justice.

Chapter 15

Technology, Forensic Evidence, and Privacy

Parul Tikia
Student of BALLB,
Maharaja Agrasen Institute of Management Studies.

Abstract

The Bharatiya Nagarik Suraksha Sanhita (BNSS), 2023, represents a paradigm shift in India's legal landscape, replacing the long-standing Code of Criminal Procedure (CrPC), 1973, with a framework optimized for the digital age. By formally incorporating provisions relating to forensic science, electronic evidence, videography, and digital record-keeping into investigations and trials, the BNSS aims to improve efficiency, transparency, and access to justice. However, this transition also brings new procedural and constitutional challenges.

This chapter provides a comprehensive comparative analysis of the CrPC and the BNSS, specifically examining the transition toward a tech-heavy evidentiary and scientific standard. It provides a clear and detailed analysis of BNSS provisions relating to electronic records, videography of crime scenes and statements, and the increasing reliance on forensic methods. Furthermore, the discussion scrutinizes the practical complexities of this rollout, identifying critical roadblocks such as regional infrastructure deficits, the necessity for standardized forensic protocols to maintain evidence integrity, and the broader implications of digital surveillance on investigative accountability.

Another important focus of this chapter is the growing collection, storage, and use of personal data during criminal investigations. It explores the data protection and privacy implications of digitised policing, continuous surveillance, and long-term retention of electronic and forensic data. The chapter evaluates whether existing legal safeguards are sufficient to protect the right to privacy while ensuring effective investigation under the BNSS framework.

The chapter further talks about the growing role of artificial intelligence and algorithmic tools in the criminal justice system including data analysis and decision-support systems. It critically examines the risks of bias, opacity, and excessive discretion associated with such technologies in the absence of clear procedural safeguards.

The chapter argues that while technological and forensic integration under the BNSS has the implicit ability to strengthen access to justice, its success depends on harmonising procedural effectiveness with data protection norms and transparency. It ultimately seeks to offer practical and critical insights into the implementation of technology-driven criminal procedure in India.

1. Introduction And Background

The enactment of the Bharatiya Nagarik Suraksha Sanhita (hereinafter referred to as BNSS), 2023[452] represents a significant legislative intervention in the history of independent India's criminal justice system. The replacement of the colonial era Code of Criminal

452 Bharatiya Nagarik Suraksha Sanhita, No. 46 of 2023 (India).

Procedure (hereinafter referred to as CrPC), 1973[453], with a new law that is tailored to address the requirements of a digital world reflects a shift in the philosophy of criminal procedure.

While the amendments to the CrPC attempt to bring in new developments in the sphere of forensic science and electronic evidence, the structural framework of the CrPC was established long before the advent of digital governance. The BNSS was part of a larger legislative package that simultaneously substituted the Indian Penal Code (hereinafter referred to as IPC), 1860[454] with the Bharatiya Nyaya Sanhita (hereinafter referred to as BNS), 2023[455] and the Indian Evidence Act (IEA), 1872[456] with the Bharatiya Sakshya Adhiniyam (hereinafter referred to as BSA), 2023[457]. The three enactments constitute an integrated framework of criminal justice revision. The provisions on mandatory forensic examination of crime scenes, videographic recording of investigation, electronic evidence collection from service providers, and audio-visual recording of witness statements constitute an attempt to rebuild, from scratch, the framework within which criminal investigation is conducted and adjudicated in India.

The rapid growth of digitalisation in the society has reshaped the nature of crimes, investigation and adjudication. As such, technology and forensic science are no longer auxiliary instruments in the search for facts but are essential components of fact-finding in the new landscape.

453 Code of Criminal Procedure, No. 2 of 1974 (India).

454 Indian Penal Code, No. 45 of 1860 (India).

455 Bharatiya Nyaya Sanhita, No. 45 of 2023 (India).

456 Indian Evidence Act, No. 1 of 1872 (India).

457 Bharatiya Sakshya Adhiniyam, No. 47 of 2023 (India).

While the application of scientific techniques enhances objectivity and reduces reliance on testimonial evidence, it also introduces challenges relating to data integrity, evidentiary management, and technological limitations. In technologically intensive cases, privacy and constitutional concerns also arise. The use of personal data collection, storage, and analysis by investigative agencies has become more prominent, and this clearly engages the right to privacy. The processes of surveillance, data retention, and decision-support systems must comply with the principles of legality, necessity, and proportionality.

2. Journey from CRPC to BNSS

The BNSS introduces structural shifts in criminal procedure that extend beyond the mere consolidation of existing laws.

A. The Inherited Framework and Its Limitations

The CrPC, which has been in force since 1973 as a consolidation and update of the colonial law, has been the governing law on criminal investigation and trial in the country over the last five decades. The basic assumptions on which CrPC was based upon the nature of evidence and the criminal investigation process were based on the technological capabilities of the times. The crime scene was a physical location, evidence was physical objects or oral statements, and the criminal investigation process was documented on paper in the police diary and charge sheet.

The basic framework of the CrPC was, and continues to be, pre-digital in nature, while the IEA has undergone several changes through various judicial decisions and legislative interventions, a significant intervention being the addition of Section 65B[458] on the admissibility of computer-generated documents.

The results of such a structural disconnect were starkly evident in the judicial decisions on the question of electronic evidence. The Supreme Court decisions in the ***Anvar P.V. v. P.K. Basheer***[459] and ***Arjun Panditrao Khotkar v. Kailash Kushanrao Gorantyal***[460] cases brought to the fore the inherent contradictions in an evidence code that was created in a pre-digital era to a criminal justice system that was rapidly shifting to a digital era.

B. The BNSS's Philosophical Reorientation

The philosophical change that has been incorporated through the BNSS has been incorporated in three areas: the nature of the investigation, the standards of evidence required for the investigation, and the technology that needs to be employed for making the investigation more efficient. Unlike the CrPC, where the investigating officers were given a lot of discretionary powers, the need for the incorporation of the scientific method has been emphasized in the BNSS. One of the first changes is that any offense which is punishable with seven years of imprisonment or more requires a forensic investigation of the crime scene by experts. This provision appears to reduce investigative discretion by making forensic examination mandatory for serious offences.

The BNSS, when read with the BSA attempts to streamline the treatment of digital evidence. By encouraging the authentication of electronic evidence at an early stage of investigation, documenting the same, and making the mandatory provision of videography of the

458 Indian Evidence Act, 1872, § 65B.

459 Anvar P.V. v. P.K. Basheer, (2014) 10 SCC 473.

460 Arjun Panditrao Khotkar v. Kailash Kushanrao Gorantyal, (2020) 7 SCC 1.

processes involved in the investigation, the system seeks to reduce evidentiary disputes pertaining to the evidence at a later stage of the trial. The new law also incorporates the use of technology to make the process more efficient. The provision for the electronic serving of summons to the accused, virtual courts under Section 530[461] and the supply of case documents to the accused electronically under Section 230[462] with the use of technology would make the process quicker and more accessible. However, the availability of technology depends on the regions.

C. Continuities and Unrealised Reforms

Nevertheless, it has been found that despite the incorporation of new technological and procedural innovations, there is considerable continuity between the new law and the procedural framework of the CrPC. For instance, there are considerable similarities between the provisions of the new law relating to arrest, bail, framing of charges, and the trial process. The BNSS has evolved on the basis of the procedural framework already established by the CrPC. The legislative process of the new law has also indicated a number of reform measures that were proposed but never fully realized. For instance, there was considerable discussion on the proposal to strengthen the support mechanisms for the victims of crime, the proposal to strengthen the witness protection mechanisms, and the proposal to fully address the concept of plea bargaining. The new law has thus introduced considerable technological and forensic reforms to the criminal procedure. At the same time, there is considerable continuity with the criminal procedure of the past.

461 Bharatiya Nagarik Suraksha Sanhita, 2023, § 530.

462 Bharatiya Nagarik Suraksha Sanhita, 2023, § 230.

3. Forensic Science Integration Under the BNSS

A. The Mandatory Forensic Examination Requirement

A major amendment that has been made under the BNSS is the inclusion of a legislative requirement for the inclusion of forensic science in the investigation of crimes. Section 176[463] requires the investigating officer to ensure that a forensic expert examines the crime scene and the investigation is videotaped if the punishment is imprisonment for a term of seven years or more. This is a major amendment from the CrPC, where no such criterion was included. As per Sections 53 and 53A[464], relating to the medical examination under the CrPC, the inclusion of scientific skill was directory but not required.

The significance of Section 176 cannot be seen only on the basis of the need for a forensic investigation but also on the philosophy of investigation. The philosophy of investigation is reflected by the fact that the involvement of scientific experts is mandatory even in the investigation of serious offenses. This is also reflected by the judicial observations that highlight the importance of the investigation of crimes on the basis of scientific evidence. In the case of the ***State of Gujarat v. Kishanbhai & Ors.***[465], the Supreme Court of India highlighted the importance of the standards of investigation and the quality of the evidence.

463 Bharatiya Nagarik Suraksha Sanhita, No. 46 of 2023, § 176 (India).

464 Code of Criminal Procedure, No. 2 of 1974, §§ 53, 53A (India).

465 State of Gujarat v. Kishanbhai, 5 SCC 108 (Supreme Court of India 2014).

Furthermore, the BNSS enables forensic experts to assist in the crime scene examination through audio-visual electronic means where the physical presence of the expert at the crime scene is not feasible. This allows the expert to supervise the collection of evidence at the crime scene through the guidance of investigating officers via video conferencing. This flexibility in the BNSS allows for the compliance of the statutory requirement. However, the use of remote forensic supervision introduces new evidentiary questions regarding the chain of custody and the expert's ability to observe minute physical details.

B. The Forensic Infrastructure Deficit

Although the requirement to conduct a forensic assessment has been provided in Section 176 the scope of the same remains restricted based on the existing scenario in India. According to the Bureau of Police Research and Development, the availability of forensic science labs varies from state to state in India.[466]

Such infrastructural challenges have a great impact on the efficiency of the investigations. The National Human Rights Commission has observed that such a delay in the forensic examination, especially in sexual crime cases, has a bearing on the prosecution of such crimes and the rights of the victims.[467] If the forensic report is not made available within a particular period of time, then the efficacy of the evidence collected is undermined, which defeats the purpose of a timely and efficient criminal justice system.

466 Bureau of Police Research and Development [BPR&D], 2023, pp. 84–91).

467 National Human Rights Commission of India. (2023). *Annual report 2022–23* (pp. 47–52). NHRC.

There is a risk that without commensurate infrastructure, the statutory mandate may face implementation challenges, potentially affecting the substantive quality of forensic inputs. This concern is further heightened by the absence of specific statutory consequences for non-compliance with the requirement, which is instead dependent on judicial scrutiny during the trial.

C. The Need for Standardised Forensic Protocols

A further challenge is the absence of nationally uniform standards governing the forensic process. Though the BNSS has provided for the forensic process under serious offenses, it has not provided standards concerning the methodology that has to be adopted during the forensic process. For example, the expertise of the forensic experts, the chain of custody, and the accreditation of the forensic labs are handled at the administrative level. As a result, the reliability of the evidence obtained during the forensic process varies.

In addition, international best practices have recommended the accreditation of the methods used during the forensic process, scientifically validating them. The International Laboratory Accreditation Cooperation and the National Accreditation Board for Testing and Calibration Laboratories (hereinafter referred to as NABL) have recommended that the labs must follow scientifically validated analytical procedures.[468] Furthermore, less than forty percent of the FSL labs are accredited by the NABL, which means a large percentage of the evidence used to solve crimes is obtained through labs that have not been scientifically validated.

---

468 National Accreditation Board for Testing and Calibration Laboratories. (2022). *Guidelines for forensic science laboratories* (NABL Doc 116). NABL.

The importance of judicial scrutiny of expert evidence is underlined by the doctrine of comparative jurisprudence. In the case of ***Daubert v. Merrell Dow Pharmaceuticals, Inc.***[469], the United States Supreme Court has mandated the gatekeeping role of the courts with regard to the reliability of expert evidence. While the Indian courts have occasionally placed emphasis on the importance of the reliability of expert evidence, the same has not been reflected in the Indian criminal procedure. The Law Commission of India has recommended the codification of the standards of forensic evidence as far back as 2003[470]; however, the absence of codified standards within the BNSS reflects a continued reliance on administrative guidelines rather than statutory forensic protocols.

4. Electronic Evidence and Digital Record-Keeping

The concept of evidence has seen a major change with the advent of digital communication, financial transactions, and social interactions. The recognition of the change to digital communication, financial transactions, and social interactions has led to the inclusion of the BNSS which has provided procedural mechanisms to facilitate the use of electronic documents during the investigation process. The BSA mainly includes guidelines regarding the admissibility of digital evidence. The legislative intent behind the law is to address the issue of the use of digital evidence, like mobile data, electronic communication, video recordings, etc., during the course of a criminal trial.

469 Daubert v. Merrell Dow Pharmaceuticals, Inc., 509 U.S. 579 (1993).

470 Law Commission of India. (2003). Report no. 185: Review of the Indian Evidence Act, 1872. Government of India.

The rules on the admissibility of evidence of electronic records are provided in Section 63[471] of the BSA, which provides that the production of the electronic evidence is to be accompanied by a certificate issued by the concerned individual dealing with the operation or management of the concerned device. The certificate must confirm the identity of the device, that it was regularly used, and that the electronic record produced is accurate. Section 63 seeks to address the difficulties experienced in the application of Section 65B of the IEA[472], specifically as highlighted by the Supreme Court in ***Anvar P.V. v. P.K. Basheer*** [473] and ***Arjun Panditrao Khotkar v. Kailash Kushanrao Gorantyal*** [474]. However, it remains difficult to obtain certification where the evidence is stored with a foreign service provider.

Another important issue is the preservation of the integrity of electronic evidence. Electronic evidence is susceptible to being copied, altered, or manipulated without leaving any discernible trace, which raises concerns regarding the integrity of the chain of custody. A verifiable chain of custody requires documentation of all processes from the seizure of evidence to its production before the court. The BNSS mandates the videography of certain investigative procedures, which includes the preservation of audio-visual evidence. However, there are no specific statutory regulations regarding the handling of electronic evidence. According to international best practices, as codified in the UNODC Criminal Justice Assessment Toolkit[475] and the Council of

471 Bharatiya Sakshya Adhiniyam, No. 47 of 2023, § 63 (India).

472 Indian Evidence Act, No. 1 of 1872, § 65B (India).

473 Anvar P.V. v. P.K. Basheer, (2014) 10 SCC 473 (India).

474 Arjun Panditrao Khotkar v. Kailash Kushanrao Gorantyal, (2020) 7 SCC 1 (India).

475 United Nations Office on Drugs and Crime. (2011). Criminal justice assessment toolkit: Electronic evidence and computer crime (Module 3). UNODC.

Europe's Budapest Convention on Cybercrime[476], specific validated forensic tools should be used to produce an exact copy of the evidence.

Further, BNSS increases the powers of the state to access information from service providers. Under section 105[477], there is authority granted to senior police officers to demand information from service providers for the purpose of criminal investigation. This section increases the powers of the state in dealing with cybercrime and electronic communication.

5. Mandatory Videography and Procedural Transparency

A. Requirements for Videography in Terms of Content and Scope

The BNSS has introduced the mandatory aspect of videography as a vital tool to enhance the level of transparency and accountability in the investigation of crimes. There are a number of provisions which have collectively given shape to the framework of mandatory videography. Section 176(3)[478] has mandated the investigating officers to ensure the videographic documentation of the examination of the crime scene and search/seizure operations in the investigation of serious offences. Section 183[479] has mandated the audio-visual recording of statements in cases involving offences against women and children. Section 103[480] has retained the aspect of independent witnesses in search operations

476 Council of Europe. (2001). Convention on cybercrime (ETS No. 185). Council of Europe.

477 Bharatiya Nagarik Suraksha Sanhita, No. 46 of 2023, § 105 (India).

478 Bharatiya Nagarik Suraksha Sanhita, No. 46 of 2023, § 176(3) (India).

479 Bharatiya Nagarik Suraksha Sanhita, No. 46 of 2023, § 183 (India).

480 Bharatiya Nagarik Suraksha Sanhita, No. 46 of 2023, § 103 (India).

while introducing the aspect of videographic documentation. Section 530[481] has provided a framework for the application of audio-visual technology in judicial proceedings.

The rationale for such provisions is to ensure an unbiased and updated record of the investigation process. The process of investigation was typically recorded in written reports and a diary maintained by police officers in the earlier system of the CrPC. Such reports have been challenged in courts on several occasions when allegations of coercion and unethical practices during the search procedure have been made. Videographic documentation helps the court to better assess the process of investigation and provides a visual record of the investigation process. It also helps the accused to question the process of investigation.

B. The Statement Recording Improvement

Section 183, BNSS[482] marks a departure from the position under Section 164 of the CrPC[483]. Under the previous law, a statement made to the police or a statement made to a magistrate was required to be recorded in writing. The magistrate was required to certify that the statement was made voluntarily. The question of voluntariness was determined on the basis of competing accounts of the parties. This area of uncertainty is sought to be addressed by requiring audio-visual recording of statements. The original recording is required to be retained in court custody, while a copy is required to be made available to the accused along with the charge sheet. This reduces the scope for selective disclosure. The accused is thereby able to access the recording for the purposes of their defence. Recognition of technology-assisted

481 Bharatiya Nagarik Suraksha Sanhita, No. 46 of 2023, § 530 (India).

482 Bharatiya Nagarik Suraksha Sanhita, No. 46 of 2023, § 183 (India).

483 Code of Criminal Procedure, No. 2 of 1974, § 164 (India).

procedures by courts, as evident in the case of ***State of Maharashtra v. Dr. Praful B. Desai***[484], has been recognized as providing judicial legitimacy to audio-visual procedures.

C. Limitations and Risks

While the potential of the mandatory videography is to increase transparency in judicial procedures, it is not without its limitations. The first limitation is in regard to the recording of evidence. It is only possible for the camera to record evidence that is within its lens, and it is also possible for those in charge of recording evidence to have control over it. Hence, videography can only be effective in enhancing transparency in judicial procedures to the extent that it is comprehensive. The second limitation with respect to the effectiveness of videography in enhancing transparency is with respect to the recording itself. While the original recordings are to be preserved in court custody provides a measure of protection against tampering with the recording, there is no guarantee that the recording itself is not altered before presentation in court. The BNSS does not prescribe standards such as cryptographic authentication and digital signatures, which are commonly used in video verification in forensic science. This indicates that the effectiveness of the mandatory videography framework remains contingent on the development of stronger technical standards.

484 State of Maharashtra v. Dr. Praful B. Desai, (2003) 4 SCC 601 (India).

6. Privacy and Data Protection Concerns

A. The BNSS Context and Constitutional Data Privacy Right

The framework that governs the analysis of the BNSS rules can be found in the decision in ***Justice K.S. Puttaswamy v. Union of India***[485] (hereinafter referred to as Puttaswamy Case), where it held that a person's right to privacy as a fundamental right under Article 21 of the Constitution. It is clear that the Court has settled that the principles of legality, legitimate goal, and proportionality are to be followed in any action that concerns data privacy. Informational privacy encompasses an individual's right to exercise control over the collection and sharing of personal information. In the context of criminal investigation, various categories of personal information may be collected, such as call data records, information related to electronic communications, biometric identification, DNA profiling, and videographic recording of investigation procedures. These categories of personal information underscore the need to examine investigative processes against the constitutional parameters established in Puttaswamy Case.

B. Data Protection Framework and Investigative Processes

The Digital Personal Data Protection Act, 2023 Act (hereinafter referred to as the DPDP Act)[486] establishes an overarching framework for the processing of personal data in India, which includes data processed in the course of public functions. In the context of criminal investigations, the interaction of BNSS with the data protection regime

485 Justice K. S. Puttaswamy (Retd.) & Anr. v. Union of India & Ors., (2017) 10 SCC 1 (India).

486 Digital Personal Data Protection Act, No. 22 of 2023

raises concerns regarding the proper balance between investigation and data protection. The processing of data for the purposes of investigation is subject to a regime of law that attempts to strike a balance between the requirements of law enforcement and the requirements of the Constitution.

The policy debates, as reflected in the report of the Justice B.N. Srikrishna Committee[487], emphasize the importance of data protection principles such as purpose limitation, data minimisation, and retention of personal data. However, the extensive exemptions provided to law enforcement agencies in the DPDP Act have raised concerns about the applicability of these principles in the context of investigation, and this is one area that is still pending in the current legislation.

7. Surveillance, Data Retention, and Constitutional Safeguards

A framework for the acquisition and retention of information relating to persons in the context of criminal investigations has been provided in the BNSS. Under the provisions of sections 349 and 106[488], electronic data and the electronic devices themselves can be retained for considerable periods of time until the completion of the trial and appellate court proceedings. This enables law enforcement agencies to retain information relating to persons for considerable periods of time. There are no provisions in the BNSS for the deletion of the information or return of the information after the completion of the trial and appellate court proceedings. This is crucial in the context of

487 Srikrishna, B. N. (Chair). (2018). A free and fair digital economy: Protecting privacy, empowering Indians — Report of the Committee of Experts on Data Protection (ch. 8). Ministry of Electronics and Information Technology.

488 Bharatiya Nagarik Suraksha Sanhita, No. 46 of 2023, §§ 106, 349 (India).

the right to informational privacy and the data minimisation and data storage limitation principles as established under the GDPR[489].

The larger framework in which data is accessed and monitored is also an added factor for concern. The investigative powers vested in Section 105[490] to collect electronic data from service providers are subject to an existing framework that is largely based on executive approval under legislation such as the Information Technology Act of 2000 and the Indian Telegraph Act of 1885, without any prior judicial approval.[491] Although the Supreme Court recognized the intrusive nature of monitoring in the case of ***People's Union for Civil Liberties v. Union of India***[492], the absence of judicial oversight has been identified as a significant gap in the existing framework.

Additionally, BNSS entails an expansion of the scope of sampling, including DNA sampling, where appropriate. This raises questions regarding the constitutional provisions on personal liberty under Article 21 as well as provisions regarding self-incrimination under Article 20(3) of the Constitution. The Supreme Court has held that the coercive use of such measures as narcoanalysis and polygraphy without consent is a violation of constitutional provisions, as seen in the case of ***Selvi v. State of Karnataka***[493].

---

489 General Data Protection Regulation, art. 5(1)(e), Regulation 2016/679, 2016 O.J. (L 119) 1 (EU).

490 Bharatiya Nagarik Suraksha Sanhita, No. 46 of 2023, § 105 (India).

491 Indian Telegraph Act, No. 13 of 1885, § 5(2) (India); Information Technology (Procedure and Safeguards for Interception, Monitoring and Decryption of Information) Rules, 2009, r. 3 (India).

492 People's Union for Civil Liberties v. Union of India, (1997) 1 SCC 301 (India).

493 Selvi v. State of Karnataka, (2010) 7 SCC 263 (India).

8. Artificial Intelligence (AI) and Algorithmic Tools in Criminal Justice

The digitization of criminal investigations has led to an increase in the use of AI technologies in criminal investigations. Facial recognition technologies, predictive policing technologies, online monitoring technologies, and AI technologies used to analyse online evidence are increasingly being used in criminal investigations. Although it has been argued that AI technologies have the potential to increase the efficiency of criminal investigations and to identify patterns in criminal investigations, there is no clear framework to use AI technologies in criminal investigations in India. The provisions related to AI technologies have not been included in the BNSS.

The use of AI in the criminal justice system is associated with various risks and concerns, particularly in terms of fairness and biases. Investigations might reflect biases and unfair outcomes if it is based on data collected from past policing practices. If such data is biased towards certain social groups in society, it is likely to reflect similar biases in outcomes in investigations. Various international case studies have identified various risks associated with the application of AI in the criminal justice system. For instance, in ***Loomis v. Wisconsin***[494], risks associated with the application of AI in the criminal justice system have been identified in association with the controversy involving the COMPAS risk assessment tool. In India, the constitutional principles enunciated in the case of ***Maneka Gandhi v. Union of India***[495] and ***Puttaswamy Case*** have held that any such process that is applicable to personal liberty must be fair, reasonable, and proportionate.

494 Loomis v. Wisconsin, 881 N.W.2d 749 (Wis. 2016), cert. denied, 137 S. Ct. 2290 (2017).

495 Maneka Gandhi v. Union of India, (1978) 1 SCC 248 (India).

9. Implementation and Infrastructure Challenges

The presence of a robust digital infrastructure is imperative for the successful implementation of the technology-based requirements under the BNSS. Digital connectivity is still not a common phenomenon in India, however. As of March 2024, the Internet penetration rate in rural India stood at around thirty seven percent, while in urban India, it stood at around sixty seven percent, as per data from the Telecom Regulatory Authority of India.[496] This has been a challenge for the technology-based requirements under the BNSS, such as virtual court hearings under Section 530 of the BNSS.[497]

Apart from connectivity, the effective implementation of digital forensic analysis under the BNSS also needs the overall digitization of police records and information systems. Projects like the Crime and Criminal Tracking Network and Systems were conceptualized to establish a national database of crime records and improve the management of police information systems. Further, the Comptroller and Auditor General's assessment has shown that the overall implementation of such projects is still pending in some states, with substantial deficiencies in the digitization of First Information Reports and case records, as well as discrepancies in data quality and compatibility among systems.[498]

496 Telecom Regulatory Authority of India. (2024). *Annual report 2023–24* (p. 12). TRAI.

497 Bharatiya Nagarik Suraksha Sanhita, No. 46 of 2023, § 530 (India).

498 Comptroller and Auditor General of India. (2023). *Report on implementation of CCTNS (Crime and Criminal Tracking Network and Systems) project* (paras. 4.1–4.9). CAG.

A further challenge concerns institutional capacity. Many of the police stations, especially in rural areas, do not have the capacity to deal with digital and forensic evidence. Without adequate training in digital and forensic evidence handling, the effective operationalisation of the BNSS's technological provisions may be limited across several jurisdictions.

10. Normative and Reform-Oriented Recommendations

A. Strengthening Forensic Infrastructure

A major area for reform is the improvement of the forensic infrastructure in support of the requirement for mandatory forensic examination as provided in Section 176 of the BNSS. The forensic science lab infrastructure varies considerably in its current setup, and many states suffer from the lack of sufficient staff in the forensic labs.

B. Data Protection in Criminal Investigations

The increasing trend of the use of digital evidence, therefore, underlines the need to have more specific rules regarding the collection and use of personal data during the investigation of crimes, even though the DPDP Act has provided a broad framework for the governance of data, the exemptions provided to law enforcement agencies are broad, and a specific framework must be put in place for the collection, storage, and use of data, including principles like the principle of purpose, principle of data minimisation, principle of storage limitation, etc.

C. Regulation of Artificial Intelligence in Criminal Justice

As the investigative agencies are increasingly adopting these algorithmic tools for data analysis and crime detection, a regulatory mechanism for the use of artificial intelligence in criminal justice is called for. This regulatory mechanism should require the disclosure of the AI-based tools used for the investigation, test the reliability of the tools, and ban the automated decision-making process for matters relating to individual liberty.

D. Judicial Oversight of Investigative Surveillance

The expansion of the investigative powers for accessing communications data and digital records has created concerns about the proportionality of the investigative measures. The requirement of a judicial authorisation for the adoption of intrusive investigative measures, particularly the access to personal communications data, is therefore recommended to bring such measures into conformity with these constitutional requirements.

E. Standardised Evidence Handling and Chain-of-Custody Protocols

Procedural guidelines for the management of evidence are also necessary due to the use of digital evidence. There is a need for guidelines on the chain of custody of digital evidence, such as the use of validated forensic instruments for managing the evidence, as stipulated by NABL accreditation standards and best practices.

11. Conclusion

The BNSS marks a significant shift in the legislative framework governing Indian criminal procedure. The nature of the investigation procedure, which was mandated by the CrPC has undergone considerable change with the imposition of the mandatory requirement of forensic investigation in the investigation of serious crimes, the scope of the acceptance of electronic evidence, the videography of the investigation procedure, and the audio-visual recording of the statements.

At the same time, the chapter also dealt with some of the structural challenges which may have an impact on the effective implementation of the reforms. Viability is a key problem since different states have different forensic facilities required to comply with the statutory examination under Section 176 BNSS.

There are also concerns with regard to privacy and data protection, especially with the increasing use of digital evidence. The wide exemptions granted to law enforcement agencies under the DPDP Act also raise concerns with regard to the adequacy of the rules on the use of investigative data by law enforcement agencies, especially with the use of algorithmic tools of investigation.

Ultimately, the shift from the CrPC to the BNSS is an aspect of a larger constitutional shift wherein the growing capabilities of the state must be balanced with the need to protect constitutional rights. The effectiveness of the BNSS will depend not only on the effectiveness of the criminal investigations it facilitates, but also on its capacity to operate within the constitutional principles of privacy, fairness, and accountability.

Chapter 16

Digital Forensics in the Bnss Era: Electronic Evidence, Videography Mandates and Privacy Tensions in India's Criminal Justice System

Avesh Malik
Ph.D. Research Scholar, Dr. B.R. Ambedkar National Law University, Sonepat, Haryana.

Abstract

The Bharatiya Nagarik Suraksha Sanhita (BNSS) introduced major changes in the Criminal Justice System of India which includes the incorporation of digital forensics and technology driven investigative techniques. The significance of electronic evidence, requirement of videography of the crime scenes and the growing privacy concerns within the framework of new criminal laws are examined in this chapter. It analyses how the digital records, including call data records (CDR), CCTV footage, social media content and electronic communications are central to criminal investigations and prosecutions conducted these days. With a special focus on procedural protections and review of case laws, this chapter assesses the legal requirements controlling the gathering, preservation, verification and admissibility of such evidence. The chapter also covers the effects of mandatory requirements to record the search, seizure, arrest, etc. While these measures aim to enhance transparency, accountability and public confidence, certain challenges are emerging related to data storage, technological capacity, evidentiary integrity and potential misuse. Further, the increasing conflict between the constitutional right to privacy and the effectiveness of investigations is an area of emphasis. The chapter also examines whether current legal safeguards against capricious intervention are sufficient in a time of increased surveillance, data retention and digital profiling. Thus, the chapter provides a fair evaluation of the advantages and disadvantages of technology in criminal proceedings by placing digital forensics within larger constitutional and ethical discussions. It makes the case for a technologically advanced, institutionally sound and rights conscious strategy to guarantee that technological advancements uphold rather than compromise the rule of law.

1. Introduction

The unprecedented increase in the creation and use of the electronic data is reconstructing the hitherto based on traditional method of collecting evidence, the Indian Criminal Justice System. This overhaul is epistemic rather than being merely technological in the way as to how the evidence is collected, analyzed and validated in the legal process. All these developments have transformed the evidentiary landscape which makes the digital forensics all more important in the administration of criminal justice in the contemporary world.

The Bharatiya Nagarik Suraksha Sanhita (BNSS) introduced major changes in the Criminal Justice System of India which includes the incorporation of digital forensics and technology driven investigative techniques. There is a higher significance of electronic evidence, including the videography of the crime scenes in the contemporary criminal jurisprudence which is accompanied by the growing privacy concerns within the framework of new criminal laws. The new criminal laws reflect how the digital records, including call data records (CDR), CCTV footage, social media content and electronic communications are central to criminal investigations and prosecutions conducted these days. It needs a special focus on the assessment of the legal requirements controlling the gathering, preservation, verification and admissibility of such evidence.[499]

The BNSS has made the forensic examination of certain offences mandatory along with the mandatory requirements to record the search, seizure, arrest, etc.[500] While these measures aim to enhance transparency, accountability and public confidence, certain challenges are emerging related to data storage, technological

---

499 Singh, R. N., & Kaur, N. (2025). Modern trends in the criminal justice system in India. *The Infinite, 2*(9), 78.

500 BNSS, s. 176(3): "On receipt of every information relating to the commission of an offence which is made punishable for seven years or more, the officer in charge of a police station shall, from such date, as may be notified within a period of five years by the State Government in this regard, cause the forensic expert to visit the crime scene to collect forensic evidence in the offence and also cause videography of the process on mobile phone or any other electronic device"; BNSS s.105: "The process of conducting search of a place or taking possession of any property, article or thing under this Chapter or under section 185, including preparation of the list of all things seized in the course of such search and seizure and signing of such list by witnesses, shall be recorded through any audio-video electronic means preferably mobile phone and the police officer shall without delay forward such recording to the District Magistrate, Sub-divisional Magistrate or Judicial Magistrate of the first class".

capacity, evidentiary integrity and potential misuse.[501] Further, the increasing conflict between the constitutional right to privacy and the effectiveness of investigations is an area of emphasis. The author aims to provide a fair evaluation of the advantages and disadvantages of technology in criminal proceedings by placing digital forensics within larger constitutional and ethical discussions. It makes the case for a technologically advanced, institutionally sound and rights conscious strategy to guarantee that technological advancements uphold rather than compromise the rule of law.

2. Electronic Evidence: From CRPC tO BNSS

The electronic evidence and its framework were introduced in the Indian Evidence Act, 1872 specially by the Information Technology Act, 2000 (hereinafter referred to as the 'IT Act')[502] when it provided a special regime for the admissibility of electronic records through sections 65A and 65B in the Indian Evidence Act, 1872 (hereinafter referred to as the 'IEA'). The Digital records are different from the traditional documentary evidence in the way that they are highly susceptible to mutations which makes it important to have additional safeguards so that the authenticity of these digital records can be ensured.

As per section 65B of the IEA, any electronic evidence produced in the form of evidence must be accompanied by a certificate including therein the manner of production of the electronic record, the device involved in the data creation or storage and the steps undertaken to ensure that the record remained authentic and untampered. There have been multiple decisions of the Supreme Court explaining the

501 Joshua, E. (2025). Navigating the legal challenges of cybersecurity and forensic evidence in the digital era. *Law Nectar, 4.*

502 Act No. 21 of 2000.

importance of such certificate and whether such certificate is mandatory in case of electronic evidence to make it admissible.[503] However, there have been many challenges in fulfilling the requirements of producing these certificates and its mandatory nature has been often challenged. It was indeed a loophole due to which accused would be let away merely on this procedural requirement the absence of which made some direct electronic evidence inadmissible and lack of other evidence made the court to acquit the accused.

In *State (NCT of Delhi) v Navjot Sandhu*[504], the Supreme Court adopted a flexible approach while allowing the admission of electronic evidence without strict compliance with Section 65B requirements. However, this flexibility was overruled in *Anvar P.V. v P.K. Basheer*[505] when the Supreme Court held that Sections 65A and 65B of IEA constitute a complete code in itself. This decision was reaffirmed in *Arjun Panditrao Khotkar v Kailash Kushanrao Gorantyal*[506], which clarified that it is mandatory to produce the certificate as per section 65B of IEA unless the original device itself is produced.

The transformation in 2023 through the BNSS and The Bharatiya Sakshya Adhiniyam (BSA) retains the basic framework of the old laws i.e., Code of Criminal Procedure (CrPC), 1973 and IEA but increased the reliance on the electronic evidence significantly. The use of such evidence in the CrPC was working in the form of a discretion for the investigating agencies and was merely incidental. However, BNSS makes it a mandatory requirement to have forensic centred approach specially for offence punishable with seven years imprisonment or more.

503 See Anvar P.V. v. P.K. Basheer, (2014) 10 SCC 473 and Sonu @ Amar v. State of Haryana, (2017) 8 SCC 570.

504 (2005) 11 SCC 600.

505 (2014) 10 SCC 473.

506 (2020) 7 SCC 1.

This change further highlights the importance of the requirement of certificate as hereinabove mentioned in section 65B of IEA.

Key Changes in the new Criminal Laws in the context of Electronic Evidence:

I. Expanded Definitions

The definitions of 'Document' and 'Evidence' in BSA incorporated the aspects of electronic data. BSA defines "document" by including electronic or digital records like e-mails, server logs, Mobile phone data and semiconductor memory outputs.[507] The definition of "Evidence" now includes "statements given electronically" in the form of oral evidence and "electronic or digital records" in the form of documentary evidence, thus broadening the scope beyond IEA.[508]

II. Primary Evidence Status

In the context of electronic records, four new explanations are introduced under section 57 of the BSA while defining the 'Primary Evidence'. These explanations are introduced to eliminate the difficulty in admitting some electronic evidence which were hitherto covered under the definition of secondary evidence in IEA. The difficulty was to have a mandatory requirement of the certificate under section 65B of IEA for certain electronic evidence. This is a major change which aims to resolve the ambiguities from the case of *Anvar P.V. v. State of Kerala*[509] easing judicial reliance on digital proof. These explanations (Explanation 4 to Explanation 7) clarified the position of certain digital data by specifically granting them the primary evidence status,

507 S. 2(1)(d) of BSA.

508 S. 2(1)(e) of BSA.

509 (2014) 10 SCC 473.

thus eliminating the prior need of certification which was required for these evidence as well as per section 65B of IEA. These evidences are as follows:

a. When an electronic record is created or stored, **'simultaneously or sequentially'**, in multiple files, each such file is the primary evidence. (Explanation 4)

b. When such record is **produced from proper custody**, it will be considered as the primary evidence unless it is disputed (Explanation 5)

c. Where a **video recording** is **simultaneously stored** in electronic form and **transmitted or broadcast or transferred to another**, each of the stored recordings is primary evidence. (Explanation 6)

d. Where an electronic record is **stored in multiple storage spaces** in a computer resource, each such storage is primary evidence which even includes any temporary files. (Explanation 7)

III. Admissibility Rules

Secondary electronic evidence is governed by Section 63 of BSA (contemporaneous to section 65B of IEA). For its admissibility, there is a requirement of a contemporaneous certificate to be submitted along with the electronic record. This certificate must be signed by the device operator and an expert describing the generation of the record, its accuracy and integrity.[510] The format of certificate is also given in the Schedule of BSA in two parts i.e., Part A which is to be filled by the party and Part B which is to be filled by the expert.

All these developments introduced firstly by IT Act, 2000 and then by new criminal laws of BNS, BNSS and BSA underscore a shift

510 See s. 63(4) of BSA.

from traditionalism towards evidentiary formalism with an objective of ensuring reliability in evidence collection, production and admission. However, it also creates several challenges specially in cases which involve third-party data.[511] The BNSS intensifies these challenges by expanding the scope of digital investigation without providing a corresponding procedural solution.

3. Digital Forensics and the Investigative Paradigm

Digital forensics plays a vital role in gathering admissible evidence for cyber-stalking, cyber-bullying, and image-based abuse cases in India, but gaps in victim support and evidentiary processes limit its effectiveness. Enhancing forensic integration within the *Bharatiya Nyaya Sanhita (BNS)*, *Bharatiya Sakshya Adhiniyam (BSA) 2023*, and *IT Act 2000* could strengthen victim-centred justice.

India addresses cyber-stalking under Section 78 (stalking women) of BNS, Sections 66E (privacy violation), 67/67A (obscene content), and 67B (child exploitation for image-based abuse) of IT Act, 2000. Cyber-bullying falls under Section 67 of IT Act[512] and Sections 11/13-15 (for minors) in POCSO Act[513], with BSA 2023 modernizing electronic records as primary evidence via provisions given under sections 56, 61 and 63, presuming authenticity if produced from proper custody.

511 Rakha, N. A. (2025). Cybercrime and the law: Addressing the challenges of digital forensics in criminal investigations. *Mexican Law Review, 16*(2).

512 S.67 of IT Act provides 'Punishment for publishing or transmitting obscene material in electronic form'.

513 Sexual Harassment, Use of Child for pornographic purposed and Storage of pornographic material involving child are punished as per these provisions.

Digital forensics supports chain-of-custody through BNSS 2023 provisions like Section 105 (videography of seizures) but requires Section 65B-like certificates under BSA for admissibility.Forensics traces IP addresses, recovers deleted images, and analyses metadata in stalking/bullying cases, as in *Suhas Katti v. State*[514] using Yahoo logs and IP tracking for conviction under Section 67 of IT Act. It aids victims by preserving volatile data (e.g., chats, browser history) via *tools like Cellebrite or EnCase*,[515] enabling prosecutions in image-based abuse. The operational dimension of electronic evidence is represented by what is called the 'Digital Forensics'. It incorporates a systematic process of identifying, acquiring, preserving, analysing and presenting the digital data. It is not merely limited to the recovering of the information but also in ensuring that the evidentiary value of such information can be retained.

The broader societal changes are being reflected by the increasing focus on digital forensics. The activities of crime are deeply intertwined with the digital world which ranges from complex cybercrimes to even the traditional offences like Extortion or Robbery which often leave digital footprints. Call data records, Geolocation data, CCTV footage, Smart devices including mobile phones, smart watches and Laptops or Tabs are often used to commit crimes. The use of digital forensics helps in tracing the offender through social media interactions, location of accused through his movement patterns and reconstruction of communication networks.[516] The importance of such evidence has

514 CC No. 4680 of 2004, Chief Metropolitan Magistrate, Egmore, Chennai.

515 Cellebrite and EnCase are the major tools used in Digital Forensics with the former specializing in the extraction of data from mobile devices followed by its analysis while the latter is used in the industrial world for analysis of computer, disk forensics and e-discovery. Both of them help in providing end-to-end capabilities in investigation covering multiple types of data.

516 Casey, E. (2011). *Digital evidence and computer crime* (3rd ed.). Academic Press.

also been highlighted by the Judiciary. For example, In *Tomaso Bruno v State of Uttar Pradesh*[517], the Supreme Court observed that "Adverse inferences may be drawn where available electronic evidence is not produced".

The above discussion reinforces the belief that investigative agencies should utilize all the technological tools to strengthen their cases. The new BNSS has already mandated the forensic investigation of offences punishable with seven years' imprisonment or above.[518] But at the same time, BNSS itself reflects the infrastructural limitation in the same provision by prescribing a period of five years when it would be mandatory in every state. The state can also use the forensic facility of another state if it is not available in the concerned state where investigation is being conducted. Thus, the effectiveness of such mandates depends in the institutional capacities. In addition to the infrastructural shortcomings, there is a significant lack of expertise among the law enforcement agencies to handle the digital evidence. It is imperative to maintain the integrity of the digital evidence to utilize its effectiveness and improper handling can seriously compromise this integrity and ultimately leading to exclusion of such evidence during the trial.[519] Further, there is an absence of uniform guidelines for handling the digital data as well as the standardized protocols which result in inconsistency of using such evidence across jurisdictions. The lack of such uniform guidelines leads to the ineffective use of digital forensics since it is contingent on individual competence rather than the systemic robustness.

517 (2015) 7 SCC 178.

518 S.176(3) of BNSS.

519 Kerr, O. (2005). Digital evidence. *Columbia Law Review, 105*(1), 279.

4. Videography Mandates and Procedural Accountability

BNSS introduced one of the most significant changes in the form of mandatory requirement of video recording of certain procedures during investigations of offences specially the Search and Seizure Proceedings through section 105 BNSS. These proceedings are required to be recorded through any audio-video electronic means preferable by the mobile phone and is to be forwarded to the Magistrate, executive or judicial. This reform is introduced with the objective to enhance transparency and reduce the allegations of misconduct or faulty investigation on the part of the Police or any other investigating agencies.

Such video recordings are aimed to provide a contemporaneous record of actions taken by investigating authorities and thus enhancing the credibility of the investigation as well as that of the evidence collected during the investigation. It also enables the judges to have more reliance on the direct evidence available and reducing their inclination to have the evidence corroborated by the testimony of witnesses. It also acts as a deterrent to the delinquent officials against the misconduct often done by them specially during investigations.

However, the implementation of these requirements again raises the same issue of lack of uniform standards in the practices to be followed by the agencies and the documentation to be done by them. It leads to selective documentation and improper handling can also lead to editing and omission of recordings, reducing the credibility of such evidence. The storing and managing such video data requires robust infrastructure to ensure data security and prevent the tampering of the data. It is difficult in the resource constrained settings and the implementation would not be effective. Further, videography is intertwined with another issue of privacy and dignity. The recording of individuals during their personal search or while taking possession of any article, property or thing during the search may constitute an intrusion into the personal space specially when these recordings are retained or shared without proper safeguards.[520]

5. Privacy and Surveillance in the Digital Age

The evolving digital investigation involves the issue of extent of intrusion into the Fundamental Right to Privacy as recognized by the Supreme Court in the case of *Justice K.S. Puttaswamy v Union of India*[521] under Article 21 and had also articulated a proportionality framework for evaluating state action. This proportionality framework necessitated that any infringement of this fundamental right has to be sanctioned by law while pursuing a legitimate aim and is necessary and proportionate. If it is considered in the context of digital forensics, the collection of data and surveillance practices must be subject to procedural safeguards and narrowly tailored.

These concerns of privacy have not been comprehensively addressed by the BNSS while it undoubtedly facilitated the technology driven investigation. The collection of evidence in the form of video recordings or digital data often involves the access to some sensitive personal data which includes private communications and location history. In the absence of clear safeguards and limitations, these processes have serious risk of becoming arbitrary and intrusive into the personal autonomy.

---

520 Brown, C. S. D. (2015). Investigating and prosecuting Cyber Crime: Forensic dependencies and barriers to justice. *International Journal of Cyber Criminology, 9*(1), 55.

521 (2017) 10 SCC 1.

In *People's Union for Civil Liberties v Union of India*[522], the Supreme Court laid down certain safeguards for phone tapping while recognizing its potential of being abused. However, these safeguards are inadequate in light of advanced and emerging digital technologies. The absence of data protection mechanism in the form of a robust framework further exacerbates these concerns. The individuals remain vulnerable to misuse of their private information in absence of statutory limits on the retention of the data and its use.

6. Evidentiary Integrity and Technological Manipulation

The contemporary criminal justice system is highly dependent on the digital evidence which makes it a central concern to maintain the integrity of such evidence. Digital evidence more susceptible to manipulation or alteration than the traditional physical evidence.[523] Digital data can be altered without leaving any visible mark or trace and the emerging technologies like *Deepfake* further complicates the issue by enabling the creation of content that is highly fabricated but appears realistic.

The chain-of-custody mechanism plays an important role in the process of ensuring the integrity of digital evidence. It involves the documenting of every stage of handling evidence and thus seeks to establish that the evidence produced in digital form is authentic, unaltered and reliable. However, there is a requirement of technical infrastructure and administrative discipline to maintain such documentation at each stage of evidence handling. Forensic verification

522 (1997) 1 SCC 301.

523 Brenner, S. W. (2012). *Cybercrime and the Law: Challenges, Issues, and Outcomes.* Northeastern University Press.

is another additional safeguard in this process by enabling experts to assess the authenticity of the evidence in the digital form. Courts also rely on the testimony of experts for accepting the digital evidence as reliable. But, the standards of reliability of such testimony are still underdeveloped.[524]

An Example: Best practices for preserving digital evidence in stalking cases

It requires a strict protocol to maintain the integrity, chain-of-custody and court admissibility under the current legal framework of BNSS and BSA to preserve the digital evidence in case like that of stalking. Taking an example of Stalking as an offence which is given under section 78 of BNS, victims and investigators must give the priority to documentation and non-alteration of the digital records from the very beginning when the offence was alleged to have committed. Such practices help to ensure that the digital evidence pass the test of admissibility challenges during the prosecution in stalking cases which sometimes are based entirely on the digital evidence:

Initial Seizure Steps

The devices involved must be secured as soon as possible in *faraday bags* so that there are no signals that can reach the device and no remote wiping of the data in the device. Then, the device must be put in the power off mode to stop the loss of volatile data like the running applications or logs. The entire scene of securing the device must be documented with timestamped pictures of device locations, the states of screen and cables before the handling.

524 Ghosh, R. (2025). Digital and cyber forensics: Foundations, tools, and emerging frontiers. In *Applied forensic science and law* (pp. 66–92). Bharti Publications.

Forensic Imaging

The validated tools like FTK Imager[525] or Cellebrite must be used to create bit-for-bit forensic copies with write-blockers to prevent any original changes. The originals must never be analyzed directly. The Copies must be verified through hash values at each step to confirm integrity matches.

Chain of Custody

The detailed logs of every person handling the device or record must be maintained along with the access time, purpose and location transfers. Such logs must be stored securely in an offline mode in an encrypted, access-controlled environments. The tamper-evident seals must be used and there should be multiple backups made for avoiding redundancy.[526]

Victim-Led Preservation

The screenshots of every record without any interaction must be secured along with full headers like URLs, timestamps, metadata etc. Further, the entire threads must be saved via browser tools or applications before deletion. Then, the victim must report the offence promptly to the cybercrime portals and should avoid the originals post-preservation

BSA 2023 Compliance

The evidence must be paired with the certificates under section 63 of BSA from the operators and experts which affirm the accuracy

525 Forensic Tool Imager (FTK) is a digital forensic tool widely used to extract and preserve digital data in a secure manner to maintain the originality of data during the investigation.

526 Ghosh, R. (2025). Digital and cyber forensics: Foundations, tools, and emerging frontiers. In *Applied forensic science and law* (pp. 66–92). Bharti Publications.

of the device and its non-tampering. There should be an attempt to leverage primary evidence status for electronic records to enhance the admissibility of such records in stalking like cases.

7. Comparative Analysis of Digital Forensics Laws: UK, US, and INDIA

The laws related to digital forensics in the United Kingdom (UK), United States of America (US) and India differ in their governance of evidence collection, their preservation and admissibility in the courts. Such difference is based on their legal traditions and the technical ecosystem. BSA in India has reformed the very old IEA and attempted to modernize the rules regarding the electronic evidence in light of emerging technological world but lacks in the standardized protocols as compared to the mature framework of UK and the federal-state hybrid system of US.[527] The comparison among the three big legal systems is being highlighted hereinafter in the form of strengths, gaps and reforms specially in the context of cyber-crimes.

UK: Regulation of Investigatory Powers Act (RIPA) 2000

RIPA in UK enables the interception and decryption of electronic data with judicial warrants which is further supported by the Police and Criminal Evidence Act (PACE), 1984 codes for Forensic imaging and chain-of-custody protocols. The admissibility of electronic records is guaranteed without any certification provided the integrity of such records is proved through the testimony of experts, thus emphasizing the proportionality under article 8 of European Convention on Human

527 Gupta, G., & Husain, A. (2023). Digital evidence in police investigation: A comparative analysis of challenges faced in India, the UK and the United States. *Journal of Victimology and Victim Justice*, *6*(2), 133–145.

Rights (ECHR)[528]. Further, the ACPO guidelines standardize the tools like *EnCase* for preserving the volatile data.[529]

US: Federal Rules of Evidence (FRE) 901/902

The FRE Rules 901 require that the electronic record is authenticated via the testimony of experts or the hash verification. However, self-authenticated records like certified government data bypass such requirement under rule 902(13).[530] The unauthorized access is criminalized by CFAA (18 U.S.C. § 1030)[531] and there are Daubert Standards for scientific reliability which is enforced by the Regional Computer Forensics Labs (RCFLs) of the Federal Bureau of Investigation (FBI). Fourth Amendment protections are prioritized

---

528 Art. 8 of ECR: "Everyone has the right to respect for his private and family life, his home and his correspondence; There shall be no interference by a public authority with the exercise of this right except such as is in accordance with the law and is necessary in a democratic society in the interests of national security, public safety or the economic well-being of the country, for the prevention of disorder or crime, for the protection of health or morals, or for the protection of the rights and freedoms of others."

529 The foundational procedures are covered under PACE and the detailed technical standards of Forensic imaging are provided by the ACPO (Association of Chief Police Officers) to ensure its admissibility.

530 Rule 902(13): "A record generated by an electronic process or system that produces an accurate result, as shown by a certification of a qualified person that complies with the certification requirements of Rule 902(11) or (12)" is self-authenticating and require no extrinsic evidence of authenticity in order to be admitted.

531 This Act (Computer Fraud and Abuse Act) of US provides the punishment for Fraud and related activities in connection with computers.

by warrants for Communications Service Providers (CSP) data which are mandated by the Stored Communications Act.[532]

India: BSA 2023 and IT Act 2000

It is mandatory to produce certificates under Section 63 of BSA to produce secondary copies of electronic records. Some records have been given primary evidence status via new explanations under section 57 of BSA, as discussed hereinabove. However, the lack of standardized protocols for chain-of-custody and documentation makes the record vulnerable to tampering. Section 69 of the IT Act, 2000 enables interception of data [533] but Indian legal system lacks dedicated and specific forensic acts unlike US or UK. Cyber Cells in India is underutilizing the available tools of digital forensics which is exacerbated by training gaps, ultimately leading to low conviction rates.

8. Role of Independent Forensic Experts in Indian Courts Today

A pivotal role is being played by the Independent forensic experts in the Indian criminal justice system these days in light of the increasing importance of digital evidence in the contemporary times. These experts give their testimony which is considered as an expert opinion

---

532 The Stored Communications Act (SCA), 18 U.S.C. §§ 2701–2712 mandates the warrants for law enforcement agency to require the disclosure of electronic communications content from the Communications Service Providers (CSPs). Such warrant must be issued by the court upon the showing of a probable cause that a crime has been committed and evidence of the concerned crime will be found in the data requested.

533 S.69 of IT Act, 2000 provides for "Power to issue directions for interception or monitoring or decryption of any information through any computer resource".

admissible under section 39 and 45 of BSA[534] since they give their opinion regarding the complex digital and scientific evidence. The reliability is ensured by their involvement in cyber-crimes but the challenges of underutilization and credibility remain intact. Recent reforms have more inclination towards bolstering their autonomy in light of low conviction rates.

Legal Recognition

Section 39 of BSA admits expert opinions on science, art, foreign law, identity of handwriting or finger impressions when courts require such specialized knowledge. The experts must be the one who are specially skilled in the said fields to have their opinion as relevant under section 39 of BSA. Further, section 39(2) of BSA makes the opinion of the examiner of electronic evidence relevant when the court has to form an 'opinion on any matter relating to any information which is transmitted or stored in any computer resource or any other digital or electronic form'. Section 329 of BNSS also permits certain government scientific experts to submit reports directly without personal attendance in courts, thus streamlining proceedings. Such Government Scientific experts include the Director, Deputy Director or Assistant Director of a Central Forensic Science Laboratory or a State Forensic Science Laboratory.

Role in Proceedings

The role of experts in the field of Digital Forensics, during the legal proceeding in courts, extends from authenticating the digital evidence via hash verification and chain of custody analysis, to rebutting the tampering claims in certifications of section 63 BSA. The Indian

534 These provisions make the opinion of various experts along with the grounds on which such opinions are based, as relevant.

Courts have been increasingly relying on these experts post the landmark judgements of Supreme Court in the case of *Selvi v. State of Karnataka*[535] related to narco-analysis tests and *Anvar P.V.*[536] related to electronic evidence.

Challenges Faced

The most concerning challenge related to these experts is the lack of their independence from the Police interference. There is an over-reliance of Police on forensic labs and its influence on the labs often leads to biased results. Further, there is a very limited use of forensics in the criminal investigations with judges often raising questions on the qualifications of these experts in the absence of any national level certification.

Reforms and Trends

Recent guidelines in 2025 are pushing the autonomous bodies like the National Forensic Sciences Universities (NFSU) for certified independent forensic experts, their training and introducing courses on digital forensics.

9. Conclusion

The new Criminal laws introduced in 2023 in the form of BNS, BNSS and BSA, replacing the Indian Penal Code (IPC), 1860, The Code of Criminal Procedure (CrPC), 1973 and the Indian Evidence Act (IEA), 1872 marks a transition phase and a significant overhaul specially in the area of Digital Evidence and Forensics. These laws represent a major step forward towards the modernization of the Criminal

535 AIR 2010 SC 1974.
536 (2014) 10 SCC 473.

Justice System of India. They seek to enhance the transparency and reliability of evidence by certain mandates in the form of videography of investigative procedures and integrating digital forensics in the investigation and court proceedings. However, various challenges are also accompanying these reforms such as relating to privacy and institutional capacity.

There is a need of a cautious and balanced approach towards integrating the modern reforms in the system while ensuring that the basic fundamental rights like privacy are kept intact. The technological advancements must be utilized to their highest potential with an aim to improve the efficiency of investigation without crossing the boundaries of Constitutional rights. This requires a harmonious gathering of institutional strengthening, legislative refinement and judicial oversight. Finally, the success of the Digital Forensics in the era of new criminal laws largely depends on the ability of the Indian Legal System to reconcile the Innovations in technology with the fundamental principles of justice and fairness.

Chapter 17

Digital Criminal Procedure under the Bharatiya Nagarik Suraksha Sanhita: Electronic Evidence, Videography, and Virtual Courts in Practice

Abhyudaya Singh
Assistant Professor, India International University of Legal Education and Research (IIULER), Goa, & Ph.D. Scholar at Himachal Pradesh National Law University (HPNLU), Shimla

Vaibhav Pandey
Student of BBA LL.B (Hons.) student,
Amity University Uttar Pradesh, Lucknow.

Abstract

The BNSS marks a significant change to India's criminal procedure and rules regarding the use of electronic evidence; videography for documenting crime scenes and investigations; and online court proceedings and teleconferencing technologies as part of conducting trials. These reforms reflect a normative shift toward transparency and processing efficiency, as well as enhancing accountability through technology. However, the implementation of these reforms generates numerous complex doctrinal and operational issues related to admissibility and authenticity of electronic evidence, data integrity, chain of custody, and privacy protections; as well as access to technology disparity.

This chapter critically examines the rules governing electronic records, including the authentication of electronic records and their admissibility into evidence, as well as how mandatory videography affects the investigative independence of law enforcement agencies and constitutional protections against compulsory self-incrimination and coerced confession. This chapter will also critically analyze the procedural legitimacy of virtual courts and their effect on open access, effective representation and the right to due process in the administration of justice. Through a doctrinal and policy analysis methodology, the research argues that while the BNSS legislation attempts to modernise how criminal cases are tried, it will only achieve its full potential by ensuring that the introduction of technology into the adjudication process is aligned with due process protections, that the courts are prepared to receive and use new technologies, and that all courts have similar judicial interpretations of how electronic evidence can be used in a case.

1. Introduction: Digital Transformation of Criminal Procedure

India's Criminal Justice System is about to undergo a major change with the creation of the Bharatiya Nagarik Suraksha Sanhita, 2023, which will completely replace the Code of Criminal Procedure (CrPC) of 1973. This new law will not only make some updates, but will bring in very different ways of handling cases through the use of new technologies such as digital records, video recording of evidence during investigations and the use of virtual courts. These changes to the system are part of the global trend towards using digital technology to deliver justice more efficiently and accountably, and to increase the level of transparency in the justice delivery system. The previous version of the CrPC relied heavily on long-standing methods of conducting criminal cases, using paper-based records and oral evidence as well as in-person hearings. In contrast, the new BNSS will establish a new way of managing the filing and decision-making processes for criminal cases, based on digital processes that will begin with registering the first information report (FIR) and continue to completion and disposition of a case. The Ministry of Home Affairs has stated that the reforms will improve access to justice by reducing delays and backlogs in the system.

However, using technology in criminal law has created complicated legal issues including how electronic evidence will be proven to be real; how will we keep these records; what will happen to the records if they are destroyed or lost; and how do we provide equal opportunity for people to use the same digital systems? The issues also present serious constitutional and procedural problems. Courts now must find a balance between technology as a tool for efficiency versus protecting basic rights; in particular, Article 21 refers to providing a person with his or her right to a fair trial.

This chapter uses a doctrinal and policy-based approach to explore three major areas of the developing framework of criminal procedure. First, it discusses how evidence is governed by the evidentiary rules relating to electronic records and examines their admissibility and reliability in court. Second, it looks at the constitutional implications of requiring all investigators to use videography during investigations, particularly with respect to issues of privacy, due process, and improper use. Finally, it evaluates the legal viability and institutional feasibility of virtual courts as an alternative means of adjudication. The main argument of this chapter is that the Bharatiya Nagarik Suraksha Sanhita is a progressive and necessary reform for the purpose of modernising criminal procedure. However, the success of this legislative change will depend on ensuring that it is implemented in a manner that is both careful and constitutional, by aligning the innovative procedures provided for under this law with the guarantees of fundamental rights, and by ensuring that judicial and investigative institutions have the technical capacity, infrastructure, and training necessary to implement these reforms fairly, efficiently, and accountably.

2. Statutory Framework of Digital Criminal Procedure Under Bnss

The BNSS lays out an integrated digital procedural architecture. It requires audio and video documentation during search and seizure operations, and requires submission to the Magistrate. This is a move towards institutionalizing videotape documentation for post-mortem examinations, and allows for electronic communication and video conferencing throughout the trial process. In addition, it allows for the accused to receive electronic copies of all relevant documents, thereby enhancing the transparency of the process[537].

This framework is based on existing legislation including the Indian Evidence Act 1872 where sections 65A and 65B govern the admissibility of electronic evidence and the Information Technology Act of 2000 which provides for the legal recognition of both electronic records and digital signatures. Together, these statutory provisions

537 Aishwarya Chourasia, *Recording of Search and Seizure Through Audio-Video Electronic Means Under Section 105 of the BNSS*, Aashayein (Jan. 20, 2025), www.alec.co.in.

create a legal basis for incorporating technology into criminal procedure. These laws will work together to provide legal validity and procedural reliability to both legal systems and ensure that the procedural integrity of digital evidence exists. The combination of these laws will provide a comprehensive, integrated, and coherent structure for the regulation and support of digital criminal processes throughout the entire justice system[538]

The BNSS defines a framework for incorporating digital technologies into the criminal justice system. Unfortunately, it doesn't include sufficient rights for defendants during this era of rapid technological advancement. Although electronic evidence continues to be utilized and recognized, defendants do not have certain key protections under the BNSS, such as a right to independent forensic review and ability to receive competent legal counsel. The BNSS creates an unbalanced structural dynamic between the prosecutor and defense, as technology disproportionately benefits the prosecutor without corresponding benefits to the defense. Defendants are challenged when attempting to contest the authenticity or reliability of electronic evidence against them. This imbalance points to further systemic normative issues within the BNSS, placing into question the extent of state-sponsored technological advancement in criminal justice in light of the importance of having strong procedural protections. Digital innovation must occur in conjunction with established concepts of fairness, due process and equal protection of the law.

Privacy obligations for personal data handlers add another layer of complexity to the regulatory frameworks that govern how to use

538 A. Jain, *Admissibility of Electronic Evidence Under the Indian Evidence Act, 1872*, Manupatra (Sept. 22, 2023), available at: https://articles.manupatra.com/article-details/ADMISSIBILITY-OF-ELECTRONIC-EVIDENCE-UNDER-THE-INDIAN-EVIDENCE-ACT-1872

personal data. The Digital Personal Data Protection Act (Ministry of Law and Justice, Government of India, 2023) identifies certain exceptions, particularly for law enforcement purposes, thus allowing law enforcement agencies to use personal data as part of their investigations; however, it does not provide any definitive guidelines as to the amount of personal data that can be collected or how long personal data may be retained during a criminal investigation. This lack of clarity leaves an indefinite line between the protection of an individual's right to privacy and the practical requirements needed by law enforcement agencies in their criminal investigations. As a consequence, there are questions regarding the proportionality, necessity, and accountability of personal data used by law enforcement agencies, which ultimately may affect the level of judicial review and the standards of evidence needed to obtain a conviction against an accused individual. Furthermore, the lack of clearly defined safeguards may lead to matters being determined in ways that differ from one another due to lack of enforcement consistency between individual cases, which leads to an excessively large gap between individuals' right to privacy, and law enforcement's ability to properly perform criminal investigations.[539]

539 Hogan Lovells, *India's Digital Personal Data Protection Rules Update*, Lexology (Nov. 17, 2025), available at: https://www.lexology.com/: https://www.lexology.com/library/detail.aspx?g=06a5c11c-6f5d-4aec-8d07-851cf89d992d#:~:text=The%20rules%20will%20become%20effective,manner%2C%20as%20detailed%20further%20below.&text=The%20DPDPA%20applies%20exclusively%20to,formally%20notified%20to%20the%2

3. Electronic Evidence: Admissibility, Authentication, and Privacy

3.1 Nature and Scope of Electronic Evidence

Different types of electronic evidence can be being found in the digital world. Types of digital evidence would include CCTV, mobile devices, GPS recordings, e-mail, social media & transaction records. Electronic evidence differs from traditional documentary sources of documents because it is highly volatile, easily altered & requires the use of technology to interpret. As a result, these differences require the development of different types of laws & forensic protocols in order to establish norms for admissibility.

3.2 Section 65B and Judicial Interpretation

Section 65B of Indian Evidence Act can be directly referenced when trying to determine what types of electronic evidence will be admissible in court. It should be noted that when presenting any electronic record to a court, that it must be accompanied by a certificate indicating the authenticity of the evidence, as well as that the device used to record the evidence was properly functional during the event recorded.

The role of judicial interpretation in clarifying the application of a provision through landmark judgments has been critical. The Supreme Court of India made significant determinations regarding the admissibility of electronic evidence in *Anvar P.V. v. P.K. Basheer*[540]. The Supreme Court of India held that an electronic record can be accepted as evidence if it meets Section 65B of the Indian Evidence

540 *Anvar P.V. v. P.K. Basheer*, Civil Appeal No. 4226 of 2012 (S.C. Sept. 18, 2014), *available at:* https://aphc.gov.in/docs/imp_judgements/Anvar%20PV%20case.pdf.

Act. This judgement broke from previous practices that noted strict adherence to procedures in admitting types of evidence to general rules about evidence. The Court also made it clear that a certificate required by Section 65B (4) of the Indian Evidence Act must accompany the electronic record and is fundamental to its being admitted as evidence. This certificate must be provided by an individual who has a reasonable amount of knowledge regarding the operation of the device or system that generated the electronic record and must guarantee the authenticity and integrity of the electronic record. In addition, regardless of relevance or probative value, electronic evidence will not be permitted in court unless there is a corresponding certificate attached to it.

The Arjun Panditrao Khotkar v. Kailash Kushanrao Gorantyal[541] case confirmed the principle and allowed greater flexibility regarding when the certificate must be produced. The Court stated that enforcement of procedural requirements should not prevent the achievement of substantive justice. These decisions illustrate a major problem with the use of digital evidence: it is typically admitted based upon procedural compliance and not based upon substantive reliability. Consequently, in practice, where evidence has been excluded due to failure to comply with the requirement to produce, the prosecution's case has been greatly weakened by the exclusion of relevant evidence.

3.3 Authentication and Chain of Custody

The use of proper forensic methods, verifying hash values and maintaining a secured chain of custody is essential for establishing the authenticity of digital evidence. Proper acquisition, handling,

541 D. Gandhi & N. Garg, *Electronic Evidence*, SCC Online Blog (June 7, 2021), available at: https://www.scconline.com/blog/post/2021/06/07/electronic-evidence-2

and presentation of digital data throughout the forensic process must demonstrate that the original digital data has remained unchanged from when it was acquired to when it is presented in a court of law. In State (NCT of Delhi) v. Navjot Sandhu[542] the Delhi high court acknowledged the relevance of the chain of custody by evaluating the reliability and authenticity of electronic records on a holistic basis. As of yet, there are no established national standards on how to deal with electronic records evidentiary practices, and as such, evidentiary practice remains inconsistent based on jurisdiction.

3.4 Privacy and Constitutional Concerns

In K.S. Puttaswamy v. Union of India[543], the Supreme Court of India held that collecting electronic records raises privacy issues. The Court said that all government actions infringed on an individual's right to privacy and that every such infringement must meet the standards of legality, necessity and proportionality. In general, digital investigations include large volumes of personal data, including personal communications, geolocation and other forms of metadata. The lack of specific legal protections for such actions increases the risk of violating existing laws. The broad and volatile nature of the methods used to conduct digital surveillance also increases this concern. In addition, the lack of clear exclusionary rules for the use of illegally obtained evidence creates uncertainty about what evidence can be deemed legally sufficient to establish guilt or liability. As a result,

542 *State (NCT of Delhi) v. Navjot Sandhu*, Appeal (Crl.) Nos. 373–375 of 2004, (2005) 11 S.C.C. 600 (India), discussed in *Ruling of Navjot Sandhu Case to the Extent of Admissibility of Electronic Evidence as Secondary Evidence Overruled*, SCC Online Blog (Sept. 20, 2014), *available at:* https://www.scconline.com/blog/post/2014/09/20/ruling-of-navjot-sandhu-case-to-the-extent-of-admissibility-of-electronic-evidence-as-secondary-evidence-overruled/

543 AIR 2017 SUPREME COURT 4161.

illegally possessed digital evidence may still be admitted into evidence in a criminal proceeding, which reduces procedural fairness and creates a weak basis for protecting privacy rights guaranteed by operational or statutory law[544].

4. Videography in Criminal Investigation: Transparency vs Rights

4.1 Legislative Intent and Evidentiary Value

Video recording of search and seizure, as well as post-mortem, is mandated by the BNSS. The purpose of the reform is to enhance transparency, prevent the fabrication of evidence and provide an objective record of investigative activities. Videography can provide multiple functions including: bolstering evidence for prosecution; allowing for scrutiny of evidence by defence; and providing oversight for the courts. Therefore, videography acts both as a mechanism of evidence and accountability.

4.2 Constitutional Implications

Doubts have been raised about whether mandatory videotaping violates the Constitution's protection against self-incrimination (Art. 20(3) of Constitution of India). The Supreme Court of India ruled that the involuntary extraction of testimonial evidence violates fundamental rights in Selvi v. State of Karnataka[545]. Although videography does

544 Khushi Malviya, *K.S. Puttaswamy v. Union of India: Landmark Case on Right to Privacy*, CLATalogue/Lawctopus (Oct. 28, 2024), available at: http://lawctopus.com/clatalogue/clat-pg/ks-puttaswamy-v-union-of-india-landmark-case-on-right-to-privacy/.

545 *Selvi v. State of Karnataka (2010)*, available at: https://www.drishtijudiciary.com/constitution-of-india/selvi-v-state-of-karnataka-2010.

not compel an accused to give testimony at the time it happens, the constant video recording of investigators can have an indirect and potentially coercive effect on an accused by creating a perpetual psychological pressure on the accused during the investigative process that could lead them to act or behave differently in relation to whether they wish to exercise their right to remain silent. Because videography may appear to be procedurally neutral, it will be necessary for courts to determine if the indirect impact it will have on an accused would infringe upon their constitutional protections. The effect of this technology will require thorough judicial scrutiny to ensure that its use would not diminish the fundamental safeguards found in Art. 20(3) of Constitution of India.

4.3 Practical and Institutional Challenges

There are many obstacles to be overcome in order to implement videography as required in the law. An overwhelming number of police stations do not have adequate video recording equipment; nor do most police stations have effective methods to safely store recorded footage. Bureau of Police Research and Development's (BPR&D) most up to date Data on Police Organizations 2024 show 18,284 sanctioned police stations (as of January 1st 2024) in Indian States and Union Territories collectively. This total includes police stations in rural and urban areas as well as special-purpose police stations such as Women's Police Stations and Cyber Crime Cells, plus those that oppose crime towards vulnerable persons. Of the 18,284 police stations, 9,127 are located in rural areas; 5,492 are in urban areas; and 3,665 are classified as special-purpose police stations[546]. Additionally, a significant number of police

546 Government of India, Ministry of Home Affairs, *Ranking of Police Stations 2025* (2025), *available at:* https://www.mha.gov.in/sites/default/files/2025-12/FinalReportEng_22122025.pdf.

stations lack standard operating procedures (SOPs) regarding the use of video recording equipment. This lack of SOPs raises concerns about the selective recording of persons and events, thereby compromising both the integrity and the completeness of the recorded footage. The lack of standardization in the recording process can also create inconsistencies that may affect the reliability of recorded footage being used as evidence in court. To successfully implement videography as required by law, it is critical that police departments establish clear procedural guidelines, invest in building capacity through training, and implement sound monitoring mechanisms. Each of these actions will serve to ensure that police departments operate with increased accountability, maintain evidentiary standards, and produce footage of persons and events through videography that will serve the purpose for which they were created by law.

5. Virtual Courts and Digital Trial Process

5.1 Legal Recognition and Institutional Framework

With the express authorization in the Bharatiya Nagarik Suraksha Sanhita (BNSS), virtual court proceedings are now legitimate under law, giving them authority to hold trials (in addition to other proceedings) via video conferencing. This statutory authority further supports and bolsters the Supreme Court of India e-Courts initiative and the more general ICT policy framework (Information and Communication Technology) that seeks to update the administration of justice. Virtual courts were created as a response to the need for a quick and efficient way to resolve disputes due to the disruption caused by the COVID pandemic, but are now an established part of the judicial system. The continuing rise of virtual court proceedings reflects a shift toward technology-based forms of resolution. The ultimate goal of virtual proceedings is to expedite the resolution of cases that have historically caused delays in the justice delivery process and to improve access to justice for litigants, lawyers, and other stakeholders, particularly those located in rural, remote or underserved communities in India, thereby creating a justice system that is more efficient, inclusive and responsive to the needs of citizens.

5.2 Open Court Principle and Fair Trial

Under the principle of open justice, court proceedings should be made available to the public. Virtual courts present challenges to this principle because access to them is frequently restricted to participants who have the required technology to be able to participate in the court hearing by way of video. In the case of State of Maharashtra v. Praful B.[547] Desai the Supreme Court found that video conferencing was a permitted method of carrying out a fair hearing; however, the format of video conferencing used in the case did not foresee the large-scale digital use of video conferencing for trials or the broader implications of this new method of conducting trials. Some issues have also been raised as to how effective a process video conferencing is in terms of cross-examination of witnesses, assessing the reliability of a witness who has provided their evidence via video conferencing and the possibility of other people influencing or coaching witnesses who are providing their evidence through virtual means[548].

---

547 (2003) 4 S.C.C. 601.

548 *State of Maharashtra v. Dr. Praful B. Desai*, (2003) 4 S.C.C. 601, *available at:* https://www.drishtijudiciary.com/indian-evidence-act/State%20of%20Maharashtra%20v.%20Prafulla%20B.%20Desai%20(Dr.)%20(2003)%204%20SCC%20601.

5.3 Digital Divide and Access to Justice

A virtual court system will not operate at maximum efficiency in the future due to the digital divide. Reliable internet access and technology infrastructure differ greatly throughout the United States; for example, according to the (TRAI), in many rural areas, internet access has still not grown as fast as in urban locations. Consequently, this disparity in service level has a direct impact on all participants in the judicial system: the defendant, the attorney, and the actual courts. Because of the lack of digital resources available to many participants, the ability to participate in virtual court proceedings may reduce, causing delays in the disposition of cases and the compromise of procedural fairness. If the digital divide continues to create access and usage disparities in different geographical regions, it may ultimately result in a diminished equality of justice for all citizens and the creation of a structural disadvantage for those people that live in low-connectivity areas. If there is ongoing dependence on virtual courts in this environment, the judicial systems may become unbalanced due to the relationship between access to technology and access to the judicial process.

6. Doctrinal Tensions, Comparative Insights, and Implementation Gaps

6.1 Efficiency vs Due Process

The Bharatiya Nagarik Suraksha Sanhita's (BNSS) main goal is to improve the efficiency of procedures and fix the backlog of criminal cases in the criminal justice system. This goal is a way of improving access to justice; however, achieving the goal should not come at the cost of providing all accused persons the opportunity to receive a fair trial. The need for balancing the provision of speedy criminal trials and fairness in trials is also an ongoing constitutional requirement.

In Hussainara Khatoon v. State of Bihar[549], the Supreme Court of India recognized that the right to a speedy trial is part of the right to life and personal liberty set forth under Article 21 of the Constitution of India. However, the Supreme Court of India also stated that expeditious proceedings cannot be conducted in a manner that violates a defendant's rights to fair treatment and due process of law. Thus, while the BNSS may contain measures that would allow for some streamlining of criminal procedure, the implementation of the measures contained within the BNSS must be done carefully so that the rights of those accused of crimes are afforded adequate protection under the law and that the delivery of justice under the law is done in an equitable manner, in an transparent manner, and in accordance with law.

6.2 Inconsistency in Judicial Interpretation

The Indian Evidence Act, Section 65B, has experienced inconsistent legal interpretation between numerous courts, causing uncertainty towards its range and reach. For example, The Supreme Court in Anvar P.V. v. P.K. Basheer[550] established a strict standard for compliance with certification requirements; while reaffirmed and clarified in Arjun Panditrao Khotkar v. Kailash Kushanrao Gorantyal (2020) afterwards. Nevertheless, the practical ambiguities continue to exist, especially with respect to the procedural thresholds for admitting electronic evidence. The Courts have also warned against the use of overly technical requirements to inhibit the furtherance of justice in a digital world. As a result, until we see the development of new laws and

549 S.A. Nair, *Hussainara Khatoon v. Home Secretary, State of Bihar*, Manupatra (Aug. 23, 2022), *available at:* https://articles.manupatra.com/article-details/HUSSAINARA-KHATOON-V-Home-Secretary-STATE-OF-BIHAR

550 *Anvar P.V. v. P.K. Basheer*, Civil Appeal No. 4226 of 2012 (S.C. Sept. 18, 2014).

judicial procedures to expedite these processes, the legal framework will remain open-ended, creating hurdles for Courts, practitioners, and litigants[551].

6.3 Comparative Perspectives

The United Kingdom provides operational guidance for the management of electronic evidence through resources such as Crown Prosecution Service directives that detail how to collect, manage and present electronic evidence; however, the standards for accepting the electronic evidence into court is determined by the statutes of the law and common law rules ensuring that the electronic evidence will be judged against the larger evidentiary law instead of against a completely separate system of judicial processes. With regard to providing presumptions of authenticity to electronic records under the Evidence Act of Singapore, a party's ability to demonstrate such presumption creates efficiencies in the lessening of the burden of proof upon such party when relying on digital records and thus expediting the judicial process.

India, however, employs a much more rigid regulatory framework than the United Kingdom or Singapore, specifically with regard to the certification requirements set forth in Section 65B of the Indian Evidence Act. While the certification process is meant to ensure the accuracy and reliability of electronic records, the rigidity of the procedural requirements to satisfy the certification requirements has resulted in inconsistencies in how different courts have interpreted the

551 Aryan Bhattacherjee & Ondrajit Adhikari, *Arjun Panditrao Decision: The Time to Revisit S. 65B of Indian Evidence Act – A Scientific Legal Analysis*, LiveLaw (Sept. 8, 2020), available at: https://www.livelaw.in/columns/arjun-panditrao-decision-the-time-to-revisit-s65b-of-indian-evidence-act-a-scientific-legal-analysis-162590

certification requirements through varying applications of the law. As opposed to an overall lack of a legal framework, the challenges that exist in India deal more with the lack of uniformity in the administration of the law, than the lack of a cohesive legal framework.

The need for developing institutional capacity is highlighted by the development of the Bharatiya Nagarik Suraksha Sanhita (BNSS), while e-Courts Mission Mode Project's initiatives framed progress in digitalization; Nevertheless, shortcomings in infrastructure, technical capability and stakeholder training still exist to create barriers to effectively utilizing these resources. Therefore, developing these areas by providing targeted training to judges, law enforcement and legal practitioners will be critical to achieving the overall goal of modernizing India's criminal justice system.

7. Conclusion and Recommendations

India's criminal justice system has made a monumental leap towards digitisation with the BNSS. The electronic evidence, videography, and virtual courts included in the BNSS indicate a progressive approach to justice delivery. The analysis found large doctrinal and operational deficiencies, such as a complicated evidentiary framework with inconsistent application, videography requirements without standard implementation processes, and virtual courts possibly increasing existing inequities to accessing justice.

A number of changes must occur to fix these problems. Section 65B should be simplified to remove wrongful procedural barriers. There should be a national Standard Operating Procedure (SOP) on videography with implementation and enforcement. Investment in digital infrastructure must give priority to rural and lower tier courts. Develop and expand more judges and police officer training programs to create more jobs. There should be new privacy protocols specifying electronic evidence. Above all, a successful digital version of criminal procedures must comply with the Constitution. Technology enhances the fairness and integrity of the criminal justice system. The B.N.S.S. provides a structure for the success of implementation and continuing support with close oversight by the judiciary.

Chapter 18

Witness Protection in India - From Judicial Recognition to Statutory Framework Under the BNSS, 2023

Dr. Deepti Singla
Assistant Professor of Law, Amity University, Punjab.

Abstract

In India, witness protection had been undefined and unclear over many years. People were supposed to come out and speak the truth but they had minimal guarantee of safety. This was transformed in Mahender Chawla v. Union of India (2019). The Apex Court noted that nobody is able to testify freely when his life is at stake. The Court associated witness protection has been provided under Article 21 of the Constitution and that is why witness protection has become an integral part of the rights to life, personal liberty and fair trial. Section 398 of the Bharatiya Nagarik Suraksha Sanhita (BNSS), which formed a legal basis for modern witness protection mechanisms, subsequently reinforced this judicial recognition.

In spite of these developments, there are major gaps in reality. The continuing issue of hostile witnesses establishes that there exists an extensive gap between law and reality. Most witnesses do not become hostile willingly, but due to the fear, intimidation, the influence of social pressure or the lack of protection. This challenges prosecutions and, in some instances, collapses cases. It has become more of an issue in the digital era, where the anonymity is challenging since personal data can be traced and the traditional protection mechanisms are not as effective. In comparison, the United States and the United Kingdom jurisdictions embrace comprehensive strategies, which involve long-term rehabilitation and witness identity protection.

The chapter examines the history for providing witness protection in India, the reasons and impact of hostile testimony and the drawbacks of the existing legal system. It further takes into consideration emerging technological issues and makes comparative insights to suggest a more holistic and humanitarian approach. Nevertheless, the efficacy of the justice system is not merely a matter of law, but the ability of witnesses to testify without any fear and live a dignified life.

1. Introduction

The Indian criminal justice system, developed during the colonial British rule in India, is founded on an adversarial system (or accusatorial system). In this system, the truth is established by presenting and evaluating evidence before an impartial court. In this context, the witness testimony plays a central role. It offers first-hand testimonies that help courts in re-creating events. Oral testimony, in contrast to documentary evidence or forensic evidence, can be subjected to intimidation, coercion and psychological pressure. This vulnerability contributes to the increasing trend of the hostile witness phenomenon, when a person withdraws or changes their previous statements significantly, during the trial. Although law allows such witnesses to be cross-examined, their hostility is often not simply an issue of conflicting evidence, but a reflection of significant structural deficiency.

As judicial practice shows, the adverse impact of witness intimidation on fairness in trials cannot be underestimated. The Apex Court in *Zahira Habibulla H. Sheikh v. State of Gujarat*[552] demonstrated how the injustice in the Best Bakery case was happened due to coercion of eyewitnesses. Likewise, in another case of *State v. Manu Sharma*[553], the Court recognised the effect of hostile testimony on the integrity of the trial. The lack of appropriate witness protection procedures makes it possible to suppress truth. Such cases demonstrate that it is not a single event, but rather is a systemic problem affecting the entire criminal justice system. Hostile testimony has even resulted in acquittals in serious crimes including organised crimes, corruption and sexual offences. This compromises conviction rates and negates the confidence of the people. Although the courts have focused on the civic responsibility of individuals to help in the delivery of justice, it should be accompanied by an analogous duty on the part of the State to protect and safeguard them.

Earlier, India did not have a set of comprehensive laws about the protection of witnesses. Action was mainly improvised and based on court orders like in-camera proceedings or interim police custody. One of the greatest transformations came with the establishment of the Witness Protection Scheme, 2018, which offered systematic methods for threat evaluation and protection. It was declared constitutional in the case of *Mahender Chawla v. Union of India*[554], In this case, the Court made witness protection as an integral part of the right to life and personal liberty under Article 21 of the Constitution. Furthermore,

552 (2004) 4 S.C.C. 158.

553 (2010) 6 S.C.C. 1

554 (2019) 14 S.C.C. 615

Section 398 of the BNSS was another significant development towards the transformation of a discretion-based system to a statutory-based system.

However, in the modern world, witness vulnerability has gone beyond physical threats. New risks come in the form of digital traceability. The growing use of systems like Aadhaar and digital communication networks leave continuous data trails. This complicates the aspect of anonymity and weakens conventional protection mechanisms. Against this background, the chapter explores the issue of crisis of testimony in India through study of emergence of hostile witnesses, development of legal safeguards and weaknesses of the existing legal framework. It aims at evaluating whether current mechanisms suffice to cope with these challenges and the way in which a more efficient and human-friendly system can be made.

2. Evolution of Witness Protection Mechanisms in India

Until 2018, the Indian system of witness protection was in disarray and was predominantly left to personal judgment, since there were no clear and binding laws that established the rights of witnesses or what the State could or could not do. The only sort of protection available was reactive and established on a case-by-case basis, for example ordering in-camera proceedings or police protection or shifting the trial location. These measures were case-specific and therefore lacked continuity and they could differ significantly across jurisdictions. This led to undermining the issue of witness safety as a peripheral issue instead of a central part of the criminal justice process that puts witnesses at risk, particularly in high profile cases, with intimidation or coercion.

Understanding this structural weakness, different groups of experts proposed holistic reformation. It is pertinent to mention that the Law Commission of India in its 14th, 154th and 178th report has consistently underlined the need for a statute that would guarantee that the identity of the witness would remain anonymous[555]. Likewise, witness hostility was cited by the Malimath Committee Report[556] as a primary cause of a low rate of convictions in the country and thereby encouraged the establishment of a formal witness protection programme. Nevertheless, in spite of these suggestions, a long period of years passed before legislation was enacted that left the issue of protection of witnesses to judicial action and administrative discretion.

2.1 Judicial Recognition of Witness Protection as a Constitutional Concern

The historic change in the legal status of witness protection happened because of judicial action, wherein the Apex Court gradually recognised the protection of witnesses as an inseparable part of the constitutional right to a fair trial. Without adequate protection, the Court stated that a witness commonly turns hostile and this compromises the justice system[557]. It underscored that a fair trial is impossible if witnesses cannot testify without fear, intimidation or pressure.

555 Law Comm'n of India, *14th Report: Reform of Judicial Administration* (1958), Also see: Law Comm'n of India, *154th Report on the Code of Criminal Procedure, 1973* (1996) & Law Comm'n of India, *178th Report on Recommendations for Amending Various Enactments* (2006).

556 Gov't of India, Ministry of Home Affairs, *Committee on Reforms of Criminal Justice System (Malimath Committee Report)* (2003).

557 *Mahender Chawla v. Union of India*, (2019) 14 S.C.C. 615.

2.2 The Witness Protection Scheme, 2018

In the year 2018, the Government of India formulated the first scheme on witness protection, which laid down a standard mechanism to assess threats to witnesses and provide necessary protective measures. Several measures have been adopted in the scheme for protection including police protection, relocation, in-camera hearings, video-conferencing and anonymity. In addition to these, there is a gradation system through which the threat to witnesses is assessed and a district level competent authority consisting of the District and Sessions Judge along with police and prosecution officials. These district-level authorities scrutinises applications, evaluates threat analysis and issues necessary directions on protection measures, ensuring judicial oversight in policymaking. One of the significant protections is the preparation of the Threat Analysis Report whereby the police evaluate the nature and extent of risk. Such threat analysis report forms the basis for protection decisions that aim to facilitate fairness and impartiality.

The Court furthermore reinforced the Witness Protection Scheme, 2018 and directed it to be rolled out nationwide in the meantime until appropriate legislation was enacted[558]. This decision not just bridged the legal vacuum but also changed witness protection from a policy issue to a constitutional obligation, demonstrating the role of the courts to safeguard procedural fairness in the absence of the law.

2.3 Limitations of the Witness Protection Scheme, 2018

Despite its progressive design, the Witness Protection Scheme, 2018 faced several structural and operational limitations. One of the biggest concerns was the lack of adequate financial resources, as many States

558 Ministry of Home Affairs, Gov't of India, *Witness Protection Scheme* (2018).

were unable to adequately operationalise witness protection funds, thereby limiting the implementation of resource-intensive measures like relocation and long-term protection. Moreover, the Scheme overly relied on local police for both threat assessment and execution of protection measures, thereby raising concerns about fairness and impartiality, particularly in intricate cases.

Another central concern was that the 2018 scheme was unable to keep up with digital threats. The growing reliance on systems such as Aadhaar along with digital communication networks leave behind a trail of digital footprints that makes it challenging to be anonymous even after relocating. In addition, the scheme did not have strict enforcement mechanisms or penalties of noncompliance, which compromised accountability and created discrepancies in the implementation across States.

A comprehensive rehabilitation plan was also lacking in the scheme. It was primarily concerned with physical protection in the short-term (during investigations and trials), whereas it originally did not consider the long-term requirements of psychological assistance, financial support and social inclusion. This loophole made the witness protection measures less feasible and effective.

2.4 From Policy Framework to Statutory Mandate

The limitations of the Witness Protection Scheme, 2018 accentuated the necessity of a more powerful and legally enforceable framework that eventually led to the introduction of witness protection within the structure of criminal procedure law. Section 398 of the BNSS marks a shift from a judicially recognised policy to a statutory mandated system. However, it also raises some new issues about uniformity, enforcement and institutional capacity, which are discussed in section 4 of the chapter.

3. Witness Protection in Special and High-Risk Cases

It is also essential to note that witness protection is much more complicated in the situations related to terrorism organised crime and other severe offences, where the threats are often systemic and include not only the witness but also their relatives. Such a situation places the criminal justice system in a great dilemma as it should strike the right balance between witness protection rights and the right to a fair trial in accordance with Article 21 and thus forms a constitutional tension between protection and procedural fairness. In spite of the general framework provided by the Section 398 of the BNSS, the nature of protection in high-risk cases is mostly subject to special statutes and to judicial interpretation.

3.1 Statutory Provisions for Anonymity and In-Camera Proceedings

The Indian law offers certain protection based on special legislation meant to regulate the threats arising in high-sensitivity cases. Section 44 of the Unlawful Activities Prevention Act, 1967 (UAPA) authorises courts to mask the identity and addresses of the witnesses in the case of terrorism, whereas the National Investigation Agency Act, 2008 (NIA Act) permits in-camera hearings and prevents the disclosure of confidential information. These protections include pseudonym (using fake names), removing or hiding personal information and restricting access to proceedings by the public. On the one hand, such provisions contradict the principle of open justice, but on the other hand, they are justified by the reasons of witness protection and true testimony.

Simultaneously, they should pass the test of proportionality, since unnecessary restrictions can also affect the accused's ability to effectively challenge evidence, which likewise highlights that the said protections do not primarily fit within the scope of the BNSS framework.

3.2 Judicial Development of the Redaction Doctrine

The courts have established a doctrine of redaction with the view of striking a balance between the rights of witnesses and the right to fair trial. In *Waheed ur Rehman Parra v. Union Territory of Jammu and Kashmir*[559], the Apex Court has affirmed that fair-trial rights do not require the open disclosure of witness identity when such a disclosure will pose a safety risk, but at the same time said that the accused should be provided with enough material to prepare a defence. The Court took a proportionalist stance, disclosing only the necessary information about the person, but not complete disclosure. This ensures that the identity of a witness is not compromised yet he or she can be questioned fairly in court. Nonetheless, this is not clearly expressed in the BNSS and therefore, it is still left to the courts to exercise their discretion to implement this rule.

3.3 Individualised Assessment and Rejection of Blanket Protection

In judicial decisions, it is emphasised that witness protection must be based on a case-to-case risk assessment, as opposed to a blanket protection approach. Practically this would imply that the case of every witness is considered individually, as opposed to considering all the witnesses as being equal. In *Mohammed Asarudeen v. Union of India*[560], the Court stated that any protective action should be supported by the

559 2022 SCC OnLine SC 145.

560 2025 Supreme (SC) 886.

articulated reasons, which should be in writing. Such considerations must take into account the nature of the crime, the level of risk and circumstances surrounding the case. This helps keep protection fair and balanced without affecting the right of the accused to a fair trial as well as ensures transparency. Nonetheless, Section 398 BNSS itself do not mandate these criterions and therefore, their consistent application is a matter of judicial interpretation and administrative discretion.

3.4 Organised Crime Legislation and Presumption of Threat

Laws on organised crime, including the Maharashtra Control of Organised Crime Act, 1999 (MCOCA), recognise the risky situations that witnesses have to encounter. In certain situations, it also enables the courts to make the assumption of a threat and take pro-active measures against it without the necessity to present detailed evidence on a case-by-case basis. This is critical particularly in the case of organised criminal networks. Simultaneously, these kinds of presumptions should be properly balanced with procedural fairness so that the accused could be able to effectively challenge the evidence. Since the BNSS does not explicitly say when to use these presumptions, the courts may decide cases differently in similar cases.

3.5 Expansion of Protection for Vulnerable Witnesses

The scope of witness protection has been gradually increasing to include vulnerable categories like children. The Protection of Children from Sexual Offences Act, 2012 (POCSO) has introduced child friendly procedures, non-intimidating environments and limited interface with the accused. In *Smruti Tukaram Badade v. State of Maharashtra*[561], the

561 2022 SCC OnLine SC 78

Apex Court also instructed to set up Vulnerable Witness Deposition Centre to make the process of witnessing safe and decent. These advances indicate a transition to the recognition of psychological vulnerability as well as a physical risk, though such mechanisms have not yet been incorporated into the BNSS in a wholesome and integrated manner.

3.6 Balancing Fairness and Protection - Emerging Judicial Philosophy

The Indian courts have taken a more balanced approach by attempting to have a balance between witness protection, the right of the accused to a fair trial and the principle of open justice. It is based on proportionality, case-by-case evaluation and procedural protections like redaction to conceal personal information and in-camera hearing. Though this new judicial perspective enhances its practical application, its dependence on individual case decisions is a fundamental flaw of the BNSS framework. Section 398 recognises the problem on a statistical level, but fails to formulate the principles by which such balance is to be achieved, leaving most of witness protection to judicial discretion instead of comprehensive legislation.

4. Structural Limitations and Implementation Challenges of Witness Protection Under Bnss, 2023

The implementation of BNSS is a significant change to the criminal procedure in India as it officially institutionalised the practice of witness protection in the legal framework. Section 398 provides this concept with legal support and a constitutional obligation to fair-trial rights in the constitution in Article 21. Nonetheless, effectiveness of any legal reform is not just a question of recognition but also a question of the designing and implementation of this reform. On a more detailed analysis, it is observed that both the legal structure and the reality on the ground create limitations that affect how well witnesses are actually protected.

4.1 Statutory Mandate and Legal Character

Firstly, Section 398 is an enabling rather than a developed right. Although it imposes a responsibility on state governments to develop witness-protection programs, it does not provide an express and enforceable right of individual witnesses or even standardised norms. Consequently, the nature and quality of protection differ with the manner the state enforces its scheme. This flexibility as opposed to uniformity undermines consistency and makes the overall efficiency of the framework less effective.

4.2 Institutional Continuity and Structural Adaptation

Building on this, the institutional design under the BNSS largely continues the framework established by the Witness Protection Scheme, 2018. Authorities still rely on existing mechanisms such as the Competent Authority model involving judicial and police representatives. While this continuity helps preserve administrative experience, it also means that earlier structural weaknesses remain unaddressed. The reform, therefore, appears to formalise an existing system rather than fundamentally transform it.

4.3 Federal Structure and Implementation Disparities

This reliance on state-led implementation further shapes how witness protection operates in practice. Since law and order fall within the jurisdiction of state governments, Section 398 results in a decentralised model. Although this allows adaptation to local conditions, it also leads to uneven implementation. Differences in administrative capacity and infrastructure mean that witnesses in different states may receive varying levels of protection, raising concerns about fairness and equal access to justice.

4.4 Enforcement Gaps and Institutional Dependence

Alongside these structural concerns, the framework also faces important enforcement gaps. Section 398 does not clearly define accountability mechanisms or uniform procedures, which creates uncertainty in implementation. A major issue is the continued reliance on police authorities for both threat assessment and protection. While this may be practically necessary, it raises concerns about neutrality, especially in cases involving powerful accused persons. In some situations, visible protection measures such as escorts may even increase exposure instead of ensuring safety, highlighting the need for more independent and specialised mechanisms.

4.5 Digital Risks and Traceability

These challenges are further complicated by changes in the digital environment. In today's system, identity is closely tied to digital records through mechanisms such as Aadhaar and online authentication. Even when witnesses are relocated, their biometric identity and digital footprint remain unchanged. Everyday activities like mobile usage, banking and online verification create data trails that can expose their identity. This makes traditional protection methods less effective and shows that the law has not yet fully adapted to the realities of digital traceability.

4.6 Financial Constraints and Resource Inequality

In addition to technological concerns, financial capacity plays the key role in describing the effectiveness of witness protection. Although protection funds exist, their allocation and use vary across states due to differences in resources and priorities. This affects access to key measures such as relocation, secure housing and on-going support. As a result, witnesses facing similar risks may receive different levels of protection depending on location, reinforcing inequalities within the system.

4.7 Procedural Delays and Witnesses Vulnerability

The problem is further intensified by delays in criminal trials. When proceedings take a long time, witnesses remain exposed to pressure and intimidation for extended periods. This increases stress, financial burden and the likelihood that they may withdraw or change their statements. Such delays weaken not only witness confidence but also the overall effectiveness of the justice system, showing how closely procedural efficiency is linked to witness protection.

4.8 Absence of Long-Term Rehabilitation

Even where immediate protection is provided, support often ends once the trial is over. The current framework pays limited attention to long-term rehabilitation, leaving witnesses to rebuild their lives on their own. Those who are relocated may struggle with employment, housing and social adjustment, along with psychological stress. Without continued support such as counselling and financial assistance, protection remains incomplete and fails to address the full impact of participation in the justice process.

4.9 Transitional Nature of the BNSS Framework

Taken together, these issues show that while Section 398 is an important step forward, it represents a transitional stage rather than a complete solution. The framework establishes a legal foundation but still depends on stronger institutions, clearer standards and better implementation. Unless these gaps are addressed, witness protection may remain effective in principle but limited in practice. The future of the system lies in bridging this gap between legal intent and lived reality.

These structural and practical limitations highlight that while the BNSS provides an important legal foundation, it does not fully address the complexities of witness protection in practice. The gaps in enforcement, institutional design and long-term support raise an important question about whether alternative models offer solutions that are more effective. In this context, a comparative study of global witness protection frameworks becomes useful in understanding how similar frameworks respond to similar challenges and what lessons can be drawn for the Indian framework.

5. Comparative Perspective

It is based on the limitations that a cross-comparison of the witness protection systems in the world can be used to highlight the advances as well as drawbacks of the Section 398 of the BNSS. The examples of a successful witness protection witnessed in states like the US and the UK show that real witness protection depends not just on legal acknowledgment but also on effective institutional scheme, sound coordination and continuous support. Through these systems, we see efficiency of witness protection is not only the result of legislation but also implementation.

5.1 US - Centralised and Identity-Based Protection

In the US, witness protection has been implemented in the form of the Federal Witness Security Program that is under the Witness Security Reform Act, 1984. The main characteristic of this model is holistic identity change where the eyewitnesses and their relatives are relocated, given different names and offered with new documents and job prospects. This practice prioritises anonymity and it is supported by long-term financial and rehabilitative support[562]. The program is centrally operated, which ensures that there are consistent standards, confidentiality and accountability. Conversely, Section 398 of the BNSS does not provide identity change or centralised administration and is primarily concerned with physical protection.

5.2 UK - Coordinated and Flexible Protection

The UK adheres to a balanced approach in the form of the Protected Persons Service, backed by the Serious Organised Crime and Police Act, 2005[563]. Instead of permanent identity change, the system gives priority to procedural anonymity in trials[564]. Under the Coroners and Justice Act, 2009, the courts can grant anonymity orders, which permit witnesses to adopt pseudonyms, distort their voices and restrict the amount of information disclosed about themselves. This type of balanced approach safeguards witnesses without contradicting the standard of open justice. The arrangement is in the form of coordination of both national and local powers in a structured system something

562 U.S. Marshals Serv., *Witness Security Program (WITSEC) Overview*, available at: https://www.usmarshals.gov.

563 U.K. Home Office, *Serious Organised Crime and Police Act Implementation Framework, available at:* https://www.gov.uk

564 U.K. Ministry of Justice, *Witness Anonymity and Court Protection Measures Guidance*, available at: https://www.gov.uk.

that state-based system of India does not clearly define. Section 398 of the BNSS does not provide any procedural safeguards of this kind, but instead relies on judicial discretion and other laws.

5.3 Key Differences with the Indian Framework

The main difference is the intensity of the institutional level of coordination and long-term support systems. The US and the UK both operate under centralised or coordinated systems that ensure a consistent protection. Section 398 of BNSS leaves the implementation to individual states, leading to uneven effectiveness across States. The international models primarily focus on long-term rehabilitation, witness identity protection, financial aid, relocation and reintegration, which are the key elements missing in the Indian scheme. The Indian framework is mainly concerned with short-term security measures like police protection and relocation, with little focus on keeping identities safe and supporting witnesses after the trial.

In general, although India has achieved noteworthy development with the 2018 Witness Protection Scheme and the statutory acknowledgment of the scheme in Section 398 of the BNSS, the framework is still in its stages of development. The fact that it is not centralised, does not protect identities and does not offer long-term rehabilitative support set it apart from more established systems. This comparison shows that witness protection needs stronger coordination, clear standards and a holistic approach.

6. Recommendations

The analysis of witness-protection policies in the BNSS indicates that even if the statutory recognition is a crucial step, the effectiveness of these policies will depend on the strength of institutions, appropriate implementation and the ability to respond to modern demands. To address the existing structural and operational limitations, the following recommendations are put forward

6.1 Establishment of a Centralised National Authority

There should be a centralised National Witness Protection Authority that would ensure that all states have the same standards. This authority would help in streamlining the implementation, creating clear instructions and monitor compliance, therefore would reduce inconsistencies created by decentralised implementation and reinforce the comprehensive accountability.

6.2 Creation of a Dedicated National Witness Protection Fund

Adequate witness protection requires a long-term financial investment, which is currently uneven across States. To ease the limitation posed by the local budgetary restrictions, a special fund should be created with joint funding by the Central and State governments to provide access to protective measures fairly and reliably.

6.3 Integration of Technological Safeguards

In the era of digitalisation, witness protection should not be limited to physical protection. The framework must also include the protection measures like encrypted communications, secured information systems, identity obfuscation/masking, limited access to sensitive data because they are essential in alleviating risks created by digital traceability .

6.4 Independent and Multi-Agency Threat Assessment

Assessment of threats should not only be limited to the police authorities. The introduction of a more balanced paradigm that would involve the judicial officers, the administrative bodies and independent professionals would contribute to a more objective and credible approach, which would develop a higher level of trust in the system, especially in the case of sensitive or high-risk cases.

6.5 Expansion to Long-Term Rehabilitation

The protection of witnesses ought not to be limited to the end of the trial process. It should also include long-term rehabilitation initiatives such as counselling, financial support, training and reintegration support so that the witnesses can be able to reconstruct their lives after undergoing the justice process (which involves investigation, trial and judgment).

6.6 Institutional Training and Sensitisation

Constant training of police officers, judicial officers and administrative officials is necessary. Moreover, sensitisation programmes can also improve their understanding about the requirements of vulnerable witnesses and help ensuring that the protective measures are applied consistently and effectively.

6.7 Strengthening Awareness and Accessibility

There is also a high percentage of witnesses who do not know about the protections. Therefore, Legal Services Authorities should take a proactive approach in terms of information circulation and simplifying processes. An increased outreach would mean that witnesses would be aware of their rights and could easily access protection.

7. Conclusion

The witness protection in India has seen a clear shift in ambiguous court-oriented protection towards a more organised legal protection. The Witness Protection Scheme[565] was the first organised effort to recognise the need of witness protection to a fair trial. This is further consolidated by section 398 of the BNSS that formally introduces witness protection into the criminal procedure law. All of these measures together represent a constitutional commitment to ensuring that witnesses can involve in the justice system safely, confidently and with dignity.

However, reality on the ground shows that legal recognition alone is not sufficient. The system is still affected by unequal inter-state implementation, limited resources, reliance on police reports, inordinate delays and increasing digital threats. Practical experience of countries like the US and the UK has proven that witness protection requires more than merely temporal security, but also organised systems, identity protection and long-term supporting efforts. The BNSS framework is one of the major developments in India and it is still developing. Its efficacy depends on strong institutional support, proper implementation and the ability to respond to the new realities so that idea of witness protection works in practice, not just in law.

565 Ministry of Home Affairs, Gov't of India, *Witness Protection Scheme* (2018).

Chapter 19

Online Proceedings and Virtual Courts Under the Bharatiya Nagarik Suraksha Sanhita, 2023: Legal and Practical Challenges –An Empirical Study from East Khasi Hills District

Yophika Grace Thabah
Assistant Professor, Shillong Law College.

Monomita Mitra
Law student, Shillong Law College.

Abstract

The increasing reliance on online proceedings and virtual courts signifies a substantial transformation in India's criminal justice system, particularly following the enactment of the Bharatiya Nagarik Suraksha Sanhita, 2023 (BNSS), which formally acknowledges electronic modes of conducting criminal proceedings. Although virtual courts are projected as instruments for improving efficiency, accessibility, and continuity of justice, their integration raises complex legal and practical concerns that warrant empirical scrutiny. This chapter proposes an empirical socio-legal study of online criminal proceedings in the East Khasi Hills District of Meghalaya, with specific reference to courts operating in Shillong. It aims to examine how virtual hearings are implemented within the BNSS framework and to assess their implications for procedural fairness, access to justice, effective legal representation, and the protection of the accused's rights at the district court level. Employing a qualitative research methodology, the study is based on semi-structured interviews with judicial officers, practicing advocates, public prosecutors, and court personnel, supplemented by doctrinal analysis of statutory provisions and policy guidelines governing electronic proceedings. The chapter critically analyses whether the increasing use of virtual courts aligns with constitutional principles and the practical realities of criminal adjudication in non-metropolitan settings. By grounding its analysis in empirical data from a district-level jurisdiction, this chapter aims to contribute nuanced, context-sensitive insights to the evolving discourse on digital criminal procedure under the BNSS and to suggest measures to ensure that technological integration reinforces, rather than undermines, fair trial guarantees.

1. Introduction: The Digital Transformation of Indian Criminal Justice Systems

The Indian criminal justice system has undergone the largest changes since the colonial period[566]. A major step forward in this process was the introduction of the Bharatiya Nagarik Suraksha Sanhita (BNSS) 2023, replacing the Code of Criminal Procedure 1973 (CrPC). This represents a strategic move towards developing and implementing a modernised, technologically advanced legal framework[567] The

566 Jaiswal et al., Evolving Paradigms of Criminal Law in Contemporary India: Challenges, Reforms, and the Quest for Justice in a Digital Age, 3(34) LawFoyer Int'l J. Doctrinal Legal Rsch. (2025).

567 Gangwar, Challenges of BNSS 2023, Knowledgeable Research (2025), https://doi.org/10.57067/d1prsg54.

introduction of the BNSS does not represent simply a new and updated administrative approach to the operation of the Indian criminal justice system, but rather it represents a new statutory approach to the application of criminal law and procedure in India. In fact, the BNSS explicitly allows, and in some cases obliges, the use of digital approaches to criminal procedure, court operations, and evidence collection.

The development of a modern Indian judiciary has been a long-term effort underway for over a decade; it has accelerated dramatically in response to the global COVID-19 pandemic. The temporary measures implemented to maintain the flow of justice during this crisis have evolved into a permanent institution of the Indian judiciary[568]. The primary purpose of the transition to remote hearings and electronic filing is to solve three long-standing issues within the Indian criminal justice system: (1) the issue of judicial delays; (2) the issue of the high transaction costs associated with litigation; and (3) the issue of limited access to justice for people living in remote parts of India. By enabling remote appearances and electronic document submission, the BNSS will facilitate the efficient processing of court cases. However, the shift away from traditional physical courtroom settings and toward remote hearings through the internet is a fundamental shift in jurisprudence. Implementing a highly developed digital environment is fraught with challenges. Beyond simply mandating the transition to virtual courtrooms through legislation, there must be a complete overhaul of the infrastructure supporting the criminal justice system, a change in the system's

568 Richard Susskind, Online Courts and Online Dispute Resolution (2023), https://doi.org/10.1093/9780192864727.003.0015.

legal culture, and answers to numerous legal questions concerning defendants' rights and the reliability of evidence[569].

Although virtual courts are viewed by many as essential tools to improve operational efficiency, expand access to the criminal justice system, and ensure the continued delivery of justice, their inclusion in everyday practice raises numerous difficult legal and practical questions that require systematic empirical research. Much of the current academic literature focuses on metropolitan high courts or apex judicial bodies. One of the most glaring gaps in the existing literature is a lack of knowledge about how these far-reaching national mandates for the digitalisation of criminal proceedings operate in non-metropolitan, or rural, regions of India. As part of this study, the views of individuals who work at the "front lines" of the criminal justice system — judicial officials, prosecuting attorneys, defence counsel, and court staff — will be examined. It is hoped that this analysis will offer a critical evaluation of the BNSS framework for conducting hearings remotely and assess the practical and legal obstacles that hinder its effective implementation in the East Khasi Hills region. Legal Framework of Online Proceedings under BNSS 2023

The BNSS 2023 establishes a solid statutory foundation for the digitalisation of criminal proceedings[570]. Unlike the former CrPC, which was essentially silent on the utilisation of technology, the new Sanhita embeds digital methods into the very structure of the trial and investigation process.

569 Wang, Online Litigation Challenges and Countermeasures to Traditional Litigation Rules, (2024), https://doi.org/10.12677/ojls.2024.125426.

570 D. Varghese, Electronic Communication under the Bharatiya Nagarik Suraksha Sanhita, 2023 and Bharatiya Nyaya Sanhita, 2023 (2025), https://papers.ssrn.com/sol3/Delivery.cfm?abstractid=5096623.

1.1 Facilitating Statutory Provisions for Video Hearings

The key changes brought about by the BNSS include the legalisation and legitimisation of the use of virtual courtrooms and remote participation for hearings. The legislation will allow video conferencing, enabling the accused, witnesses, and legal counsel to participate in hearings, potentially reducing the need for physical attendance at court and the associated logistical challenges. For example, Section 183 of the BNSS provides for the recording of confessions and witness statements electronically; however, there may be questions about the reliability and voluntariness of such statements when recorded electronically.

In addition, the Sanhita allows courts to require accused persons to appear before them electronically, thereby improving the efficiency of trials involving the accused. The introduction of virtual hearings is described as one of the most important statutory developments that facilitates the universal application of virtual courts[571].

1.2 Digital Recording of Police Investigations

The BNSS further requires that technology be used during an investigation to ensure transparency and preclude the manipulation of evidence. Under Section 185 (which corresponds to Section 105 in other discussions), the BNSS requires that searches and seizures be electronically recorded via audio/video means. In essence, this section was designed to provide a contemporaneous and tamper-proof record of police activities. Nevertheless, in order to satisfy the practical requirements of investigators to document their investigations using handheld mobile devices, presents considerable technical and ethical challenges.

---

571 Yadav, Digitizing Justice: The Case for Dedicated Online Dispute Resolution Legislation in India, SSRN (2024), https://doi.org/10.2139/ssrn.4840167.

1.3 E-Filing of Documents and Serving Electronic Notices

Similarly, the BNSS promotes the e-filing of documents and the digitisation of court records[572]. It also recognises the service of electronic notices and summons through digital platforms, aiming to accelerate processing time and ensure the presence of all parties. The BNSS establishes the legislative framework as a pivot toward the creation of a digitised criminal justice system, which incorporates electronic records into the normal practices of evidentiary matters.

2. Judicial Foundations

The progression to digital adjudication under the BNSS is not simply a product of recent legislative policy; rather, it represents the statutory codification of the Supreme Court of India's interpretations over the last twenty years regarding progressive approaches to virtual hearings. The Supreme Court has demonstrated a measured acceptance of virtual hearing practices; it has balanced the advantages of increased efficiency afforded by technology against the rigidity of procedural due process requirements in substantive law.

2.1 Virtual Presence Doctrine

The main legal structure for electronic evidence was established by the Supreme Court in State of Maharashtra v. Dr Praful B. Desai (2003)[573]. The fundamental jurisprudential issue at hand concerned whether the recording of a witness's testimony via video conference met the requirements of the previous provisions of the Code of Criminal Procedure, 1973 (Sections 273 & 308 of the BNSS) — namely, that evidence must be obtained in the "presence" of the

572 Shahi, Online Kachaheri, Int'l J. for Sci. Tech. & Eng'g (2025), https://doi.org/10.22214/ijraset.2025.71662.

573 State of Maharashtra v. Dr. Praful B. Desai, (2003) 4 SCC 601

accused. The Supreme Court broadly interpreted the requirement for "presence", stating that "presence" did not require the parties to be physically present. The Supreme Court stated that video conferencing is a modern scientific method that allows the court to view and listen to a witness contemporaneously and to assess their demeanour during the hearing. The Supreme Court's decision essentially overturned the concept of criminal trials being based solely on physical presence and laid the foundation for the creation of Section 530 of the BNSS, which provides statutory approval for all trial phases to be conducted via audio/video electronic means.

2.2 Institutionalisation of Virtual Courts and the Pandemic Pivot

The COVID-19 pandemic forced the judiciary to establish virtual courts as a permanent fixture. In the Suo Motu writ In Re: Guidelines for Court Functioning Through Video Conferencing During COVID-19 Pandemic[574], the Supreme Court utilised its extraordinary power under Article 142 of the Indian Constitution to officially create virtual courts. Stating that "technology is here to stay," the Supreme Court directed all High Courts to draft specific guidelines for video conferencing. Notably, the Supreme Court outlined the limitations of technology, noting that while video conferencing can be very effective for appeals and remands, its use for recording evidence at trial requires stricter procedural safeguards to prevent witness coaching and ensure the integrity of cross-examination. The Supreme Court's concerns about the use of technology directly influenced the implementation of the strict structural safeguards currently required under the BNSS and applicable High Court regulations.

574 In Re: Guidelines for Court Functioning Through Video Conferencing During COVID-19 Pandemic, (2020) 6 SCC 1.

2.3 Trauma-Informed Justice and Vulnerable Witnesses

In Re: Children in Street Situations[575], the Supreme Court has used virtual courts to protect vulnerable witnesses from the intimidating nature of physical courtrooms. The Court developed a Standard Operating Procedure (SOP) for recording the testimony of child witnesses and victims of trafficking. The Court emphasised that virtual procedures should continue after the end of the pandemic and that trial courts shall normally take statements of vulnerable witnesses remotely through designated points to ensure in-camera protection and child-friendly practices. The Supreme Court's trauma-informed justice approach complements the BNSS's framework, which strongly encourages the use of electronic means to protect the identities and emotional wellbeing of sensitive witnesses[576].

2.4 Limitations of Digitalisation: Protection of Due Process

Although the Supreme Court has been generally positive about technology in court processes, it has always drawn a clear distinction between investigative excesses that infringe on individual liberties. In cases examining police conduct, such as Satender Kumar Antil v. Central Bureau of Investigation[577], the Supreme Court has reaffirmed that the police apparatus may not circumvent mandatory procedural safeguards. For example, the Court has ruled that serving statutory notices for appearance via informal digital channels (e.g. WhatsApp) without following traditional and prescribed modes of service will be

575 In Re: Children in Street Situations, 2022 SCC OnLine SC 189

576 Sharma et al., From Policy to Practice: Integrating Trauma-Informed Victim Support in India's BNSS Era, Int'l Rev. Victimology (2025).

577 Satender Kumar Antil v. Central Bureau of Investigation, (2022) 10 SCC 51.

considered invalid. The Court's position highlights a significant limit of the BNSS regime: while digitalisation can enhance the efficiency of adjudication, it cannot be used by investigative agencies to bypass constitutional safeguards to prevent arbitrary government action.

2.5 Access to Justice vs. Procedural Orthodoxy

Perhaps the clearest expression of the philosophical tension underlying virtual courts is found in Justice D.Y. Chandrachud's dissent in Santhini v. Vijaya Venketesh (2018)[578]. In this case, the majority ruled that video conferencing should not be used for a standard procedure for matrimonial disputes based upon concerns regarding the individual's right to privacy; however, the dissent argued that limiting justice to a physical space has the potential to severely limit the ability of marginalized groups to access the justice system- specifically, those who are economically disadvantaged, or live in rural/remote locations. Thus, the dissent has essentially defined the philosophy of technology as a means to democratize access to the court systems, and this philosophy has been utilised as the primary basis for the Bharatiya Nagarik Suraksha Sanhita (BNSS), which has validated the use of digital infrastructure to assist in bridging the gaps created by geography and logistics.

3. The Legislative and Regulatory System in Meghalaya

Virtual courts have not been implemented solely under the auspices of the BNSS, but rather as part of a multi-layered, three-stage evolution of regional regulatory instruments that transformed the system from an emergency response into a structured institutional process.

578 Santhini v. Vijaya Venketesh, (2018) 1 SCC 560.

3.1 Emergency Response

Initially, the switch to online proceedings was facilitated by the High Court of Meghalaya Circular dated 7 January 2022[579], which represented a largely emergency administrative response to the COVID-19 Pandemic. Although the circular ensured the continued provision of justice during the pandemic, it lacked long-term procedural safeguards and was never intended to provide a permanent regulatory framework for the operation of virtual courts.

3.2 Structural Regulation

The establishment of the High Court of Meghalaya (Video Conferencing) Rules, 2020[580], provided the first formal legal authority for video conferencing in the state for the purpose of hearing matters. These Rules were significant because they provided legitimacy, established procedural requirements, and granted formal approval for virtual proceedings, thereby ensuring that such proceedings would be considered valid as if they had taken place in person. However, empirical evidence indicates that the Rules' success was heavily dependent on existing infrastructure and broad judicial discretion.

3.3 Institutional Consolidation and the BNSS Era

The final and definitive shift toward the full implementation of virtual courts occurred with the implementation of the District Courts of Meghalaya for the Use of Electronic Communication and Audio-Video Electronic Means Rules, 2025[581]. This instrument was built upon previous efforts to strengthen the overall system by providing direct

579 High Court of Meghalaya, Circular dated Jan. 7, 2022.

580 High Court of Meghalaya (Video Conferencing) Rules, 2020.

581 District Courts of Meghalaya for the Use of Electronic Communication and Audio-Video Electronic Means Rules, 2025.

empowerment to trial courts, while aligning local procedures with the BNSS. As a result, the Rules enabled virtual criminal proceedings to be practised efficiently at the district level- the level at which most remand, bail, and trial proceedings occur.

4. Research Methodology

The purpose of this research is to identify the operational realities of how the BNSS works and how Local High Court Rules work at the micro level. The research focuses on the specific socio-legal context of the East Khasi Hills District in Shillong, India. Primary Data were obtained using Semi-Structured Interviews with the following Stakeholders:

- Judicial Officers: To assess adjudication challenges and evidentiary assessments.
- Bench Assistants/ Court Staff: To determine administrative burdens and physical infrastructures.
- Public Prosecutors: To assess state representation and case disposal as well as investigative accountability.
- Advocates/ Lawyers: To assess defence rights, client confidentiality and access to justice.

Empiricism will be used, in addition to doctrinal analysis of the BNSS's statutory provisions and the policy guidelines governing electronic proceedings, to supplement primary data collection.

5. Empirical Findings: The Operational Realities of Virtual Courts

Although the BNSS has ambitious statutory objectives for the creation of virtual courts, many systemic barriers hinder their implementation in practice. These barriers are exacerbated in India due to significant regional disparities in infrastructure and digital literacy. At the operational level, the data provide a clear distinction between the theoretical efficiencies proposed by digital processes and the actual operational realities in the East Khasi Hills District.

5.1 Infrastructure and Connectivity: The Building Blocks of Digital Justice

The ability to conduct virtual hearings depends entirely on the availability of reliable, high- speed internet connections and stable power supplies. Much of the literature has identified connectivity constraints as a major bottleneck to the digitisation of the judiciary[582]. Unreliable internet and power outages can cause sudden loss of connectivity and abrupt termination of proceedings, potentially delaying the trial or compromising its fairness.

Additionally, establishing a secure e-court platform is capital-intensive, requiring not only the initial costs of hardware and software but also ongoing costs for maintaining the system, investing in cybersecurity, and continually improving the digital forensic capabilities of police and prison services. However, empirical evidence indicates that severe and recurring systemic impediments exist in Shillong. In general, bench assistants stated that "technical failures are frequent" during virtual court proceedings. They specifically identified the following as common types of recurrent technical problems: "network

582 Richard Susskind, Online Courts and Online Dispute Resolution (2023),

problems", "server is down", and "frequent electricity shutdowns". Similarly, judicial officers corroborated the bench assistants' findings, specifically citing connectivity problems and internet outages as the most recurrent operational challenges in conducting online hearings.

5.2 Space Problems and Court Administration

Reviews of current e-court systems indicate widespread problems with e-filing workflows and the dependability of judicial platforms. Technical errors in executing tasks and complex e-filing procedures may increase transaction costs for lawyers and parties involved in the proceeding, leading to missed deadlines and procedural defaults. The lack of a uniform, user-friendly interface across the various High and District Courts adds an additional layer of complexity.

Conversely, the transition to a hybrid justice model has created challenges with physical space. Court personnel emphasised a critical logistical barrier: District Courts have small courtrooms and limited space to store case files and equipment. This suggests that while court processes are migrating to the cloud, the physical equipment needed to access them is causing overcrowding in traditionally paper-based courtrooms.

In addition to physical space issues, hybrid operations have significantly increased the court staff's workload. A clear gap exists in terms of training for managing virtual court operations. When asked if they received training for managing virtual court operations, all of the bench assistants uniformly replied "none". This lack of training, combined with infrastructure deficits, has led court personnel to recommend ending virtual court operations.

https://doi.org/10.1093/9780192864727.003.0015.

5.3 Prosecutorial and Systemic Effectiveness

Although there are technical challenges associated with implementing virtual proceedings, they provide the prosecution and the judiciary with unique opportunities to create efficiencies. Virtually all public prosecutors (estimated 0-25%) reported that virtual hearings significantly or moderately improved the rate at which cases were disposed of by the court. One of the main advantages of using virtual proceedings is that it greatly reduces the time required to transport accused persons to and from the courtroom.

Judicial officers specifically noted that the use of video proceedings had created significant efficiencies in obtaining testimony from official witnesses. The virtual proceedings have enabled the efficient disposition of cases involving official witnesses; for example, when forensic experts testify in multiple courts on the same day, they can now do so from their own offices rather than travel to each courthouse.

Digitalisation of the court process serves an important role in creating a more transparent and accountable process. In addition to the efficiencies it has created for both the prosecution and the judiciary, prosecutors have noted that *"the mandatory audio-video recording provides for more accountability and transparency of the investigative agencies"*, which can lead to higher- quality trials. The audio-video recording of the investigative process is also seen as a way to reduce instances of custodial abuse and the fabrication of evidence[583].

583 L. Podor, Courts in a Digital World - The Concept of 'Justice Without Walls', SGEM World Science Scholarly Society (2024), https://doi.org/10.35603/sws.iscah.2024/fs01.03.

6. Legal Challenges: Procedural Justice and Defence Rights

While the introduction of virtual proceedings represents a number of advances in efficiency and cost-effectiveness in the administration and prosecution of the criminal justice system, it raises legal and constitutional issues that affect the rights of the accused. Although the administration and prosecution of the justice system emphasise the efficiency of the BNSS and virtual court rules, defence attorneys in Shillong express several concerns about procedural justice. Defence lawyers have stated that one of the core elements of criminal adjudication is the effective defence of the accused, and that this process is being fundamentally changed by digital mediation[584].

One of the principles of procedural justice is the right of the accused to be physically present at his/her trial, and to engage in private and effective consultations with legal counsel. Defence lawyers have raised concerns that the use of virtual hearings and remote appearances could limit the accused's ability to have private, real-time consultations with their lawyer. Additionally, the lack of face-to-face interaction between the parties to a proceeding may violate the long-standing legal principle of immediacy, which requires that the parties be able to hear each other directly. This violation of immediacy could limit the court's ability to assess the demeanour of the witnesses and accused. Defense lawyers have also raised concerns regarding the "publicity" of trials. While virtual courts could theoretically allow anyone to access them, the practical obstacles to accessing a digital link would likely limit the public's scrutiny of judicial proceedings, which is a fundamental aspect of the right to a public trial.

584 Akmaldzhanovna, Online Hearings and the Right to Effective Defence in Digitalised Trials (2022), https://doi.org/10.1007/978-3-031-13952-9_9.

6.1 Right to Effective Counsel and Attorney-Client Privilege

The constitutional right to effective legal representation involves the right to communicate privately and confidentially with one's client. The empirical data collected indicate that the use of virtual formats for the delivery of legal services severely limits the privacy and confidentiality of this communication. Defence lawyers have indicated that their representation of clients using virtual formats is usually either "Moderately effective" or completely "Ineffective." Defence lawyers' ineffectiveness in representing their clients through virtual formats primarily arises from "difficulty in providing meaningful representation," "inability to assess the physical condition of the client," and "communication difficulties." Importantly, the virtual platforms courts use for hearings typically do not accommodate private, spontaneous attorney-client communications. As one defence counsel bluntly stated, "virtual hearings are almost entirely about the court hearing and rarely about the private communication between the attorney and client." Consequently, defence counsels are compelled to rely on alternative forms of communication with their clients that are not necessarily secure, such as conducting "private consultations before" the hearing, or communicating with their clients "via WhatsApp messages" during the hearing. These alternative forms of communication threaten the sanctity of the attorney-client privilege and create a unique procedural disadvantage for the defence[585].

585 J. Teague, Two Rights Collide: Determining When Attorney-Client Privilege Should Yield to a Defendant's Right to Compulsory Process or Confrontation (2021), https://presnellonprivileges.com/wp-content/uploads/2021/12/58-2-Teague-Two-Rights-Collide.pdf.

6.2 Cross Examination & The Threat of Tutoring

The right to confront and cross-examine adverse witnesses is a key component of the adversarial justice system. All of the interviewed advocates preferred the physical mode over the virtual hearing for this phase of the trial.

Cross-examination is identified as the "most sensitive part of a trial, and the way the cross-examination is recorded will have an effect on the fairness of the trial, the tactics employed by counsel, and the assessment of credibility." In the physical courtroom, the judge and counsel can assess the witness's demeanour, body language, and surroundings. However, with virtual hearings, this assessment is limited, and there is a "serious risk of tutoring the witness off camera." Furthermore, counsel indicated that they experience difficulty demonstrating to remote witnesses the physical or documentary evidence at trial, which disrupts the smooth and efficient execution of their cross-examination strategy. Overall, these factors can lead to the "denial of a fair hearing, the denial of cross-examination, issues regarding how the trial was recorded and how the evidence was accepted."

6.3 The Digital Divide and Access to Justice

A major concern identified in the comparative literature is that technology will further exacerbate pre-existing social and economic barriers[586]. Many litigants, especially those from rural or marginalised communities, do not have the necessary hardware, internet access/or digital literacy to fully participate in virtual court proceedings[587]. Unless

586 Popova, Impact of Digital Technologies on Criminal Procedure in Russia and India: Comparative Legal Aspect, 2(1) Int'l J. L. in Changing World (2023).

587 Vinayagam, A Comparative Analysis of Virtual Court System in India and International Countries, Int'l Sci. J. Eng'g & Mgmt. (2025), https://doi.org/10.55041/isjem04641.

targeted access programs and supportive measures are developed to address this issue, the trend toward virtual courts can create a new barrier to justice for individuals who are already most susceptible to injustice[588].

The empirical data indicate that this is a serious issue in the East Khasi Hills District. Advocates were very explicit when noting that the transition to digital trials "can disproportionately harm economically disadvantaged defendants because of the lack of devices, inability to access the internet and lack of knowledge." When the exercise of fundamental legal rights depends on digital literacy and high-speed broadband, it creates the opportunity for the justice system to become a tiered system that inherently discriminates against vulnerable populations.

7. Admissibility of Evidence & Constitutional Right to Due Process

The BNSS relies heavily on electronic evidence and e-documents. Nonetheless, the validity of electronic evidence's authenticity and integrity remains a subject of much debate. Some critics argue that the standards for admitting electronic evidence under the new laws are often ambiguous, creating the possibility for evidence to be tampered with or manipulated[589]. The lack of reliable methods for verifying electronic evidence and the threat of cyberattacks on electronic document exchanges pose substantial risks to the reliability of the judicial process. To mitigate these threats, it is essential to establish

588 Pandey, Access to Justice Through Virtual Courts in Current Indian Scenario (2023), https://doi.org/10.55662/saler.2023.801.

589 Wahab, Shortcomings of the Bharatiya Sakshya Adhiniyam, 2023: Challenges for Courts, Prisons, and Police, 6(5) Int'l J. for Multidisciplinary Research (2024), https://doi.org/10.36948/ijfmr2024.v06i05.28780.

strict protocols for the chain of custody and enhance forensic science's ability to verify the accuracy of evidence.

Despite various operational and infrastructural hurdles to establishing virtual courts, the respondents view the underlying legal framework for virtual proceedings as constitutionally sound, provided specific procedural measures are strictly enforced.

7.1 Substantive Fairness, Not Form; Digital Proceedings

The constitutionality of digital court proceedings is measured against Article 21 of the Indian Constitution, which provides that no person shall be deprived of their life or personal liberty except in accordance with the procedure established by law. Practitioners in the study demonstrated a thoughtful understanding of the Supreme Court's case law. In particular, they referred to the Supreme Court's extension of the definition of "procedure established by law" in Maneka Gandhi vs. Union of India (1978)[590], to include a "fair, just and reasonable procedure"; thus, practitioners indicated that "the test is substantive fairness — not physical format." Accordingly, "online adjudication can comply with constitutional due process standards, however, only as long as procedural fairness is preserved substantively and not merely formally." Thus, the legal community views virtualisation not as an inherently unconstitutional activity, but as an operational model requiring very strict, substantive regulation. Judicial officers also expressed this viewpoint, noting that virtual formats provide an appropriate balance "of the Judges and magistrates, therefore, no issue of prejudice arises as everything remains the same, only the method of appearance is different."

590 Maneka Gandhi v. Union of India, AIR 1978 SC 597.

7.2 Admissibility of Electronic Records Under the Bhartiya Sakshya Adhinayam, 2023

The integration of electronic records and virtual testimony is governed by evidentiary principles that recognise electronic records as admissible, subject to stringent authentication requirements. Advocates note that the Supreme Court of India has definitively established that evidence may be taken via video conferencing without violating fair trial principles, so long as three key conditions are fulfilled: "Identity of the witness is verified," "An opportunity for cross-examination is given," and "The proceedings are properly recorded." Advocates in Shillong further assert that these protections have been incorporated into local practice. For example, "Before virtual hearings, the identity of the person (witness/accused) must be verified through official identification documents, which becomes part of the record."

7.3 Distinction between Operational Risks and Inherent Legal Flaws

The integration of electronic records and virtual testimony is governed by evidentiary principles that recognise electronic records as admissible, subject to stringent authentication requirements. Advocates note that the Supreme Court of India has definitively established that evidence may be taken via video conferencing without violating fair trial principles, so long as three key conditions are fulfilled: "Identity of the witness is verified," "An opportunity for cross-examination is given," and "The proceedings are properly recorded." Advocates in Shillong further assert that these protections have been incorporated into local practice. For example, "Before virtual hearings, the identity of the person (witness/accused) must be verified through official identification documents, which becomes part of the record."

7.4 Distinction between Operational Risks and Inherent Legal Flaws

Defence Counsel presented legitimate objections to virtual testimony — specifically the possibility of "off-camera prompting," the "reduced ability to observe subtle demeanour," "technical disruptions impacting spontaneity," and "inequality of connectivity" — but analytically categorised them as "operational risks — not inherent legal flaws." Ultimately, the judicial evaluation of a witness's testimony is based upon its substantive merit. As one advocate stated, "Courts evaluate credibility based on the content of testimony, not merely the physical presence of a witness." If "transparency is maintained among Judges, accused persons and victims, then it will be viewed as legally valid."

8. Conclusion and Recommendations for Policy

The transition to virtual courts, pursuant to the provisions of the Bharatiya Nagarik Suraksha Sanhita, 2023, presents a strategic juncture for the criminal justice system in the East Khasi Hills District. Consistent with the empirical data obtained from Shillong, the implementation of the BNSS and the relevant High Court Rules has established a robust hybrid model that provides significant administrative advantages. The system has significantly improved prosecutors' efficiency, reduced delays in the transport of accused, and provided the flexibility required for official witnesses. Moreover, the mandatory audio-video recording of all proceedings creates an additional layer of transparency and accountability in the investigative process[591].

591 R. Singh & N. Kaur, Modern Trends in the Criminal Justice System in India (2025), https://theinfinite.co.in/wp-content/uploads/2025/09/Modern-Trends-in-the-Criminal-Justice-System-in-India.pdf.

The systemic benefits of technology in the administration of justice in India will certainly improve the system's efficiency; however, fundamental rights must always take precedence over such improvements. The data obtained from the study clearly demonstrate that the existing digital infrastructure across the majority of rural areas in India is severely vulnerable to "Frequent" disruptions, including severe "network problems" and frequent electricity blackouts. Furthermore, the virtual format of the hearings will significantly limit lawyers' ability to provide effective defence representation due to restrictions on private attorney-client communications and the increased likelihood of witnesses being coached during cross- examination.

For virtual hearings, remands, and digital adjudication to be both constitutionally robust and fair, the BNSS framework needs to be backed by localised administrative support and targeted investment.

On this basis, the following policy recommendations based upon the socio-legal analysis of the East Khasi Hills District are made:

Investment in the Physical Court Infrastructure: In order to meet the digital demands of the courts, they need to be adapted to include digital capabilities. Therefore, there is an immediate requirement for a "new court building with the appropriate infrastructure", including sufficient courtroom space for both physical records and the latest digital equipment. Additionally, the courts require uninterrupted power supplies and dedicated high-speed broadband connections that are not susceptible to fluctuation of the general regional network.

1. **Secure Digital Communication:** The integrity of the attorney-client relationship must be preserved through the establishment of secure, encrypted "private consultation rooms" (breakout rooms) in the virtual court software that will enable advocates to consult with their clients seamlessly during proceedings.

2. **Stringent Procedural Safeguards for Cross Examination:** In order to prevent the possibility of off-camera coaching of witnesses, judicial guidelines must provide for dynamic camera angles (including views of the witness's entire room) during cross examination, along with a strict "prohibition against witness tutoring".
3. **Capacity Development and Training:** The introduction of digital technologies into the court must also be accompanied by capacity development among human resources. Mandatory training programs on the use of digital technologies must therefore be introduced for all court personnel — who currently report receiving "none" — so that "court employees who are technically competent in modern technology" will be available.
4. **Bridge the Digital Gap:** In order to ensure equal access to justice, district legal services authorities must establish public access centres or "e-Sewa Kendras" in the most remote subdivisions of the district to provide economically weaker sections of society with the electronic devices and high-speed internet connection needed to meaningfully participate in virtual hearings.

Finally, the use of technology as envisioned in the BNSS has the potential to greatly enhance the administration of criminal justice in India; however, as emphasised by practitioners in Meghalaya, the technology itself cannot guarantee substantive justice. It is therefore essential that the government ensures the digitalisation of the courts provides a means to reinforce, rather than undermine, the right to a fair and just trial through the implementation of robust procedural measures and the rectification of the many obvious deficiencies in the infrastructure

Chapter 20

Undated Cases in Indian Courts and their Impact on Substantive Procedure in BNSS

Rudra Bhelloria
Student of 0FBA LLB,
Maharaja Agrasen Institute of Management Studies, Delhi

Abstract

The Indian Judiciary Lifeline software, the Case Information Software (CIS) is moving towards version 4.0 with an aim to enhance the district judiciary. The CIS and National Judicial Data Grid (NJDG) have fundamentally reshaped the tracking of cases listed in Indian courts. However, there is a significant issue of undated cases. Undated cases are those cases that have next listing dates less than the current date. As per the NJDG data 5% of pending cases are undated. There are over

24.5 lakh undated cases, and 21 lakhs are criminal cases among them. Bharatiya Nagarik Suraksha Sanhita, 2023 (BNSS) sets a substantive procedural standard, and unjustified delays caused due to undated cases can amount to a violation of the accused's rights. Therefore, when CIS and NJDG show undated cases, they potentially breach the BNSS timelines. High Courts have issued circulars requiring all trial courts to update and tag undated cases on the NJDG to ensure that every case has a definitive 'next date'. The Hon'ble e-Committee of the Supreme Court of India has launched the JustIS mobile app for court management which alerts judges about undated cases. This paper aims to bring forward the government-led initiatives in bringing down the number of undated cases and argues beyond that by providing further suggestions such as; (i) need of validation rules in CIS/NDJG that blocks saving of 'next date' earlier than the current date or on court holidays, (ii) monthly 'date-integrity' audit for criminal courts, (iii) integrating a flagging feature for public to report the undated cases from the case-status interfaces for quick rectification. With government-driven reforms, these non-legislative technological designs can significantly reduce the undated cases and improve the criminal justice system.

1. Introduction

Digitisation of case records and cause lists through CIS and NJDG has transformed how pendency, delays and case flow are measured in the Indian judiciary. For the first time, real-time dashboards give High Courts, district courts and policymakers granular visibility into age-wise pendency, stage-wise delay and other key indicators across civil and criminal dockets. However, the same data architecture exposes a structural weakness of the existence of large numbers of "undated cases" in which the "next date" field is blank, stale, or earlier than the current date. From a rights perspective, undated cases are not a mere data-quality issue but they also have direct implications for the constitutional guarantee of a speedy and fair trial under Article 212F[592] and the statutory timelines introduced by BNSS. When the

592 India Const. art. 21.

official information system itself loses track of when a case is next listed, neither the court nor external stakeholders can reliably ensure compliance with investigation and trial timelines, undermining accountability. This paper argues that undated cases must be framed as a form of structural delay, and that the design of CIS/NJDG and allied tools should embed safeguards to prevent their occurrence.

2. Meaning of "Undated Cases"

Official manual on "Case Management through CIS 4.0" prepared under the e-Courts Mission Mode Project explains that if daily proceedings are not updated in CIS on a particular date, or are entered after the replication cut-off, the corresponding matters are reflected as "Undated Cases" on NJDG3F[593]. In practical terms, an undated case is one in which the "next date" field in the case record is either blank, corresponds to a past date, or has not been synchronised to the central NJDG server. NJDG dashboards now display "Undated Cases" as a distinct alert category alongside "Excessive Dated" matters and "Cases Listed Today" at multiple aggregation levels. The presence of such dashboards reflects an institutional recognition that date-integrity is central to credible case management and that undated matters signal either a failure of data entry processes or deeper issues in listing and scheduling.

Circulars issued by various High Courts have expressly treated undated cases as a serious lapse on the part of both courts and nodal officers. A detailed order of Tripura High Court4F[594] notes that

593 e-Committee, Supreme Court of India. (2024). Case Information System (Version 4.0)

594 High Court of Tripura. (2020, September 11). *Updating CIS, uploading and replication of data and filing up of "Delay Reasons"* (Circular No. F.4(37)-HC/ Vol. II/ 2019-20/18185)

data from NJDG revealed cases shown as listed on Sundays and a pool of undated cases and directs that no case should be reflected as undated since that defeats the purpose of an automated information system designed to promote transparency. The same circular instructs presiding officers to use the JustIS mobile app5F[595] to instantly check the status of undated cases in their court, and mandates daily replication of CIS data to NJDG by system staff. Circulars from time to time are also being issued in this regard on updating of undated cases in the National Judicial Data Grid (NJDG) portal, requiring district courts to cleanse their data and ensure that every case carries a valid next date. These directions situate undated cases not just as a technical anomaly but as an administrative failure incompatible with the goals of the e-Courts project.

Undated Cases are Structural Delay

By design, CIS manuals incorporates a "Delay Reasons Module" which requires courts to enter structured reasons when progress in a case is stalled for instance, non-appearance of the accused or a stay order from a higher court6F[596]. Undated cases fall outside this module because they are not explicitly tagged to a recognised delay reason instead, they represent a collapse of the scheduling function itself, where the system does not know when the matter is next to be taken up. Analytically, undated cases can therefore be seen as a distinct category of structural delay and they mask the true pendency profile, render cause-list based monitoring ineffective, and create blind spots where neither internal nor external stakeholders can hold the system

595 e-Committee, Supreme Court of India. (2022). *JUSTIS: Mobile app for judicial officers: User manual.*

596 e-Committee, Supreme Court of India. (2024). Case Information System (Version 4.0)

to account for compliance with statutory timelines. When a significant share of pending criminal cases are undated, the normative timelines in BNSS and the constitutional right to speedy trial risk becoming aspirational rather than operational standards.

3. Violation of the Right to Speedy Trial

The Supreme Court has long read the right to a speedy trial into Article 217F[597] of the Constitution, beginning with the Hussainara Khatoon8F[598] case, which drew attention to undertrial prisoners languishing for years due to systemic delays. Subsequent judgments in Abdul Rehman Antulay v. R.S. Nayak9F[599] and P. Ramachandra Rao v. State of Karnataka10F[600] elaborated factors for assessing delay, including the length of delay, reasons for delay, assertion of the right by the accused, and prejudice caused. Further, judgement in Mohd. Muslim @ Hussain11F[601] case, the Supreme Court held that prolonged incarceration and undue delay in trial violate Article 2112F[602] and take precedence over the stringent bail limitations. While these decisions cautioned against rigid outer time-limits for all trials, they affirmed that undue delay can amount to a violation of Article 21 and may justify quashing of proceedings in extreme cases.

This jurisprudence creates a constitutional baseline against which the performance of digital case management systems like CIS/NJDG must be evaluated. If systemic features of these platforms allow large numbers of criminal cases to drift without valid next dates, thereby

597 India Const. art. 21.

598 *Hussainara Khatoon v. Home Secretary, State of Bihar*, (1980) 1 SCC 81.

599 *Abdul Rehman Antulay v. R.S. Nayak*, AIR 1988 SC 1531.

600 *P. Ramachandra Rao v. State of Karnataka*, (2002) 4 SCC 578.

601 *Mohd. Muslim @ Hussain v. State (NCT of Delhi)*, 2023 SCC OnLine SC 352.

602 India Const. art. 21.

prolonging proceedings without justification, the resulting delays can engage Article 21 even in the absence of malice or deliberate obstruction.

Procedural Timelines under BNSS

The Bharatiya Nagarik Suraksha Sanhita (BNSS), 2023 replaced the Code of Criminal Procedure (CrPC), 1973 and introduced explicit timelines for several stages of the criminal process. The Sanhitya has strictly mandated that investigation for offences punishable with imprisonment of less than seven years is generally to be completed within a shorter period, while investigations involving offences punishable with seven years or more must be completed within 180 days, with a possible extension of 90 days in complex cases13F[603]. It further seeks to curb pre-trial inertia by requiring charges to be framed within 60 days of the first hearing on such charges14F[604]. Equally significant, it also includes a provision that, once charges are framed, trials should ideally be completed within two years15F[605], with courts required to record reasons if this timeline is not met. The statute also contemplates time-bound disposal of bail applications, with some analyses noting that bail applications should ordinarily be decided within seven days, thereby addressing delays in pre-trial liberty determinations16F[606].

These BNSS timelines provides robust case management practices that can reliably track the progress of individual cases across investigation, charge framing, trial stages and final judgment. The NJDG dashboards already support stage-wise and age-wise analysis of pendency across civil and criminal cases, enabling courts and

603 Bharatiya Nagarik Suraksha Sanhita, 2023, § 193.

604 Bharatiya Nagarik Suraksha Sanhita, 2023, § 251.

605 Bharatiya Nagarik Suraksha Sanhita, 2023, § 356.

606 *Anna Waman Bhalerao v. State of Maharashtra*, (2025) INSC 1114.

policymakers to identify bottlenecks. However, this analytical power is contingent on the integrity of basic fields like the "next date," without which neither the system nor supervising judges can meaningfully monitor whether statutory timelines are being met.

Undated cases therefore present a direct challenge to implementation of BNSS. Suppose if a criminal case has no future listing date in CIS/NJDG, it is practically impossible to ensure that charges are framed within 60 days or that the trial moves towards completion within two years of charge. In this sense, undated cases are not merely a data-cleaning task but a compliance risk vis-à-vis the statutory framework, and their persistence may amount to systemic disregard of the normative commitments embedded in BNSS.

Violations of BNSS Timelines

BNSS timelines can be broadly grouped into stages of investigation, pre-trial (including filing of police reports and framing of charges), trial (examination of witnesses, evidence, arguments) and judgment. Each of these stages presupposes that the case is being listed and taken up on specific dates, which are recorded in CIS and mirrored on NJDG dashboards used by courts and the public. When a criminal case becomes undated, it effectively falls out of the monitored pipeline, as neither the next date nor the stage-based progression can be tracked reliably.

This breakdown in date-integrity is particularly problematic in serious offences where BNSS requires investigations to be completed within 180 days, with extensions tightly controlled, and where trials are expected to be completed within two years of charge. If a case has no valid future listing date in CIS/NJDG for extended periods, it becomes difficult to justify that the delay is either reasonable or properly recorded under recognised delay reasons, leading to potential violations of both statutory mandates and Article 21 jurisprudence on speedy trial.

Accountability and the Absence of Enforcement Mechanisms

Analyses of BNSS have drawn comparisons with the US Speedy Trial Act, under which specific statutory deadlines for indictment and commencement of trial are backed by enforceable sanctions such as dismissal of charges. BNSS, by contrast, primarily sets timelines without prescribing direct statutory consequences for non-compliance, instead relying on judicial oversight, administrative monitoring and constitutional remedies to give practical effect to the right to speedy trial. In this context, digital tools like CIS, NJDG and JustIS assume a critical role as de facto accountability mechanisms. They are the means by which courts can see where timelines are being breached and take corrective steps. If these tools tolerate or conceal pools of undated cases, they blunt the very feedback loops that are supposed to inform judicial and administrative interventions, thereby weakening any functional enforcement of BNSS timelines.

India already faces a chronic crisis of undertrial prisoners, with recent justice-sector analyses noting that undertrials constitute well over two-thirds of the prison population and that many remain in custody for 1–3 years or longer. BNSS timelines and Article 21 jurisprudence on speedy trial are meant, in part, to address this by expediting investigations, charge-framing, trials and bail decisions in a time-bound manner. Where a substantial proportion of pending criminal cases in trial courts are undated or excessively dated, there is a heightened risk that undertrial prisoners in those cases are effectively forgotten in the scheduling system, even if their custody is technically subject to periodic remand orders. In such situations, undated cases can be seen as a digital symptom of a deeper structural neglect that disproportionately affects the liberty of undertrials, especially those without effective legal representation.

4. Current Initiatives

e-Courts Mission Project17F[607]

The e-Committee of the Supreme Court has overseen the rollout of the e-Courts project, under which CIS has been deployed in district and taluka courts as the primary case management software. NJDG operates as a national repository of case data sourced from CIS and offers public dashboards displaying pendency, disposals, age-wise breakdowns and alerts such as undated cases and excessive dated cases. The NJDG interface clearly labels "Undated Cases" in the "Cases" alerts box, signalling that such matters warrant special attention by court administrators.

The "Case Management through CIS 4.0" emphasises that to avoid undated cases, data entry staff should begin updating daily proceedings during the hearing itself and ensure that data is replicated to NJDG before the end of the day. It recommends systematic processes in each court to prevent accumulation of undated cases, recognising that failure to do so undermines the credibility of NJDG as a transparent and up-to-date information system.

607 e-Committee, Supreme Court of India. (2023). *Digital courts: Vision & strategy: Phase III: e-Courts Mission Mode Project.*

JustIS Mobile App18F[608]

To ensure strict judicial oversight, the National Judicial Data Grid (NJDG) actively tracks undated matters and pushes this data directly to the presiding judges. Judicial Officers receive automated 'SMS Alerts' from the NJDG on their registered mobile numbers, which are specifically mapped to their respective Judicial Officer (JO) Codes. This persistent digital tracking, combined with the comprehensive dashboard of the 'JustIS' Mobile App, empowers Judicial Officers and designated Nodal Officers to personally monitor the exact volume of undated cases in their respective courts daily, ensuring that all such matters are promptly tagged with a date.

Real-Time Dashboard19F[609]

CIS 4.0 introduces a completely revamped and interactive functional dashboard designed to improve administrative efficiency. This dashboard provides Presiding Officers with a centralized, aggregated view of their daily workload, which prominently features a dedicated, real-time counter specifically for "Undated Cases". By breaking down the exact number of undated civil and criminal matters right on the home screen, the system ensures these cases are immediately visible to judges for prompt corrective action

608 e-Committee, Supreme Court of India. (2022). *JUSTIS: Mobile app for judicial officers: User manual*

609 e-Committee, Supreme Court of India. (2024). Case Information System (Version 4.0)

Delay Reasons Modules20F[610]

CIS includes a structured "Delay Reasons Module" through which courts can record reasons for delay, such as non-appearance of the accused or stays granted by higher courts, thereby allowing NJDG to present a clearer picture of why cases are pending at particular stages. The High Court requires district courts to complete data entry in this module so that the High Court and the e-Committee can segregate pendency attributable to different causes, including non-appearance or stays. In addition, the e-Committee has created a "Help Desk Module" with an escalation matrix inside NJDG through which nodal officers can report issues related to undated cases, data replication failures and data mismatches between local CIS servers and the NJDG server. This escalation mechanism allows for technical issues contributing to undated cases to be raised and resolved at appropriate levels, complementing the administrative obligations placed on presiding officers and nodal officers.

Real-Time Data Entry and Deployment21F[611]

Administrative lapses, such as failing to post daily proceedings before system replication, heavily contribute to the undated cases crisis, which has seen over 803,000 cases become undated in District and Taluka Courts. To combat this, structural directives require that daily proceeding entries commence during the calling of cases itself, with data entry staff posting the updates immediately after a case is adjourned in the court hall. Furthermore, to support this administrative burden, it is emphasized that each court must be provided with a dedicated

610 e-Committee, Supreme Court of India. (2024). Case Information System (Version 3.0)

611 e-Committee, Supreme Court of India. (2024). Case Information System (Version 3.0)

Data Entry Operator tasked specifically with clearing undated cases daily, marking delay reasons, and regularly uploading court orders and judgments.

System Generated Next Listing Date (SGNLD)22F[612]

To systematically eradicate the possibility of a case languishing in procedural limbo, a detailed automated methodology has been approved and adopted, such as the initiative implemented by the High Court of Gujarat. Under this mechanism, if a future date of listing is not manually updated in the Case Information System (CIS) on the day a matter is adjourned, the system automatically generates and allots a "System Generated Next Listing Date" (SGNLD). The criterion for allotting this automated date is carefully devised based on the different age categories of the pending matters, ensuring that no registered case is ever allowed to remain in the "undated" category.

Physical Verification and Reconciliation (APAaR-DJ)23F[613]

Under the Supreme Court's Action Plan for Arrears Reduction in District Judiciary (APAaR-DJ), courts are mandated to execute a comprehensive physical verification of all case files. This process is critical for rectifying incorrect information and involves rigorously reconciling physical court records with the electronic data displayed on the NJDG and the CIS. Through this physical reconciliation, courts are directed to systematically identify all undated cases and make concerted, immediate efforts to assign hearing dates to each matter, forcing them back onto the active judicial docket

612 e-Committee, Supreme Court of India. (2024). Case Information System (Version 4.0)

613 Supreme Court of India. (2024). *Action plan for arrears reduction in district judiciary (APAaR DJ).*

5. Proposed Reforms

Strict Validation Rules

A first line of defence against undated cases is to harden the data-entry layer within CIS and the replication logic feeding NJDG. Drawing on standard software design principles, CIS could incorporate validation rules that prevent users from saving a "next date" earlier than the current date, and from listing cases on official court holidays or Sundays unless coded as a special category such as Lok Adalat sittings. The Tripura High Court circular already treats cases listed on Sundays as a matter of grave concern and directs monitoring through CIS accounts and JustIS24F[614]. Such validation rules would convert what is currently a training-and-discipline issue into a design constraint, significantly reducing the scope for erroneous or stale dates to be stored in CIS. In combination with mandatory fields and error prompts, CIS could refuse to close a hearing without a valid future date (or a coded terminal event such as disposal or transfer), thereby eliminating a major source of undated cases at origin.

Date-Integrity Audits

High Courts could institutionalise monthly "date-integrity" audits for criminal courts, using NJDG's existing alerts on undated and excessive dated cases, combined with drill-down reports from JustIS. These audits would require each court to certify that all pending criminal matters have valid next dates recorded in CIS, subject to random verification by district judges or inspection teams. Audit reports could be integrated into the existing dashboards used by High Courts for

614 High Court of Tripura. (2020, September 11). *Updating CIS, uploading and replication of data and filing up of "Delay Reasons"* (Circular No. F.4(37)-HC/ Vol. II/ 2019-20/18185).

monitoring pendency and disposals, thereby elevating date-integrity to the same level of importance as case clearance rates. Over time, such audits would not only reduce undated cases but also create an institutional culture that treats accurate scheduling data as integral to fair trial rights and BNSS compliance.

Public Flagging of Undated Cases

NJDG and the eCourts services app already empower litigants and lawyers to track case status and cause lists, but they do not currently offer a structured way for users to report data anomalies such as undated cases, incorrect stages or mismatched party details. Introducing a "flag this case" feature in public-facing interfaces would allow advocates and litigants to alert court staff when a case appears without a future date or with obviously stale dates.

Such a feature could create a lightweight crowdsourced data-quality loop, with flags routed to nodal officers through the existing Help Desk Module and escalation matrix inside NJDG. To avoid abuse, flags could be rate-limited, require basic authentication and be confined to objective categories such as "no next date shown," "date earlier than today," or "listed on a holiday," which can be programmatically verified by court staff.

Alert Mechanism for Delay

Some courts have already adopted automated technological safeguards. For example, the High Court of Gujarat implemented a system where a System Generated Next Listing Date (SGNLD) is automatically assigned to a case if court staff fail to manually update a future date on the day of listing, completely eliminating the possibility of a case remaining undated25F[615]. Further, the Bihar Court Management Systems Committee took initiative in regards to cases in the category of "30 years and above" and "20-30 years old" in a time bound manner26F[616]. However, these could be further aligned with BNSS timelines to create automated alerts when statutory mandates are at risk of breach. For example, NJDG could generate alerts when a case approaches 60 days from the first date of hearing on charges without charges being framed, or when two years have elapsed since charge without completion of trial, distinguished by whether the delay is attributable to the court, prosecution, defence, or external factors.

The National Judicial Data Grid (NJDG) generates and sends automated 'SMS Alerts' directly to the registered mobile numbers of Judicial/Presiding Officers. These alerts notify them on a daily basis regarding the exact number of undated cases specifically those lacking a future "Next Listing Date" or where the date is older than the current date that are pending in their specific courts27F[617]. However, no such alert system is present in general nature and to clear the backlog of cases. There is significant need of a similar alert mechanisms which aligns with the BNSS procedural timelines. To be effective, such alerts must be underpinned by complete and accurate entry of dates for key procedural events, which again underscores the importance of eliminating undated cases. Reinforcing the link between date-integrity, BNSS milestones and delay reason coding would make CIS/NJDG

615 Supreme Court of India. (2024). *Indian judiciary: Annual report 2023–2024: Vol. 2. High Courts.*

616 Supreme Court of India. (2025). *Indian judiciary: Annual report 2024–2025: Vol. 2. High Courts.*

617 Centre for Advanced Research on Corporate and Insolvency Law, Chanakya National Law University. (2024). *Impact assessment of Commercial Courts Act, 2015 with reference to commercial litigation pending in State of Bihar and Jharkhand.*

not just a record-keeping tool but a proactive compliance engine for speedy trial rights.

Further, various High Court such as the the Delhi High Court28F[618], Tripura High Court29F[619], Uttrakhand High Court30F[620], Punjab and Haryana High Court31F[621], High Court of Telangana32F[622], have explicitly direct presiding officers to use the JustIS app to instantly monitor undated cases in their courts, in addition to receiving SMS alerts from NJDG whenever undated cases are detected. By integrating alerts into a handheld tool and linking them to individual judicial officers, the system attempts to internalise responsibility for cleansing undated cases at the level of each court.

6. Comparative Analysis

The BNSS introduces a rigorous normative framework of procedural timelines designed to mitigate the chronic delays historically plaguing the Indian criminal justice system33F[623]. Unlike its predecessor, CrPC, which largely lacked statutory outer limits for various trial stages, the

618 High Court of Delhi. (2025, June 25). *Regarding undated cases* (Letter No. 10645/CFM/DHC/2025)

619 High Court of Tripura. (2020, September 11). *Updating CIS, uploading and replication of data and filing up of "Delay Reasons"* (Circular No. F.4(37)-HC/ Vol. II/ 2019-20/18185)

620 High Court of Uttarakhand. (2026, January 05). *Guidelines for Digitization of Judicial Records* (Circular No.02/UHC/IT/e-Courts Phase III/ 2025)

621 High Court of Punjab &. Haryana, Chandigarh. (2014, December 24). *Directions regarding undated cases* (Circular No. 2413 Spl./C.B.6)

622 High Court of Telangana. (2021, Feburary 01). *Regarding undated cases* (R.O.C. No. 396/OP Cell/ 2021)

623 Bharatiya Nagarik Suraksha Sanhita Bill, 2023, Statement of Objects and Reasons.

BNSS mandates specific deadlines to accelerate case progression34F[624]. Key legislative imperatives include the compulsory supply of relevant documents such as the chargesheet to the accused and victims within 14 days of appearance35F[625], the filing of discharge applications within 60 days of committal, and the framing of charges within 60 days36F[626] from the first hearing on the charge. Furthermore, the BNSS strictly requires that judgments be pronounced within 30 days37F[627] of the completion of arguments, extendable to a maximum of 45 days only with recorded reasons, thereby instituting a structured, time-bound trajectory for criminal trials.

In international jurisdictions, the management of procedural timelines relies heavily on either stringent statutory limits or robust, case-specific court management systems. For instance, the United States employs the Speedy Trial Act of 197438F[628], which enforces mandatory statutory timeframes, such as requiring an indictment within 30 days of arrest and the commencement of a trial within 70 days, with strict sanctions for deviations39F[629]. Conversely, jurisdictions like the United Kingdom, Canada, and Australia lean toward flexible yet strictly monitored case-specific timetables established during early case management conferences. In the Canadian system, case management relies on establishing a comprehensive timetable for pre-determined events from a lawsuit's inception to its conclusion, while the UK's multi-track system utilizes procedural judges to set strict pre-trial and

624 Luthra and Luthra Law Offices. (2024). *A comparative analysis between the new criminal legislation and the old legislation.*

625 Bharatiya Nagarik Suraksha Sanhita, 2023, § 230.

626 Bharatiya Nagarik Suraksha Sanhita, 2023, § 251.

627 Bharatiya Nagarik Suraksha Sanhita, 2023, § 258.

628 Speedy Trial Act of 1974, 18 U.S.C. §§ 3161(b) (1974)

629 Law Commission of India. (2014). *Arrears and backlog: Creating additional judicial (wo)manpower* (Report No. 245).

trial schedules40F[630]. Consequently, while judicial delays in India are often measured in years, backlogs in these comparative systems are typically quantified in weeks and months, with countries like South Africa and Sweden maintaining exceptionally low pendency rates for cases older than one year.

The phenomenon of "undated cases" matters officially instituted but languishing in procedural limbo without a scheduled next hearing date is a structural paralysis primarily observed within the Indian system, necessitating highly specific management strategies. In India, these cases act as "invisible arrears" that bypass automated scheduling algorithms and contribute heavily to judicial stagnation. To manage this crisis, the Indian judiciary utilizes the National Judicial Data Grid (NJDG) to actively track undated matters through specialized electronic dashboards, query builders, and automated alerts sent to presiding officers41F[631]. Additionally, the Action Plan for Arrears Reduction in District Judiciary (APAaR-DJ) mandates the comprehensive physical verification of case files to identify all undated cases and requires courts to systematically assign hearing dates to force these matters back onto the active docket42F[632]. In contrast, international jurisdictions inherently prevent the occurrence of undated cases through continuous judicial oversight and rigorous pre-trial scheduling. By empowering judges to actively control the litigation plan and mandating that unreached or adjourned matters be given a new trial date immediately, these foreign

630 Centre for Advanced Research on Corporate and Insolvency Law, Chanakya National Law University. (2024). *Impact assessment of Commercial Courts Act, 2015 with reference to commercial litigation pending in State of Bihar and Jharkhand.*

631 e-Committee, Supreme Court of India. (2018). *Case Information System* (Version 3.0).

632 Supreme Court of India. (2024). *Action plan for arrears reduction in district judiciary (APAaR DJ).*

systems ensure that cases maintain a continuous procedural trajectory, precluding matters from falling into an unscheduled digital void.

7. Conclusion

Undated cases in Indian judiciary system are more than a technical nuisance, they are a structural blind spot in India's digital justice architecture that can obscure violations of BNSS timelines and the constitutional right to a speedy trial. The existing ecosystem of tools, i.e., CIS, NJDG, JustIS and the eCourts services app already provides a strong foundation for data-driven court management, but their potential is undermined when basic date-integrity cannot be guaranteed. High Court circulars, training materials and NJDG's own dashboards demonstrate an institutional awareness of the problem and an emerging set of administrative responses, including the use of JustIS alerts, delay reason modules and escalation mechanisms. Building on these initiatives, this paper has argued for multiple additional, non-legislative reforms such as stricter validation rules on next listing dates, routine date-integrity audits for criminal courts, and participatory flagging of undated cases through public interfaces, complemented by tighter integration between delay reasons and BNSS procedural timelines.

By framing undated cases as a rights issue rather than a mere data anomaly, and by treating the design of CIS/NJDG as part of the state's constitutional obligations under Article 21 and BNSS, policymakers and courts can move towards a digital case management regime in which every pending criminal matter has a clearly recorded and timely next date. Implemented together, these design and governance interventions can materially reduce undated cases, enhance transparency, and bring India's digital justice infrastructure closer to the constitutional promise of speedy and fair trials for all accused persons.

About the Book

BHARATIYA NAGARIK SURAKSHA SANHITA IN PRACTICE: KEY INSIGHTS AND CRITICAL REFLECTIONS is a scholarly work that primarily presents a collection of selected articles contributed by academicians, researchers, and experts. It primarily addresses vital issues and practical challenges emerging from the implementation of the new criminal law procedural regime under the Bharatiya Nagarik Suraksha Sanhita, 2023 (BNSS). The book offers a comprehensive examination of procedural reforms through four thematic parts: **Part I: Structural & Institutional Reforms**, which explores systemic and institutional transformations; **Part II: Police Power & Accountability**, focusing on evolving policing powers and mechanisms of accountability; **Part III: Technology & Forensic Evidence**, examining the growing role of digital processes and forensic tools in criminal justice administration; and **Part IV: Witness Protection & Other Emerging Issues**, highlighting emerging concerns and contemporary procedural issues. The work aims to ascertain key areas of similarities and changes between BNSS and CrPC; provide lucid and exhaustive elaboration of various provisions of BNSS; offer critical reflections on procedural reforms and their impact on access to justice; and integrate and harmonize issues arising in the implementation of procedural reforms.

About the Editors

Dr. Aarushi Agarwal is an Assistant Professor at the Maharaja Agrasen Institute of Management Studies, Delhi, where she has been teaching Criminal Procedure and Evidence Law for over six years. She holds a Ph.D. from Maharaja Agrasen University, Baddi, and both LL.B. and LL.M. degrees from the Faculty of Law, University of Delhi. Dr. Aarushi Agarwal is an alumna from Shri Ram College of Commerce. She has worked as an Advocate Associate with AAC law firm for five years. She holds litigation experience of more than five years in criminal, matrimonial and service matters. She has worked on various PILs on health and education related issues in association with Social Jurist NGO. Dr. Agarwal has authored and edited several significant academic works, including *"Legal Research and Moot Court with Sample Moot Memorial"* (Central Law Publications) and the *"Handbook of Research on Cyber Law, Data Protection, and Privacy"* (IGI Global, USA). Her research contributions span diverse areas such as gender justice, health inequities, and human rights, with a special focus on the rights of transgender persons in India.

Ms. Ananya Dutt is an accomplished legal academic and researcher, currently pursuing a Ph.D. in Law from USLLS, Guru Gobind Singh Indraprastha University, Delhi. A UGC NET Awardee (2019 & 2021) and recipient of the UGC National Fellowship, with specialization in Criminal and Labour Law. Presently serving as an Assistant Professor of Law at Maharaja Agrasen Institute of Management Studies, Delhi, teaching BNSS, BNS and BSA. Has also served at SRM University, Sonepat, and practiced as an Associate at PR Law Firm, New Delhi, handling civil and criminal litigation before the Delhi High Court and Supreme Court of India. Her research and publications span criminal justice reform, ADR, women's rights, and mental health law, with contributions to reputed peer-reviewed journals and law reviews.

www.ingramcontent.com/pod-product-compliance
Lightning Source LLC
LaVergne TN
LVHW100248210926
848480LV00003B/868